Reader's Digest

Wildlife Watch

Gardens & Parks in Summer

Reader's Digest

Wildlife Watch

Gardens & Parks in Summer

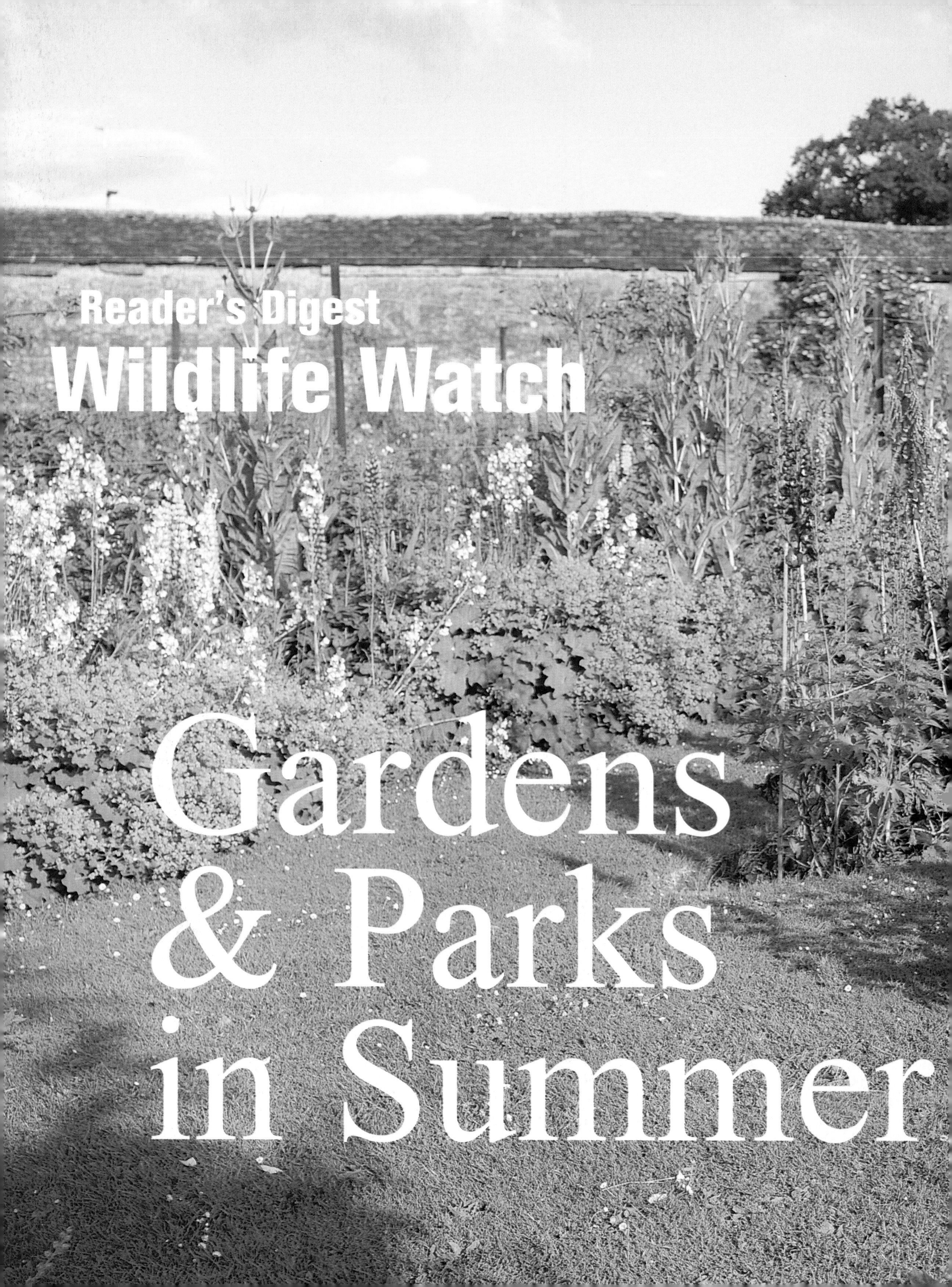

Published by
The Reader's Digest Association Limited
London • New York • Sydney • Montreal

Contents

Wildlife habitats and havens

Animals and plants in focus

Garden watch

Park watch

Introduction

Gardens are made for summer. To lie back in the warm grass while the sunlight glows through closed eyelids is one of the purest of pleasures. The air is often laden with the scent of aromatic herbs or the heavier, more sensuous fragrance of old roses, but much of the magic stems from the soft sounds of nature – the gentle rasping song of grasshoppers, the buzzing of bees foraging among the summer flowers, or the artless purity of the birdsong drifting from nearby trees and rooftops. The wings of visiting butterflies flash with exquisite colour as the insects flutter from one blossom to the next, unfurling their drinking-straw tongues to sip the sweet nectar. Delicate damselflies resemble intricate fabrications of silver and neon as they perch among pondside plants. Grey squirrels are endlessly entertaining as they bound across the grass and run up and down trees in their quest for food.

▲As dusk falls, the giant convolvulus hawk-moth may be seen on a tree trunk or wall. It uses its 75mm (3in) tongue to probe deep into tubular flowers for nectar.

◄The blackbird often nests in gardens and may rear three broods of young over spring and summer – although late-season broods are vulnerable to cold autumn weather.

A single rosebay willowherb plant can produce some 80,000 seeds each summer, so it rapidly colonises untended gardens, patches of urban wasteland and other open, neglected spaces.

Heat and dust

For garden insects – and the spiders and other creatures that prey upon them – summer is usually a time of plenty but it can also be a time of drought. After weeks with little or no rain the soil dries out near the surface and as the more shallow-rooted garden plants start to wilt, earthworms (see pages 72–73) and insect grubs burrow deeper into the ground to avoid losing vital moisture. Despite having powerful bills, rooks that nest in tall parkland trees may have trouble probing the hard ground for their usual insect food, while garden blackbirds often switch from digging out worms to combing the bushes for aphids and caterpillars, hunting alongside smaller birds such as blue tits. Between them, birds and other predators eat huge numbers of aphids and other garden pests as they feed their hungry broods (see pages 79–82).

In rural districts where they are still numerous, house sparrows (see pages 66–71) enjoy dry, dusty conditions. They can usually find plenty of grain and other seeds to eat, and they share with chickens the curious habit of dust-bathing, which helps to condition their plumage. Other animals favour damper places, such as shady churchyards (see pages 22–25), where the grass and wild flowers are often able to grow unchecked by the drought or the mower. Many churchyards are like fragments of ancient wild grassland and support a surprising diversity of wild plants and animals.

Summer nightlife

Other, rarer survivals are small urban woodlands that still retain their original plant stock (see pages 26–29). Some of these, such as Perivale Wood in west London, are protected nature reserves that provide valuable refuges for native insects, birds and mammals amid the urban sprawl.

Many of the animals that live in these woodlands forage for food in the neighbouring gardens and parks by night. They include urban foxes, which occasionally alarm householders by upsetting dustbins in their search for edible scraps. Hedgehogs (see pages 46–47) may also root around among leaf litter and other garden debris for slugs, snails and insects.

A male bullfinch is a dazzling sight but when bullfinches visit gardens they can be elusive and surprisingly difficult to see, especially during the summer breeding season.

On summer nights country gardens may be dotted with the eerie yellow-green lights of female glow-worms. They are actually beetles, although only the males have wings, which they need to find the glowing females.

Many urban woodlands contain badger setts and the animals may be attracted to nearby parks and gardens to forage for earthworms and scraps. Badgers can become regular nightly visitors.

Both foxes and hedgehogs eat earthworms, and on summer nights they may have more luck hauling them from the dew-soaked earth than the birds do hunting in the heat of the day.

Bats are also noisy night-hunting mammals but the sounds that they make are beyond the range of human hearing. Mature gardens near woodland or a churchyard may attract the long-eared bat (see pages 48–53), a specialised woodland hunter that uses its super-sensitive hearing to target insects crawling over foliage in total darkness. Other bats prey mainly on flying insects such as moths. Moths become more conspicuous to humans on warm summer nights when, attracted by house lights, they fly in through open windows. Along with other night visitors they often settle on walls and ceilings, where their subtle colours and patterns can be fully appreciated (see pages 20–21).

Migrant butterflies

By day most moths lie low, protected by superb camouflage that makes them all but invisible to predatory birds. A few moths, however, fly by day. They include the aptly named hummingbird hawk-moth, which looks just like a tiny hummingbird as it hovers on whirring wings to gather nectar from flowers. It has an extremely long tongue, which allows it to drink from very long-tubed flowers that few other insects can penetrate.

Many of the hummingbird hawk-moths that feed in parks and gardens in summer are migrants from across the Channel. They appear at about the same time as painted lady and red admiral butterflies, which also make the flight from France. It is astonishing that these delicate insects are able to make such long sea crossings, but sailors have reported seeing them in passage, flying low and fast, with a directness that is quite unlike their fluttery behaviour in gardens.

Painted ladies and red admirals are irresistibly attracted to buddleia blossoms, as are other colourful garden butterflies such as the small tortoiseshell, the peacock and the comma, making ideal subjects for garden wildlife photography (see pages 30–33). They breed in parks and gardens, laying their eggs on native plants such as thistles and, especially, stinging nettles. Few gardeners are willing to encourage these plants, but luckily many park authorities now appreciate their importance and allow them to grow in wild areas. It is always worth checking any large clumps of nettles for feeding broods of red admiral, peacock or small tortoiseshell caterpillars.

◀ Originally from India, the ring-necked parakeet has been breeding in south-east England, mainly around London, since the late 1960s. There are now several thriving colonies.

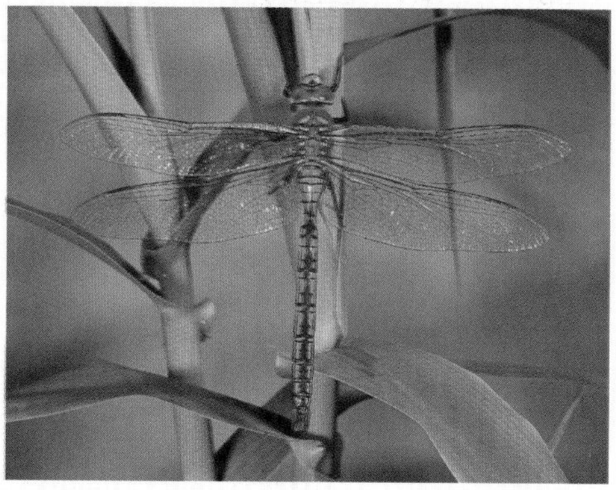

The largest British dragonfly, the emperor often hunts over the larger ponds found in parks. The male makes a dazzling sight with its brilliant kingfisher-blue body.

The fragrance of evening primrose flowers attracts night-flying moths. The plant was introduced from North America in the 17th century.

Dragons and damsels

Among the most spectacular insect visitors to parks and gardens in summer are the big dragonflies that hunt on the wing for flies and other airborne prey. Along with their smaller, more delicate relatives the damselflies (see pages 110–113), they lay their eggs in garden ponds and shallow park lakes after mating.

The mating process takes some time and pairs can often be found among pondside vegetation. Many damselflies – and some dragonflies – lay their eggs while flying in tandem, the male clinging to the female's neck as she places her eggs beneath the water, often among the leaves of aquatic plants. When the female has finished, the extra wing-power of the male helps her to break free of the surface tension, which might otherwise trap her and make her an easy target for predators.

Aerial attack

During the summer many garden birds raise a second brood of young after the first brood has fledged, and sometimes even a third. These garden breeders include residents, such as the robin and blackbird, as well as summer visitors, including the spotted flycatcher. This inconspicuous, mainly grey-brown bird gives away its identity by its aerobatic hunting technique, darting up to snatch flying insects from the air and then returning to the same perch. It will even catch bees and wasps, removing their stings by rubbing their bodies against a twig before either eating them or feeding them to its nestlings. Some flycatchers also prey on butterflies; they station themselves by a garden buddleia bush, ready to seize the insects when they fly up after feeding.

Towards the end of summer the insect supply begins to dry up and insect-eating birds leave for the tropics where they can still find plenty of food. The swifts that nest in the roof spaces of churches and old houses leave first, typically in mid-August (see pages 104–109). They are followed later by a variety of birds from wilder habitats, such as willow warblers, which often stop off in gardens to feed and build up energy for their long flight. The spotted flycatchers soon leave too, although the same birds will often return to a garden they know the following year.

Among the last to go are the house martins that breed in mud nests beneath the eaves. They gather in twittering groups on tiled, south-facing roofs, basking in the warmth that the tiles have absorbed from the September sun. If the weather holds they may stay until mid October or even later but eventually they vanish – and summer is over.

The red admiral is one of the largest garden butterflies. It arrives from Europe each year to breed on nettle patches.

Not much bigger than a large beetle, the tiny pygmy shrew has to eat almost constantly to fuel its fast metabolism. It often forages in gardens for insects and spiders.

The bird-hunting sparrowhawk has become more common in towns in recent years, nesting in park trees and frequently preying on garden songbirds.

Wildlife habitats and havens

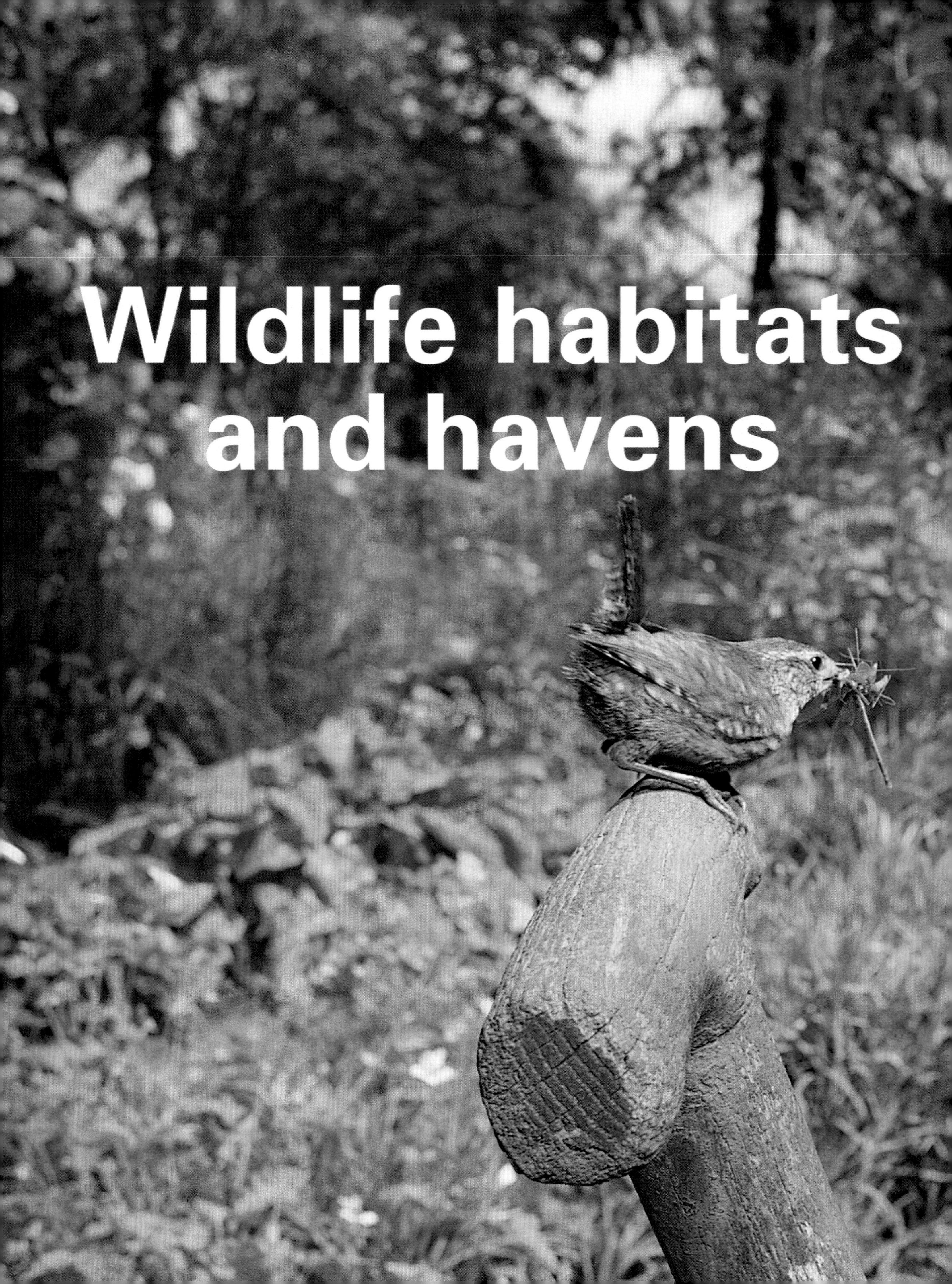

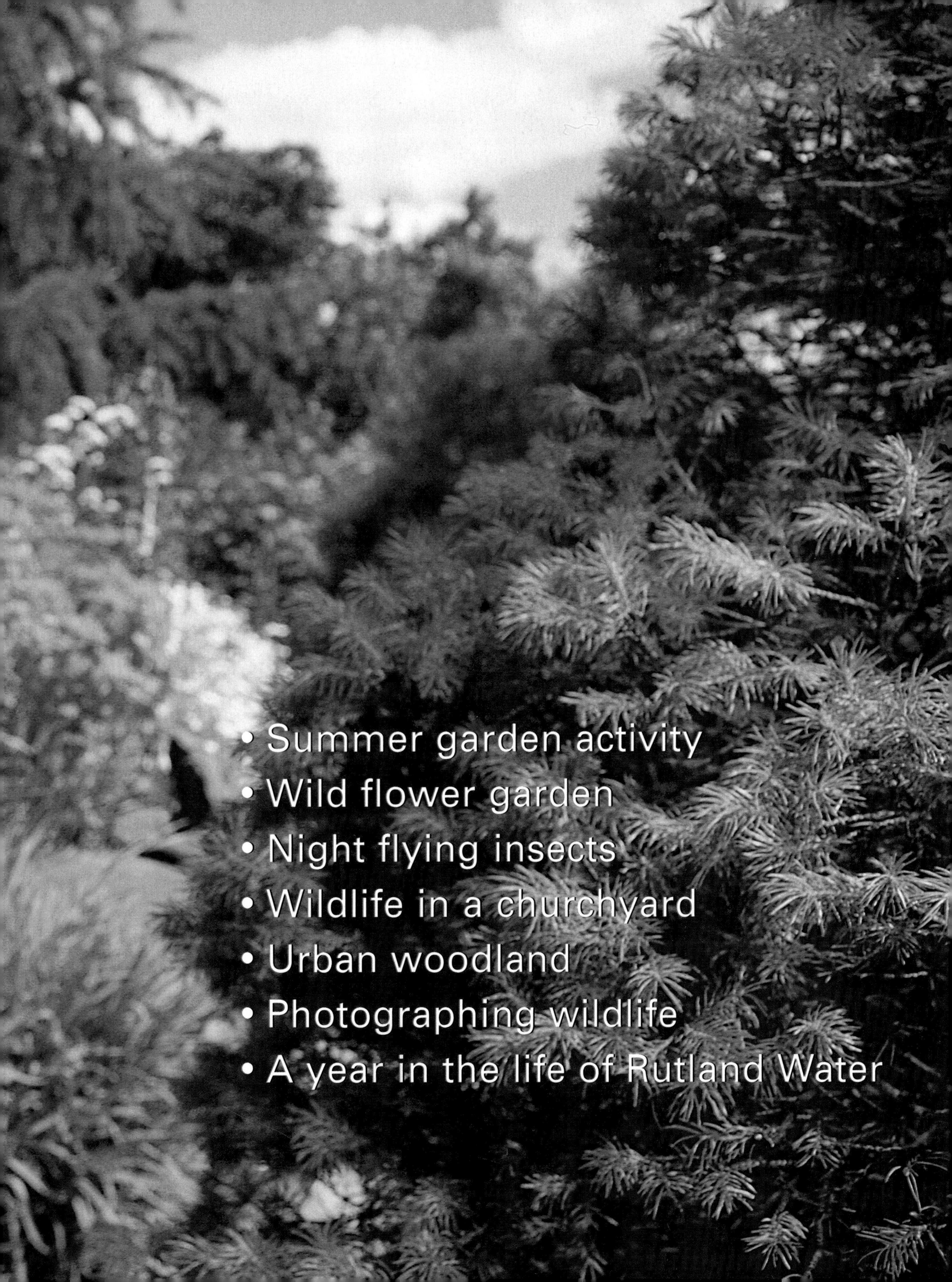

- Summer garden activity
- Wild flower garden
- Night flying insects
- Wildlife in a churchyard
- Urban woodland
- Photographing wildlife
- A year in the life of Rutland Water

Summer garden activity

Not only do dragonflies and ladybirds, frogs and blue tits enliven lawns and flowerbeds, they also help the flower, fruit and vegetable crops in the garden by feeding on plant-eating insects.

Caterpillar-hungry tits

Attracting animals and birds into the garden to feed is a natural way of preventing certain insect and invertebrate pests from becoming overwhelming, without leaving harmful pesticide residues or damaging other wildlife. Blue tits and great tits help to control both aphids and caterpillars. In spring and early summer, breeding pairs of tits gather hundreds of caterpillars to feed their nestlings. In the winter, they can be seen scouring trees and shrubs for the eggs of various aphid species, including the black bean aphid, which does so much damage to broad beans and other crops.

Tits are hole-nesters and readily occupy traditional nestboxes, but the entrance hole must be no more than 25–29mm (1–1⅛in) in diameter if it is to keep out the house sparrow. Reinforcing the entrance with metal will stop squirrels gnawing their way in. Even where nestboxes are provided, a small garden will support just one or perhaps two families of tits, as the birds are strongly territorial during the breeding season.

► A blue tit is a common sight in the garden, where it finds buds, fruits, seeds and berries to eat as well as caterpillars and insects, such as aphids. These small birds are noisy and often squabble over food and territory.

The song thrush has fewer and smaller v-shaped spots on its underparts than a mistle thrush. This one is watching for telltale signs of movement rather than listening for the rustle of snails in the grass.

Snail-eating song thrushes

In spring and summer, snails are a favourite food of the song thrush and fledglings may be seen watching their parents to learn how to break the shells on a hard surface.

Although in some places, such as the Scilly and Outer Hebridean islands and Ireland, song thrushes frequent open areas, for breeding they usually prefer gardens, parks, farmland and woods. They like to nest in dense bushes and in ivy or other creepers, so an abundance of shrubs and hedges encourages them into the garden. Hollies, elders, elms, hawthorns and conifers attract them to parks, and nests may be built on ledges, in banks, or even in holes in buildings. Nests are usually sited 1–5m (3–16ft) above the ground. No pruning or trimming should be done until the end of the nesting season.

Song thrush numbers have declined in recent years, but on fine days the loud song that gives the bird its name may still be heard, delivered from a high perch in a succession of repetitive musical phrases.

Slug-hunting hedgehogs

Hedgehogs are to be welcomed in the garden despite the fact that they eat earthworms, which perform a vital role by ventilating the soil. The reason is that the hedgehog's diet also includes slugs, caterpillars, insects and snails, all of which can damage garden plants. The hedgehogs crunch the food noisily with their sharply pointed teeth.

These mammals can be attracted into the garden by putting out a dish of dog or cat food mixed with a little water. A separate bowl of water will also help to ensure that the hedgehogs get enough fluid in dry summer periods.

A thick hedge or a compost heap that it can burrow into may encourage a hedgehog to take up residence, but care needs to be taken when digging out the compost, especially in winter when a hedgehog may be hibernating inside. Bonfire heaps should be checked for sleepy hedgehogs, too, before lighting. One way to avoid incinerating any hedgehogs is to start the bonfire nearby and transfer the garden rubbish from the pile to the fire a little at a time.

Alternatively, a rough wooden box about 25cm (10in) across, sunk into the bottom of a hedge or concealed in a pile of logs, may be adopted as a nestbox by a hedgehog.

A hedgehog is a noisy forager, snuffling among old fallen leaves and vegetation. It uses its keen sense of smell to detect prey, which consists mainly of insects and other invertebrates.

The larva of a ladybird bears little resemblance to the adult, but it shares a voracious appetite for greenfly and other small insects. A single larva can eat as many as 100 aphids in a week.

Adult ladybirds are hunters that specialise in catching and eating aphids. Their jaws are so powerful the soft-bodied aphids have no defence.

Aphid-eating ladybirds

The most familiar and well-loved of garden beetles, ladybirds eat large quantities of aphids, such as greenfly and blackfly. They feed on a variety of other small insects, too, but aphids form the bulk of their diet. After arriving on a plant, a ladybird searches each shoot for its prey, moving upwards until it finds a group of aphids. If it reaches the tip of the shoot without finding any, it climbs down again until it reaches a junction and then crawls up another branch. This systematic search ensures that it covers the whole plant.

Most adult ladybirds are easily recognised by their rounded shapes and spotted red, orange or yellow wing cases. Ladybird larvae are not so familiar, although they are just as good at hunting down and eating aphids as the adults. A typical ladybird larva eats several hundred aphids during the three weeks that it takes to mature. The larvae of the most common species – the seven-spot – are blue-black with pinkish yellow spots.

Other aphid hunters

The delicate green lacewings that are attracted to lighted windows at night are also good at controlling aphids. There are several species, plus a number of smaller, less conspicuous brown lacewings. Most have aphid-eating larvae, too. Adults chew their prey with biting jaws but the bristly, grub-like larvae pierce the aphids and drain their juices, using their curved, hollow jaws like hypodermic needles. The larvae of some green lacewing species clothe themselves with the empty skins of their prey, or other debris, making them very hard to detect.

The larvae of several hoverfly species also eat aphids. Each one destroys several hundred during its brief life, and the pale, well-camouflaged, legless larvae can sometimes be seen holding struggling greenfly in their mouths. Adult hoverflies feed on pollen and nectar, so planting flowers close to vegetable crops may attract them and encourage them to lay their eggs.

Lacewings are relentless predators. Each one may eat about 1000 aphids during its two-month adult life.

Slow-worms, frogs and toads

These three creatures all have healthy appetites for a variety of garden inhabitants. Slow-worms look like snakes but are actually legless lizards. They like plenty of grass cover in which to hunt for slugs and other invertebrates and so prefer larger, wilder gardens and orchards to small town plots. They can be encouraged into the garden by putting a sheet of corrugated iron or rubber matting on the ground in a sunny spot to absorb the sun's heat; slow-worms may lie beneath it for the warmth. They also enjoy the raised temperature inside compost heaps.

Common frogs and common toads need water for breeding, so the easiest way to encourage them is to create a garden pond. Ideally, the pond should have a shallow end in which the frogs can spawn, and a deeper end for the toads. The sides should slope gradually so that the frogs and toads can get out easily. Alternatively, a log wedged across the pond will serve as a basking platform and an escape route.

Frogs often start to breed in new ponds quite quickly, but toads prefer traditional sites and usually return to the ponds in which they grew up. Introducing a few toad tadpoles from another pond may be successful. A pond may also attract dragonflies, and these will keep down the mosquitoes that can be troublesome in the garden on summer evenings.

▲ Slow-worms in the garden are vulnerable to household pets. Cats can rapidly wipe out a small slow-worm population unless a safe retreat, such as a high compost bin, is available.

◀ Common frogs often breed in large numbers in mature suburban gardens. A pond for spawning is essential, as are refuges for summer shelter and winter hibernation. Their colour varies from dark-spotted green or brown to yellow, reddish, orange and even pink.

▼ Common toads are usually active in the garden after dark or in wet weather, searching for insects and slugs. Their shorter legs and warty skin help to distinguish them from frogs. Frogs also have a big circle behind each eye, which is absent in toads.

WILDLIFE WATCH

How can I encourage insect-eaters in the garden?

● Many major predators of garden invertebrates are themselves vulnerable to larger hunters, especially domestic cats and dogs. Provide plenty of cover, secure shelters, and hibernation and nest sites for hedgehogs, frogs, toads, lizards and birds.

Use a magnifying glass to look closely at the mouthparts of garden invertebrates. Compare the powerful crushing jaws of carnivorous beetles and centipedes with the hypodermic-like 'stylet' of an aphid, used to extract sugary sap from garden plants.

Predatory wasps

Wasps may not be most people's favourite insects but during the summer the occupants of a single common wasp nest can consume more than 250,000 insects, including many caterpillars that are harmful to garden plants. So unless a social wasp nest is located too close to the house, it makes sense to leave them alone.

Solitary wasps do not eat as many insects as the social species. They nest in rotting wood, masonry holes and even in garden canes, and adult wasps may be seen returning with their prey. They stock their nests with insects that they have caught and paralysed with their stings. In due course, the grubs eat the paralysed prey – which, since it is not dead, stays fresh until the grub kills it. Some species catch aphids, while others prefer flies or small caterpillars.

Common wasps have powerful mouthparts, which are almost as effective as their stings when it comes to dispatching insect prey. They are generally too busy hunting to be much trouble to humans.

► Centipedes emerge in the cool of the night to hunt for prey. They eat mostly worms, insects and spiders by catching them in their sickle-shaped jaws and injecting poison.

◄ A burrowing geophilid centipede has a very long, thin body, enabling it to slip through natural fissures or into the burrows of other soil animals, such as earthworms, as it pursues its invertebrate prey.

Hungry centipedes

All centipedes are carnivores, equipped with poisonous fangs that more or less encircle their heads. Although harmless to humans, they are avid hunters of a variety of creatures found in the garden, including slugs, fly larvae and eelworms, as well as other centipedes.

The two main groups of garden centipedes are the lithobiids and the geophilids. The lithobiids are shiny, mainly chestnut brown creatures that are seen scurrying away when logs and stones are disturbed. *Lithobius forficatus*, up to 30mm (1¼in) long and 4mm (⅛in) wide, is the commonest garden species. Like all lithobiids it has 15 pairs of legs when it is mature. The rear pair are much longer than the rest and function as an extra pair of sensory antennae, helping the animal to find its prey.

Geophilids are more slender and often much longer than the lithobiids, with at least 37 pairs of legs. They live in the soil, and the yellow burrowing centipede *Necrophlaeophagus longicornis* is often exposed when digging in the garden.

Caterpillar and slug parasites

Batches of golden-yellow cocoons surrounding dead caterpillars are often to be seen on sheds and fences in summer and autumn. The cocoons are those of the tiny ant-like parasitic wasp *Apanteles glomeratus*, better known as an ichneumon fly. An adult female lays up to 150 eggs in a caterpillar of the large white butterfly. The caterpillar is then eaten alive by the parasite's grubs. When fully grown, the grubs eat their way out and pupate around the shrivelled remains of the caterpillar.

Another parasite, this time of slugs, is the tiny nematode worm *Plasmarhabditis hermaphrodita*. About a third of the slug population in Britain seems to be naturally infected with this otherwise harmless parasite, but it is not normally numerous enough to kill many. However, the worms are bred commercially in huge quantities and can be bought in dried form. When reactivated with water and sprayed over slug-infested ground, the nematodes quickly infect the slugs, which die in about a week. The parasites continue to breed in the corpses. At less than a millimetre long, the young nematodes do not generally move very far in search of new hosts and continue to infect the slugs in the vicinity.

A shelled slug has a tiny, fingernail-like shell on its broad rear end – visible in this photograph – which helps to distinguish it from the plant-eating species. Shelled slugs are carnivores and include other slugs among their favourite prey.

Wild flower garden

Throughout the summer, wild flowers add splashes of vivid colour to the countryside. Cultivated varieties can reproduce this striking spectacle, and they also support a rich variety of garden wildlife.

Foxglove

A common sight in the wild, the foxglove, *digitalis purpurea,* grows in acidic soils. Its impressive spikes of purple tubular flowers grace woodland glades, heaths and banks throughout the summer. The cultivated varieties that brighten up the garden have pinkish purple (sometimes white) flowers that appear from June until September.

Although essentially a hardy biennial, the foxglove's life span is dependent upon the size of the plant. It will not flower until it has reached a certain size, and plants in low-nutrient environments take longer to reach the critical size for flowering. Once the size threshold is reached, a flower spike erupts from the centre of the leafy rosette. However, the foxglove has a contingency mechanism – if after about 12 years it is still not big enough, it will flower anyway, regardless of size.

◀ Under most conditions, the flamboyant foxglove grows leaves in its first year and flowers the following summer, producing millions of seeds.

▼ For the best results Solomon's-seal requires moist, humus-rich soil, similar to that found in its native deciduous woodlands. Clumps should be divided every few years during the autumn.

DID YOU KNOW?

Before World War I, foxgloves were grown on a commercial scale to extract a potent drug called digitalin. Minute amounts of this powerful chemical cause the heartbeat to slow and strengthen, but too much can be fatal. It is thought that excessive use of the drug contributed to the deterioration in the health of the Dutch painter Vincent van Gogh. Today, the chemical is still used, but it can be synthesised artificially.

Solomon's-seal

Arguably one of the most elegant woodland plants, Solomon's-seal is a relative of the lily and is well suited to dark, moist corners of the garden. Its arching stems carry oval, grey-green leaves, and produce white-tinged, green flowers during June and July, sometimes followed in late summer by blue-black berries.

In the wild, Solomon's-seal occurs in shady glades in ancient woodlands, especially ash woodlands, that grow on chalk or limestone soils, mainly in southern England. Now quite scarce, its natural distribution is obscured by escapes of the garden form, which is a hybrid between two wild species.

Maiden pink

A member of the carnation family, the maiden pink makes an attractive addition to borders or rock gardens. In the wild it creeps across dry, often sandy, grassland and decreasing colonies are scattered throughout England, Wales and Scotland.

Beautiful, carnation-like flowers rise above grey-green foliage between June and September. The wild type is unscented, unlike the cultivated varieties, which have had scent bred into them.

▲ The delicate blooms of maiden pink prove an irresistible attraction to butterflies and moths, which gather nectar from the flowers and, in the process, pollinate them.

Spiked speedwell

Resistant to grazing, wild spiked speedwell is dependent upon rabbits or sheep to reduce competition from other plants by eating their foliage. Following the outbreak of myxomatosis in the 1950s, rabbit populations declined dramatically and the spiked speedwell died out in many areas.

Fortunately, its spikes of intense blue-violet flowers, which bloom from June to July, had already caught the interest of gardeners, and it is widely cultivated.

► Wild spiked speedwell, now scarce, is still found in western Britain, and a rare subspecies grows in East Anglia. It responds well to cultivation, however, and tolerates a variety of soil types.

Meadow crane's-bill

The common name of this wild geranium is derived from its long, narrow seed pods, which are said to resemble the head and beak of a crane. Many different kinds of crane's-bill grow in the countryside, several of which do extremely well in the garden. Meadow crane's-bill is the most popular of these and, as its name implies, it grows wild in grassland throughout the British Isles.

The main attraction of meadow crane's-bill is its saucer-shaped flowers, which in garden varieties range in colour from violet-blue to sky blue and are laced with a network of delicate veins. The plant is attractive even when not in flower. It has deeply cut, hairy leaves that catch the dew, making the whole plant glisten in the sunlight of early morning.

◄ Growing to around 90cm (3ft) tall, meadow crane's-bill can be blown over by the wind and is best grown through a support of woven sticks. The foliage should be cut back to ground level in autumn, and the plants can be propagated by dividing them every few years in spring.

Lady's mantle

More than a dozen forms of lady's mantle occur in the wild, and they are very difficult to tell apart. Their loose spikes of tiny green-yellow flowers are produced in summer and, unusually, they are able to set seed without being pollinated, making the plants prolific.

In the garden they can be grown in full sun or partial shade. Their strong-veined, palmate leaves – that is, leaves with distinct sections – are much prized by flower arrangers. As with the crane's-bill, the fine hairs on each leaf trap beads of moisture on the surface, making them shine on a dewy morning.

► Lady's mantles are members of the rose family. They are a complex group of plants, all related to the popular garden variety that is usually known by its scientific name *Alchemilla mollis*.

◄ Columbines will grow in full sun or partial shade and after a few years may require dividing. The flowers are usually blue but may also be pink or white.

Columbine

A favourite in many gardens, the columbine has been extensively developed by horticulturists to produce a multitude of beautiful *Aquilegia* cultivars. Despite this, the attractive blue flowers of the wild native species have a great deal to offer the gardener, although it seeds freely and can be difficult to control.

Wild columbine grows in damp woodlands, marshes, fens and grassland, on chalky soils. Although by no means common, it can be found in many localities in Britain, as far north as north-east Scotland, and in much of Ireland. Some wild populations are likely to have arisen from garden escapes.

Great mullein

Conspicuous, woolly spikes of yellow flowers towering up to 2m (6ft 6in) high make this a popular plant for the back of the border. In the wild, it grows in rough grassland, on banks with hedges and along roadsides on warm, dry, sandy soils. In the garden, most well-drained soils suit it.

Commonly grown as a biennial, great mullein produces attractive, grey, downy leaves in the first year, followed by flowers and seeds in the next. It has also been used as the basis for several colourful hybrid varieties.

► Great mullein's foliage is often attacked by the large yellow-banded, black-spotted caterpillars of the mullein moth, which adds to its interest.

Red campion

The eye-catching red campion was highly regarded by horticulturists during the 16th and 17th centuries, but has fallen from favour of late. It is widespread throughout Britain in deciduous woodlands and hedgerows, on roadsides and on fertile, chalky soils, although it is less frequent in Norfolk, northern Scotland and Ireland.

Plants have rose-red, or sometimes pink or white, flowers with five deeply cleft petals and grow to almost 1m (39in) tall. Cultivated varieties can be propagated by taking cuttings from the base of the plants, or by sowing seeds thinly in open ground during spring.

► Red campion requires little attention apart from deadheading. In return, the plant produces flowers from April until November; in the far south-west it flowers from March and often continues into the winter.

Common meadow-rue

A member of the buttercup family, common meadow-rue grows in wet meadows, marshes, fens and stream sides in alkaline soils. It is common only in south-eastern and central England, as far north as the Lake District and South Yorkshire, and in central Ireland. Elsewhere it is rare.

The plant's greyish green foliage resembles that of Mediterranean rue, and its bright flowers consist mainly of yellow stamens because the pale yellow petals soon fall off. It was a firm favourite in Victorian herbaceous borders.

◄ For the best results in the garden, common meadow-rue should be grown in rich, moisture-retentive soil in light shade. The tall stems may need support during the summer months.

Cornflower

In the early 1900s, cornflowers were a familiar sight in fields of grain throughout the summer and the plant was regarded as a serious weed. However, after the 1920s they declined dramatically due to the use of new seed-cleaning techniques, and in the late 1970s the cornflower was declared a nationally scarce species.

In recent years, farm set-aside schemes, and the disturbance of dormant seed by road building, have led to its reappearance. In the garden it will grow up to 1m (39in) tall, but shorter varieties are available if more compact plants are required.

◄ The glorious blue cornflower was described in the 19th century as a 'destroying beauty' by the poet John Clare, because the plant was such a pernicious weed. Now it is recovering from near extinction.

Jacob's ladder

The name Jacob's ladder is derived from the regularly paired leaflets of this plant, which – with a little imagination – resemble the rungs of a ladder. They are said to lead to heaven, in reference to a passage in the book of Genesis. The native plant grows wild on the steep, grassy slopes of the Derbyshire and Yorkshire Dales, and at a single location in Northumberland. Plants growing wild elsewhere have almost certainly escaped from the garden.

Jacob's ladder has been grown in gardens for hundreds of years, selected for its delightful purplish blue, occasionally white, flowers with golden stamens. The flowers bloom between June and August and attract pollinating bees. With careful deadheading, however, the season can be extended. The plants grow 30–100cm (12–39in) tall, and in open, windy locations are best supported with sticks.

► A good garden site for Jacob's ladder has well-drained soil in sun or partial shade. Established clumps can be divided during autumn or spring. Alternatively, seeds can be sown in April for flowering the following year.

Sea holly

Various forms of sea holly, or eryngiums, have become very popular as garden plants, with their architectural spiky forms and powder blue flowers. The leaves of the maritime species, and varieties derived from them, are covered with a frosty or waxy coating that helps protect them from salt-laden winds. Despite looking rather thistle-like, eryngiums actually belong to the same large plant family as the carrot: the umbellifers.

As its name suggests, sea holly occurs naturally around the coast, especially on sand dunes, although it has almost disappeared from the north of England and Scotland. It grows to about 60cm (2ft) tall.

◄ All sea hollies need full sun to flower, and they are a good choice for drier gardens as they can tolerate drought. The clumps should be divided in spring. The roots of wild sea holly were once regarded as an aphrodisiac.

WILDLIFE WATCH

How can I grow summer wild flowers?

● Understanding how a plant grows in the wild is the key to success in the garden. For instance, when choosing a plant, match the plant to the soil type. Do not attempt to grow lime-loving plants in acidic, peaty soils, or acid-loving plants in chalky soils. They rarely perform well and usually die early.

If you want to grow plants that don't like your garden soil, use containers with the right type of soil. The pots can even be placed among other plants in the borders – but don't forget to water them.

● If the garden tends to be very dry during the summer months, select plants that can tolerate these conditions. Plants that grow naturally by the coast are often a good choice because many have a thick, protective leaf coating that prevents them from drying out.

Avoid plants from marshy, wet habitats unless you are prepared to water them throughout the summer, or are able to plant them in the wet, boggy margins of a garden pond.

● Never dig up plants from the wild. This defaces the countryside, is usually illegal, and cultivation is rarely successful.

Night-flying insects

On summer evenings, opening a window to let in the cool night air may also admit a host of small creatures that are attracted by the light – not just moths, but also beetles, crickets and an occasional lacewing.

Bright light attracts many airborne insects. This long-exposure photograph shows the tracks of a variety of flying insects as they dance around the light of a moth trap set up in a wild part of the garden.

On warm summer evenings, light shining through an open window or door, or an outside garden lamp, will attract hundreds of insects. Some, such as wasps, usually forage during the day and are probably fooled by strong light into behaving as though daybreak has arrived. Other species, such as caddis fly, are nocturnal creatures. Caddis fly larvae live in water, so gardens with ponds, or close to streams, attract the greatest numbers of these delicate insects.

Garden moths

Night-flying moths are commonly drawn to artificial lights and one theory for this is that they mistake the lights for navigational aids. When flying over dark open country, moths travel at a fixed angle to the moon, which ensures that they travel in a straight line. Along with most other night-flying insects, moths have compound eyes that make them very sensitive to changes in orientation. They respond to artificial light in the same way as they do to the moon, but the light is so close that they end up spiralling around it. The fact that more moths are attracted to artificial light on overcast, moonless nights seems to corroborate this theory.

One of the insects most often drawn to artificial light is the buff arches moth. A woodland species, it lives in areas where there is plenty of bramble scrub, because this is the foodplant of its caterpillar, but it also occurs in parkland and is often enticed to the lights of nearby houses. Beautiful arched buff and white markings on the forewings give the moth its name. These markings are visible even when it is at rest with its wings folded.

Outside lights attract many other species, including the green silver-lines moth and the lime-speck pug moth, which often remain in the vicinity until dawn. Individuals may tire and come to rest on garden walls and foliage in the course of the night, allowing close inspection with a torch. They are not easy to spot because they are extremely well camouflaged to avoid being seen by hungry birds during the day. The green silver-lines moth, for example, has wing markings resembling leaf veins and rests on a leaf of similar colour, aligning the markings on its wings to match the leaf.

Examining walls and tree trunks at first light often reveals a number of moths at rest.

◀ A dark patch on the front of each forewing, which can sometimes be faint, distinguishes the lime-speck pug moth from its close relatives. It occurs in mature gardens from June to September.

◀ From May to July, the green silver-lines moth is on the wing. It is common in gardens, since its larval foodplants include a wide range of trees and shrubs.

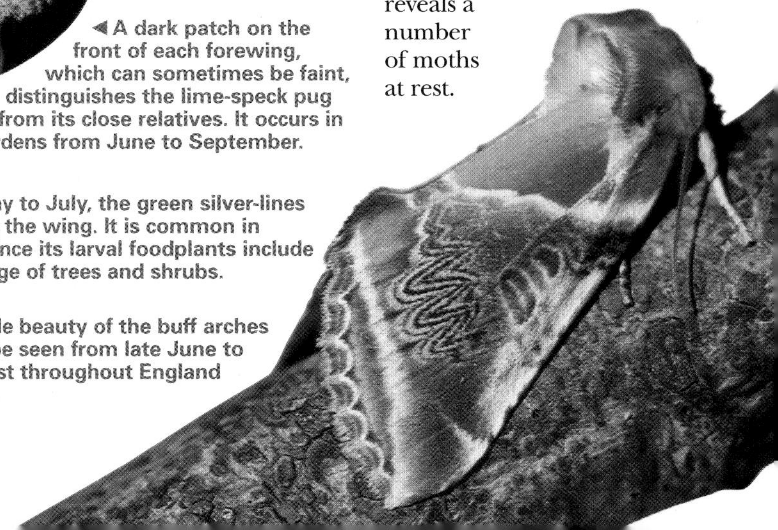

▶ The subtle beauty of the buff arches moth can be seen from late June to early August throughout England and Wales.

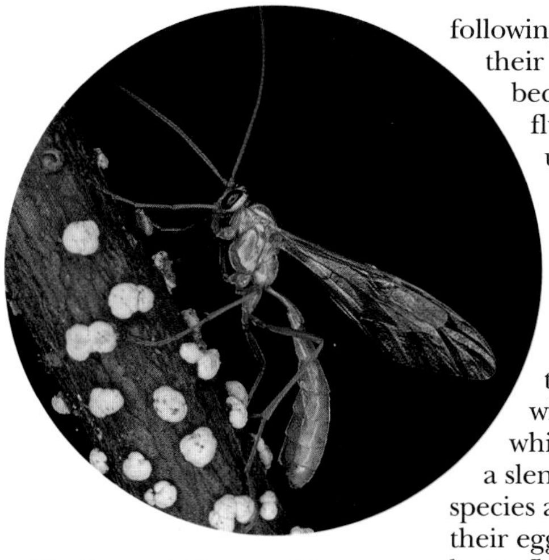
The tiny waist is one of the characteristics that shows the ichneumon fly is actually a type of wasp. Adults feed on nectar.

The larger ones soon fly off and may fall prey to early rising insectivorous birds, but smaller, less conspicuous moths may remain until the heat of the sun drives them under cover. One of these little moths, the lime-speck pug moth, can be seen all over the country from June to early September. At first glance it could be mistaken for a splash of white paint or a bird dropping – a deception that fools many of its potential predators.

Delicate lacewing
Many different species of lacewing are attracted to open, illuminated windows, especially as summer gives way to early autumn.

Some, notably the green lacewing, stay indoors throughout the winter, tucked away in quiet corners in a state of torpor, with their oval, transparent wings held in a tent-like manner over the body. Their colour changes to a pinkish brown, but as the weather improves the following spring, they regain their green colour and become active again, fluttering around lamps, usually in a bedroom.

Ichneumon fly
Although it is known as a fly, the ichneumon is actually a solitary wasp. It has two pairs of functional wings (unlike true flies, which have one pair) and a slender 'wasp waist'. Many species are parasitic, laying their eggs on moth or butterfly caterpillars so that when the grubs hatch they have a ready food supply, eating the caterpillars alive.

Ichneumon flies are often to be seen attacking their victims by day, but little is known about their habits after dark. It seems likely that some species may actively search for caterpillars during the night and are lured to light in the same way as moths.

The cockchafer is unusually 'furry' for a beetle, and has fan-like antennae. It must spread its tough wing cases before unfolding its wings to take off.

Robust cockchafer
A cockchafer crashing against a lighted window makes such a clatter with its hardened wing cases that people of a nervous disposition might think that intruders are trying to gain access to the house. This large beetle makes a loud droning sound in flight, and is on the wing from late May to early July, which accounts for its country names of 'May bug' and 'June bug'.

Cockchafers are widespread garden insects, and their root-eating grubs are often found in garden beds. Despite their rather alarming appearance and noisy behaviour, the adults are entirely harmless to humans, although they can damage garden plants by eating their leaves.

Oak bush cricket
Bush crickets are not known for their powers of flight, and are mainly insects of low herbage. The oak bush cricket, however, lives in trees. Both sexes are fully winged and capable of weak but sustained flight over short distances. Not much is known about its nocturnal habits, but it is clearly active after dark because it often visits lighted windows, and may be found resting on a bedroom ceiling in the morning.

At first glance, this delicate-looking insect could be mistaken for a stout green lacewing, but a closer look reveals its long, slender legs, particularly the hind pair, and the extremely long, whip-like antennae that distinguish bush crickets from grasshoppers. The female has a long, dagger-like egg-laying organ (ovipositor), which she uses to insert her eggs into crevices.

▲ Often active by night, the oak bush cricket's delicate green coloration is seen to best advantage by daylight. The long ovipositor of this individual, extending like a tail from the end of its body, shows that it is a female.

◀ With a fluttery flight that is not very powerful, the lacewing is seldom on the wing for long and takes frequent rests on wayside vegetation.

WILDLIFE WATCH

How can I see night-flying insects?

- Place a bright light on a long lead in the garden (making sure the wiring is safe for external use), preferably close to a white sheet suspended from a washing line.
- Moths and other insects will not stay long, so you need to sit alongside the light to observe them. Equip yourself with a good identification guide.
- Most night-flying insects respond strongly to ultraviolet light, which is beyond the range of human vision. A proper moth trap exploits this by incorporating a mercury vapour lamp, which produces a high proportion of ultraviolet light.

Wildlife in a churchyard

Country churchyards offer a peaceful, undisturbed home to a rich variety of native plants and animals, some of which are rarely found in the open countryside.

Churchyards have always been sanctuaries, havens of tranquillity isolated from the everyday bustle beyond the churchyard wall. Many have been used as burial grounds for over a thousand years, and may still inspire a sense of timelessness in a world that has changed beyond recognition over the past century.

The peaceful environs of a country churchyard provide a refuge for wildlife that has become threatened in the surrounding landscape. Such a churchyard is at its most magical in early summer, especially in the early morning when the air is clean and fresh and the dew is still lying thickly on the grass.

Although the day has hardly begun, nesting tits will already be hard at work, perhaps feeding along a boundary hedge, picking small insects from the buds. Beneath the hedge, a blackbird may be noisily shuffling last autumn's dead leaves in search of worms, insect grubs and other morsels.

Flower-rich turf

Among the eye-catching sights may be a show of cowslips, their nodding flower heads a reminder of the flower-strewn ancient pasture that was once commonplace in the countryside. Such pasture was a product of centuries of grazing, and some country churchyards may still be grazed periodically by sheep rather than mown.

If the turf has never been stripped and replanted, it may harbour more than a hundred different species of wild flower, which will produce a glorious succession of colour as the seasons pass. The earliest to appear are the snowdrop and yellow winter aconite, followed by butter-yellow lesser celandine, which can carpet sheltered corners in spring. Some churchyards are havens for the wild daffodil, also known as the 'Lenten lily', the flowers of which are far more delicate than the blooms of most cultivated varieties.

As spring turns to summer there is a subtle change from yellows to purples and blues, as plants such as the bugle,

From lichens to trees, and from ants to foxes, churchyards are often brimming with wildlife.

MEADOW SAXIFRAGE

One delicate little flower that seems to have a special affinity with churchyards, particularly in East Anglia, is the meadow saxifrage. It has vanished from much of the countryside, but often thrives in the dry, well-drained soils of churchyards. In some regions this is now almost its only habitat.

Look out for the glossy green, kidney-shaped, lobed leaves that form rosettes among the grasses. In May, flowering shoots push up to about 40cm (16in) tall to produce clusters of beautiful white flowers with tiny yellow-tipped stamens. They open fully in the sunshine, turning their heads towards the light.

speedwells and vetches come into flower. Later the deep purples of knapweeds and scabious may be seen. If the churchyard lies on chalk grassland, there may be wild thyme and marjoram, and even clumps of pale purplish common spotted or rose-pink pyramidal orchids. Southern churchyards are among the last refuges of the rare green-winged orchid, named for the green flanking lobes of its largely purple flowers, which appear in early summer.

Sadly, many churchyards have been over-tidied by regular mowing and the use of selective herbicides, turning once flower-rich swards into dense green carpets with all the appearance and interest of a lawn in an urban park.

However, some church wardens appreciate the value of the wildlife in their churchyards, and have introduced more sympathetic, wildlife-friendly mowing regimes based on the traditional hay-cutting routine. The custodians of some churchyards have even replanted the cowslips and primroses that were lost through over-zealous management in the past.

▲ The spotted flycatcher, a summer visitor, feeds by swooping from a perch to catch insects in flight, and then returning to its vantage point. Churchyards provide abundant prey, and plenty of tree or wall cavities in which to nest.

► Rough, grassy areas in churchyards attract the orange-tip butterfly. The only British butterfly with mottled underwings, it is common in early summer in England, and is spreading northwards to Scotland. The orange wing tips show this is a male.

► In midsummer the holly blue butterfly lays its eggs on the flowers of ivy and holly, which are common in churchyards.

▼ Holly bushes provide food for the holly blue's caterpillars in spring.

▲ The wood mouse is often found in churchyards, even in urban areas, but it does not normally enter buildings.

▲ After dark, bats swoop through the air, snatching flying insects and even taking spiders from the stone walls. By day, they may roost under the roof or in the tower, and some bats find that the cool recesses of churches and crypts make ideal hibernation sites in winter.

One of the special qualities of an old churchyard is the variety of lichens that encrust the surfaces of gravestones, monuments and the church itself. Some churchyards may have over 100 different species of lichen growing in them.

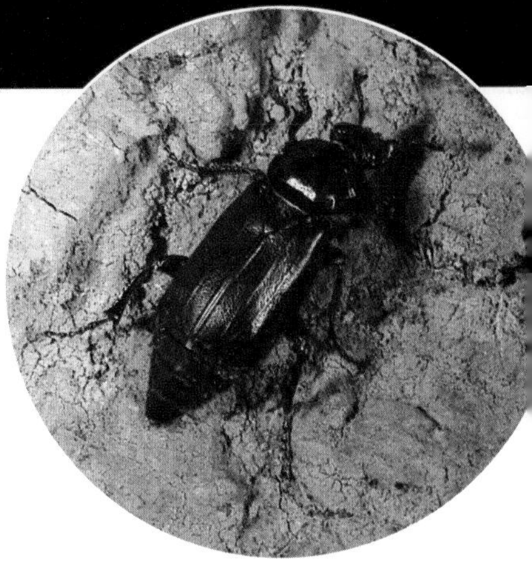

► This species of burying beetle is all black apart from the orange tips to its antennae.

Insect activity

As the day begins to warm up, the wealth of flowers attracts an increasingly active range of insects. Often the first to be seen are bumblebees, buzzing from flower to flower to gather pollen and nectar. Later the first butterflies appear, resting in sheltered glades where they can perch with their wings open to absorb the full warmth of the sun.

Two butterflies are especially associated with churchyards, suburban parks and gardens in spring and summer – the holly blue and the orange-tip. The delightful holly blue has bright, sky-blue upper wing surfaces and paler, silvery blue underwings. Holly is the spring foodplant of its caterpillars, but it also lays eggs on ivy in summer. In some years holly blues can be very numerous. These years alternate with population crashes caused by a variety of factors, including climatic fluctuations and the activities of a parasitic wasp, the grubs of which eat the holly blue's caterpillars.

The orange-tip butterfly is often seen in churchyards. The main foodplants of its caterpillar are cuckoo flower (or lady's smock) and hedge garlic (or garlic mustard). The cuckoo flower grows in damper grass, and is so named because it flowers at around the time the first cuckoos arrive in spring. Orange-tips can often be seen feeding at its pale to deep lilac-pink flowers. Only the male has bright orange tips on its wings. The female's are dark grey. However, both have exquisite mottled green-and-white underwings, which help to conceal them from predatory birds.

Churchyard birds

The usual wide range of buildings, sheltered walls, trees and shrubs in a churchyard provides many places for birds to nest and all the vegetation ensures a plentiful supply of caterpillars and other insects for the parents of hungry nestlings. As well as blackbirds, robins, great tits and blue tits, churchyards are ideal for the song thrush. This familiar yet declining bird is particularly fond of snails, and damp corners make perfect hunting grounds. Furthermore, the hard kerb stones of the graves are just right for smashing the shells of the snails to expose their juicy insides.

In winter, the berries of evergreen yews and hollies are an important source of food for thrushes, including winter-visiting fieldfares and redwings from northern Europe.

Another bird that often frequents churchyards is the spotted flycatcher, although in recent years this summer visitor to Britain has returned from its African wintering grounds in ever-decreasing numbers. It is not brightly coloured but has a distinctive, very upright stance as it sits on its favourite perch, watching for a passing insect. When it spots a fly, it darts out and snatches it in mid-air, either for itself or its young.

Swifts may nest up under the church eaves, selecting high places so that they can swoop out of their nesting cavities. On warm, clear days swifts tend to feed high in the air, gathering small flying insects as they circle slowly through the summer sky. On July evenings, however, the churchyard may echo to their wild, screaming cries as they swoop low overhead at high speed. Unlike swallows and martins, swifts leave early for their winter home in Africa. Most of them have gone by mid-August.

Emerging beetles

As the swifts career through the evening twilight, they are joined by other animals that emerge only after sunset. In May, these include the cockchafer, or May (or June) bug – a large beetle that spends most of its life as a burrowing grub feeding on grass roots. Its emergence as a flying adult marks the start of the short and dangerous final phase of its life, when it must

▲ **The brightly patterned sexton beetle is just one of the great diversity of insect species found in sympathetically managed churchyards. The insects provide prey for small birds, which in turn attract larger predators, such as hawks.**

CHURCHYARD YEWS

Many churchyards contain yew trees, some of which are extremely old. A yew at Fortinghall in Perthshire, for example, is thought to be around 3000 years old and the oldest living tree in Europe. In 1769 its girth was measured at nearly 16m (52ft), and by then it was already hollow and fragmented. The hollow in the trunk was so large that church processions reputedly passed through it.

No-one is quite sure why yews are so often found in churchyards. It appears that some of the trees pre-date the churches themselves, perhaps being associated with former pagan burial grounds – the evergreen nature of the trees, and their long lifespan, may have made them a symbol of everlasting life.

A more prosaic explanation is that they were grown to provide bows for archers, and planted in churchyards to keep them away from the village livestock.

▼ **The bright red berries of the yew are not actually poisonous, but the seeds contained within them certainly are, and so are the tree's leaves and bark.**

▼ **A yew tree, with its gnarled trunk and sweeping branches of deep green leaves, is a traditional sight in the churchyard.**

find a mate and breed. Many other beetles, including the spectacular stag beetle, have equally short adult lives, dying soon after laying their eggs.

The aptly named sexton and burying beetles live rather longer as adults. Burying beetles have an acute sense of smell and can detect the carcass of a small bird or mammal from some distance away. A pair of beetles 'bury' it by digging underneath the body so it sinks into the earth. The female lays her eggs on it and – unusually for an insect – she waits for the grubs to hatch and watches over them, even helping them to feed on the carcass.

Another beetle lurks in the gloom of the crypt – the churchyard (or cellar) beetle. This flightless, nocturnal insect is found in the coldest, dampest places underground, where it looks for vegetable scraps on which to feed.

Night hunters

The buzz of the night-flying cockchafer and other insects does not go unnoticed by a group of animals that famously haunts churchyards – bats. The combination of sheltered hunting grounds and numerous crevices for daytime roosting makes a churchyard ideal bat territory. They are more likely to be found in the church eaves than hanging in a draughty belfry. The most common species are the tiny pipistrelle, which flies at about the height of the eaves, and the long-eared bat, which prefers to hunt between the branches of trees.

In the dead of night, one more churchyard denizen is on the wing – the barn owl. Church towers used to be important nesting sites for barn owls, and their ghostly flight and eerie screeching and hissing calls probably gave rise to many stories of churchyard hauntings.

Where tower windows are screened off to deter jackdaws and pigeons, barn owls are kept out, too, but bell towers still provide places where owls can nest. From the towers they swoop low over the gravestones to catch mice and voles. They favour the more open parts of the churchyard with longer grass, because this is where rodents feed. The owls' acute hearing allows them to hunt in what seems to be complete darkness – they can pick up the faintest rustles and squeaks to locate their prey in the gloom.

Urban woodland

Within towns and cities, stretches of shady woods provide shelter for all manner of wildlife. Some individuals stray into nearby gardens while others move from garden to woodland, creating a glorious diversity of animal and plant life.

Hidden behind houses and factories, away from the noise and activity of the city, lie acres of urban woodland. Some of these green retreats have been deliberately planted as part of amenity parkland, but others are the survivors of former landscapes, fragments of ancient woodland that, in season, are bright with wild flowers, such as the bluebell and wood anemone. These old places are inhabited by a surprising assortment of wildlife, and nearby town dwellers benefit from the proximity of such secret havens as butterflies, birds and mammals such as hedgehogs venture from their wooded sanctuaries into local gardens to feed.

Urban woodlands are often dominated by the same trees and shrubs as their rural counterparts, but are subject to rather different pressures. Wild deer and rabbits are often displaced by children, dogs and cats, and without the deer and rabbits browsing and nibbling, brambles and other shrubs can grow unchecked, crowding out all but the most persistent herbs. Despite this, wood avens, red campion and herb-robert often grow in scattered patches to add colour and pattern in between the thorny tendrils.

Bramble feast

In sunny clearings, bramble blossoms – which vary from a deep rosy pink to snow white – attract a variety of nectar-hungry insects. Tiny glossy pollen beetles share this larder with the speckled wood, one of the butterflies that relishes the sun-dappled shade.

The wood mouse is one of the most common small mammals living in urban woodland. Unlike the house mouse it never becomes a domestic pest, although it occasionally finds its way into garden sheds and gnaws plants stored for winter.

Rarely seen in open gardens, this woodland species has checkered, creamy yellow markings on a brown background, making it distinctive, if somewhat modest when compared to colourful garden butterflies such as the peacock.

The speckled wood butterfly may be seen throughout the spring and summer, when a succession of short-lived 'generations' rest in sunny spots. It can be an aggressive butterfly, often engaging in aerial fights over territory. Rivals spiral upwards to the canopy until one emerges as the victor and chases off the challenger, then returns to reclaim a favoured resting spot on the bramble leaves.

Ivy sanctuary

Ivy may gain a dominating hold on the woodland floor in small roadside copses, where its evergreen tangles provide shelter for frogs and mice. The dark, glossy green foliage covers the trunks of trees in a thick layer of stems and leaves, providing the support required for the diminutive wren to construct its hidden domed nest. Remarkably tolerant of urban life, the wren goes about its business unconcerned by human trespassers, although prowling cats may cause agitation. When the male's powerful song of whirring trills explodes from the undergrowth, it is hard to believe that such a tiny bird can make such a loud noise.

If nearby householders put up bird or bat boxes to encourage wildlife into the garden, it is not always the intended occupants that take up residence. Unless tit boxes have been equipped with metal plates around the entrance holes there will always be the risk of squatters and thieves breaking in. These include other small birds, such as sparrows, which nest in the boxes, and grey squirrels and great spotted woodpeckers, which may raid the nestboxes for eggs and nestlings.

Nocturnal moths

Many moth caterpillars feed on the leaves of common woodland trees and shrubs such as oak, hazel, sallow and bramble, and this enables a

Wrens find food and sheltered places to nest in the dense undergrowth of urban woodland, and often visit neighbouring gardens to feed.

Despite the close proximity of human life, urban woodlands are a microcosm of the natural world, sheltering a complex community of interdependent species.

Honeysuckle frequently grows in woodland, where it attracts bumblebees and a variety of night-flying moths.

Hedgehogs leave their woodland refuges at night to follow surprisingly consistent routes around local gardens.

wide diversity of moth species to inhabit urban woods. Being mainly nocturnal, most will pass their lives unnoticed by humans unless the adult moths appear after dark, fluttering around nearby street lights, or against lighted windows. The night-flying swallowtailed moth, for instance, is not often seen, although it is much more common than the rare butterfly of the same name. The familiar brimstone butterfly also has a nocturnal namesake, which may visit nearby gardens after sunset.

Adult moths are sometimes regarded as the dull cousins of colourful butterflies, but this is not always so. The colours and patterns of the garden tiger moth and burnet moth are just as dazzling as those of their daytime relatives, and many common moth species – such as the buff arches, peach blossom and light emerald – have a subtle beauty of their own.

Canopy life

Much of the activity in any woodland goes unnoticed because it takes place high in the canopy. Clouds of flies swarm around the branches, and flying ants induce clumsy fly-catching attempts by starlings, chaffinches, house sparrows and even great spotted woodpeckers. Tiny caterpillars abseil down from oak leaves on silken threads, and oak bush crickets stalk about the foliage, seemingly reluctant to use their powerful hind legs to leap. The oak bush cricket has a delicate air about it, and is often knocked to the ground by high winds or a summer rainstorm.

Woodland floor

All manner of litter reaches the woodland floor. Natural debris rains down constantly, topping up the leaf fall of autumn with a steady supply of catkins, seeds, berries, twigs, honeydew excreted by aphids, the droppings of insects, birds and squirrels, and the dead bodies of insects and other small animals. Garden refuse and other detritus that finds its way into urban woodland add to the assortment that is constantly decomposing on the woodland floor, aided by fungi, millipedes, springtails, insect grubs, worms, slugs and a teeming population of soil bacteria.

The larger organisms attract hunters including rove beetles, violet ground beetles, frogs and toads, as well as a variety of ground-hunting birds, such as blackbirds, that toss aside beakfuls of leaves to expose worms and grubs. The noisy rustling and scuffling of a feeding blackbird often gives away its position, and at night the activities of foraging hedgehogs may be indicated in the same way.

INTRODUCED PLANTS

▲ Snowdrops growing wild often have an uncertain origin as garden escapes are frequently naturalised.

◀ The familiar but alien sycamore tree sets seed easily, often dominating urban woodland.

Sometimes garden plants invade nearby woodlands. Trailing runners of variegated yellow archangel, periwinkle or Russian vine sneak through back fences to become established among the wild trees.

The resulting botanical diversity can create a glorious riot of flowers throughout the year, but it can also lead to confusion over the true origin of the woodland plants. Ancient survivors, such as bluebells and primroses, may be joined by plants such as Solomon's-seal or lily-of-the-valley – species that could be natural relics from the past or may have spread from discarded garden debris. Many snowdrops were probably introduced in this way. Most garden escapes are not native plants, and although they may offer cover to wood mice or perhaps food for less choosy insects, the natural woodland plants support a much greater diversity of native wildlife.

Assortments of native and introduced trees and shrubs have become so common that many people are not aware of some species' foreign origins. Aliens include the horse chestnut, with its big compound leaves and spiny fruits, and the sycamore with its winged seeds. These can germinate in their thousands to form thickets among the native oaks, ashes, beeches and alders.

All these trees harbour countless aphids, which provide food for small songbirds and their young. Far less welcome are thickets of rhododendron and bamboo, which can come to dominate urban woodland. Conservationists spend a lot of time trying to eliminate these invasive plants.

▶ Purple honesty was introduced from Europe as a garden plant, but it often escapes from gardens into urban woodland.

▲ **The adaptable great spotted woodpecker often breeds in urban woodland, claiming its territory by drumming loudly against a dead branch or tree trunk.**

► **Black with an iridescent purple sheen on its wing cases, the violet ground beetle commonly lives under logs and stones in urban woods and parks.**

Eventually all the organic debris is recycled, whether it be a layer of fallen leaves, the body of a dead bird or a stack of dumped newspapers. More durable rubbish is another matter. Plastic packaging, metal cans and glass bottles can survive indefinitely. Opportunistic shrews and wood mice searching for food and shelter cannot resist exploring inside discarded bottles, often with fatal consequences if they become trapped inside. Half-emptied beer cans frequently lure slugs to their doom, and may become choked with their decomposing remains.

Woodland smells

In July the creamy flower spikes of sweet chestnut trees fill the air with a heady, if somewhat sickly sweet aroma. A closer look at the chestnut 'catkins' may reveal an army of tiny black beetles and hover flies that have been attracted by the smell. When the chestnuts appear they are soon discovered by squirrels, which also favour the leafy twigs of the sweet chestnut as sites for their nests, or dreys.

Another pungent woodland smell comes from the stinkhorn, a well-named fungus that has an aroma rather like rotten meat. At first, the stinkhorn resembles a large leathery 'egg', half buried in the leaf mould. The 'egg' hatches into a sturdy hollow white stalk, capped with a dark, grey-green, smelly slime that contains the spores. The putrid smell attracts flies which clamber all around the top, hoping to find food or a site for laying their eggs. In the process they pick up the slime on their feet and carry it away, spreading the spores.

More pleasing to the nose is the summer honeysuckle, the woody stems of which entwine the multi-stemmed hazel sprouting from old coppice stumps. The honeysuckle can cause spiral distortions in the hazel, which woodland craftsmen often highlight in decorative walking sticks.

Evening light

Swifts and pipistrelle bats are not the most obvious beneficiaries of urban woods, but both feed on the aerial insects that thrive in the canopy. Both species have learned to make the most of urban habitats, rearing their young in the roofs and eaves of houses. From May to early August flocks of noisy swifts chase over the treetops at dusk before relinquishing the sky to the bats, which swoop and flutter along the woodland edge.

Early summer evenings are also a good time to watch the circling song flight of the greenfinch, while the rich voice of the song thrush, with its characteristic repeated phrases, rings from many urban copses. Despite declining numbers this most musical of urban choristers is still widespread.

A grey squirrel will sometimes customise a bird nestbox for its own purposes. Squirrels may also break into occupied nestboxes to eat the eggs and nestlings, unless the boxes are made of extra tough material.

Leaf litter on the woodland floor makes a perfect moist habitat for garden snails, which range far more widely than their name would suggest.

WILDLIFE WATCH

How can I learn more about urban woodland?

- Try to unravel the origins of the trees and shrubs. Some will be non-native species, colonised from nearby garden or street plants.
- Urban woods are very attractive to passing migrant birds in spring. Listen to the dawn chorus in May, and try to notice if there are species present that never appear in nearby gardens.
- Dead and hollow trees are important breeding sites for woodland wildlife, but are often removed from urban woods for safety reasons. Nestboxes installed in nearby private gardens benefit woodland species.
- Many new urban developments have spread over the sites of existing badger setts. These will be found in remnant patches of woodland, and since the badgers are used to the presence of people they may sometimes be seen at dusk.
- Many urban woods have an associated 'Friends' group and information about it may be found in the local library. Otherwise, contact the local authority parks department, or the local wildlife trust via The Wildlife Trusts, The Kiln, Waterside, Mather Road, Newark NG24 1WT (telephone 01636 677711) www.wildlifetrusts.org

Photographing wildlife

Gardens and local parks come alive with wildlife in summer, offering the photographer some superb opportunities. With patience, skill and the right equipment, images of wildlife ranging from tiny insects to elusive mammals can be obtained.

The parks, gardens and other open spaces in cities and towns can provide excellent opportunities for photographing wildlife. Many of the larger, wilder parks act as unofficial nature reserves for native plants and animals. Even highly managed town gardens and small churchyards provide food and shelter for a variety of birds and mammals. These are nearly always tamer and more approachable than their less urban relatives, because they are used to people and have never been persecuted. Many may seem almost too familiar, but taking good photographs of species such as the robin or the grey squirrel is an excellent first step for anyone hoping to photograph wilder, more elusive animals.

A wild flower walk is a feast for the senses in more ways than one. Not only does it look glorious, but the scents may be irresistible to wildlife, as are the nectar and seeds, providing many subjects for the camera.

Summer flowers

The best subjects to start with are native plants and the insects that visit them. Plants do not fly or run away, so they offer unlimited opportunities for experimenting with lighting conditions, lenses, angles and settings. With a little imagination, common summer flowers such as ox-eye daisies can make spectacular photographs. Don't get too carried away, however, and trample or weed out the surrounding vegetation in a quest for the perfect shot. As with all forms of nature photography, it is essential to respect the wildlife, and avoid any disturbance that could compromise its survival, however common it seems to be.

Nectar-rich flowers are like magnets to butterflies such as this painted lady. For the best butterfly photographs, search early in the morning, when the insects are still slightly sluggish.

Good flower photographs can be obtained with standard photographic equipment, but using a camera support, such as a tripod or a monopod, will help achieve sharper images by eliminating camera shake. A support also encourages a more considered approach that helps with framing a shot.

Photogenic insects

Many of the native and exotic plants found in parks attract spiders and other insects. Not as wary as birds and mammals, they make fairly cooperative subjects for photography and are also highly photogenic, combining bright colours with startling body forms.

The most eye-catching are the butterflies that take nectar from plants such as lavender, michaelmas daisy, verbena, ice

◀ The spectacular elephant hawk-moth invariably makes a good picture. Search for nectar-feeding adults alighting on fuchsia and evening primrose on June evenings. The caterpillars feed on fuchsia and honeysuckle.

▲ Avoid camera shake by using a solid object, such as a sundial, as a temporary camera support. Placing a bean bag beneath the camera will protect it and allow small adjustments to be made easily to the camera angle.

plant and buddleia, but grasshoppers, beetles and spiders make interesting subjects, too. A bed of stinging nettles may harbour a brood of caterpillars – most probably those of peacock or small tortoiseshell butterflies – and on summer evenings fragrant flowers such as honeysuckle attract a variety of moths.

The problem with insect photography is getting close enough. Most camera lenses will not focus on subjects less than an arm's length away, so a supplementary close-up lens or a special close-focusing 'macro' lens is essential. Focusing is still difficult, however, because at such close ranges the margin for error is very small, especially if a wide aperture is used. Flash can be useful here, since it both 'freezes' any movement and permits the use of a smaller aperture. The flashlight also adds sparkle to the glossy bodies of insects.

A macro lens with a longer focal length – or a zoom lens with a macro setting – is often better for photographing butterflies because it permits a greater working distance, reducing the risk of scaring them off.

With a high-resolution digital camera, it may be preferable to photograph the subject from farther away, and crop the picture as necessary on a computer.

THE RIGHT EQUIPMENT

Both film and digital cameras are available in two basic types: lightweight compacts, and the bigger, heavier single lens reflex, or SLR cameras. It is possible to achieve good results with either, but an SLR makes most types of wildlife photography much easier.

SLR cameras allow the user to see exactly what is being photographed, and which parts of the subject are in focus. They can also give much greater control over focus and exposure, with manual settings that enable the automatic functions to be overridden for special conditions. Digital SLRs also respond instantly when the button is pressed, but many digital compacts suffer from a slight delay in response, which can make photographing animals very difficult.

An SLR can be fitted with different lenses, including macro lenses for high-quality close-up work, and powerful telephoto lenses for capturing good images of birds. Many zoom lenses have a useful macro setting, and may be powerful enough to target a birdfeeder. Some cameras are equipped with zoom lenses as standard, and many digital SLRs have zoom lenses that cover a wide optical range.

A tripod is vital for long-range work using a telephoto lens or long zoom. Attempting to hand-hold the camera in such circumstances nearly always results in camera shake, giving blurred pictures. A monopod may be useful at shorter range, but only for relatively static targets. For animals that move around rapidly, such as butterflies, a hand-held camera is the only option. Using flash can help.

With a film camera, first decide between print or slide film. For a talk to a local natural history society, for example, slides are essential. Then there is the question of film speed. The higher the speed, the more sensitive the film is to light, so it works with shorter exposures that are less vulnerable to camera shake. Unfortunately, the image is also more 'grainy' and less detailed. For mainly flash photography, or when using a tripod, try slow film, denoted by an ISO number of 25 to 100. For hand-held shots, 100, 200 and 400 ISO films may be better. Try a variety of film speeds to see which ones work best in different situations. Digital cameras do not have this problem, but those with fewer than 3 million pixels may also give poor 'grainy' results, especially if the image is cropped or 'digitally zoomed'. Most digital SLRs employ 5 million pixels or more, which allows some cropping with no significant loss of image quality.

Professional photographers often use very heavy tripods to eliminate camera shake. A lighter tripod can be made more stable by hanging a heavy bag from the centre column.

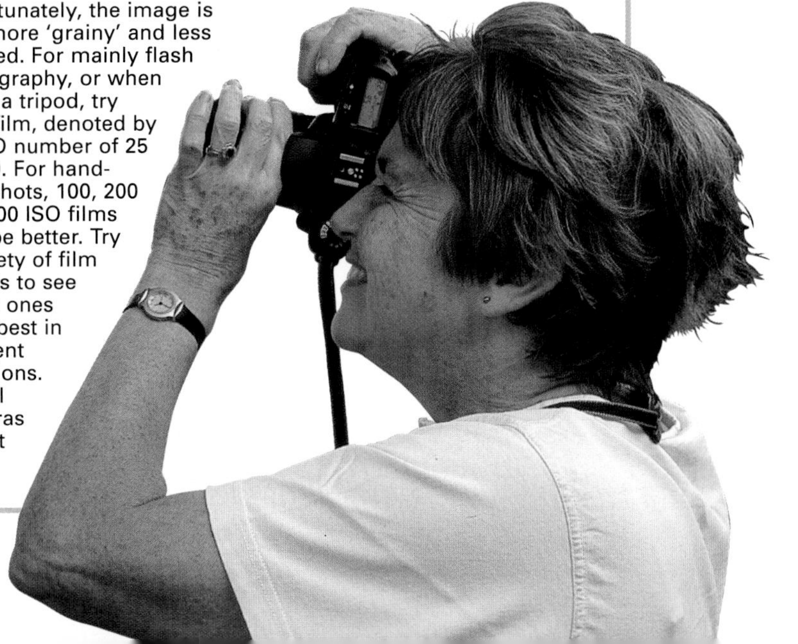

An SLR camera gives complete control over focus, allowing the subject to be isolated from its background for more impact.

Pond life

A pond often provides a rich source of subjects for photography, including dragonflies, pond skaters, frogs and toads, as well as the plants they live on and among.

Photographing frogs takes patience, because sudden movements are likely to make them dive underwater. It may be some time before a pair of eyes breaks the surface again, but this in itself can make a good picture. As with insects such as butterflies, the exercise provides good training in stealth and precise focusing.

Photo-essays

Common frogs provide great scope for making a photo-essay of a single species. The sequence could include a male calling with an inflated vocal sac, mating males and females with spawn, close-ups of the spawn, shots of tadpoles feeding and their different stages of metamorphosis into young froglets.

The hatching of a dragonfly can also make a wonderful close-up photo sequence. Early in the morning or late in the day, when it is not too warm, dragonfly nymphs emerge from the water by crawling up the stems of pond plants. As the outer skin of the nymph splits open, the adult begins to emerge. At first the wings are crumpled, but gradually they expand to their full size and dry out, allowing the insect to fly off. In order to take the entire series at the same scale, remember not to fill the first frame with the nymph. This will allow plenty of room for the complete dragonfly.

Caught on camera in the first frame of a photo-essay, a dragonfly begins its dramatic emergence by hauling itself free of its wingless nymphal skin after crawling out of a pond.

Perched on its empty skin, the newly emerged adult dragonfly is at first flightless and completely vulnerable. Its wings are still folded up, and its body is soft.

The wings expand and stiffen as blood is pumped into them. The whole process can take an hour or more, so a solid camera support and plenty of patience are very important.

Getting close to the subject can involve some contortions, and often has to be carried out in slow motion to avoid scaring the creature away.

BE PREPARED!

Photographing any wildlife can be frustrating if you run out of film or digital card memory. Carry a spare film or card ready for instant use.

Birds and mammals

Parks often have ponds or lakes populated by a wide variety of both native and exotic ducks, geese and other waterfowl. Fish in the pond may also attract herons.

Some of the tamer birds may come close enough to be photographed with a medium-length telephoto or zoom lens, which will not need a support if the light is good. For the best pictures, however, a lens with a focal length of 300mm or more (on a 35mm camera) or its digital equivalent is best. A tripod may be necessary to support it, but a shoulder stock can be adequate in good light. Use close-ups to cut out the artifical surroundings, and remember that ornamental wildfowl often have their flight feathers clipped on one side to stop them flying away.

Parks are also inhabited by a variety of smaller birds such as tits, finches and thrushes.

Hedgehogs are most active at night or twilight when flash lighting is essential. Some hedgehogs react to the bright light by rolling into a ball.

BIRDFEEDERS

◀ A birdfeeder will attract birds to within camera range, but a telephoto lens is often essential if the bird is to fill more than a fraction of the frame.

▲ Taking good photographs of birds is often a matter of patience, so a comfortable position indoors can be a definite advantage.

▲ Squirrels are among the few wild mammals that are conspicuously active by day. They often raid birdfeeders, showing an ingenuity that can make an excellent subject for a photo-essay.

Providing food, putting up nestboxes, building a pond and growing flowers favoured by butterflies all help to attract wildlife to the garden. It is important to avoid the use of insecticides because they destroy the insect life that forms the food supply of insect-eating birds.

A birdfeeder will attract birds – especially in winter and spring, when other food sources are scarce – and make them easier to photograph using a tripod-mounted camera fitted with a telephoto lens. The camera can be focused on the feeder in advance, so when a bird comes to feed, simply pressing the shutter secures the shot. Using the house as a hide, sit in the shadows and aim the camera through a partly open window to avoid distortions in the window glass.

Think carefully about the positioning of a birdfeeder. Check whether it will be lit by the sun to provide good pictures, and pay attention to the background. If necessary a permanent object, such as a brightly painted gate, can be hidden by potted plants.

Hanging a feeder in a tree may also attract squirrels. However, if squirrels are scaring away the birds from a pole-mounted feeder, they can be deterred by covering the pole with a smooth plastic tube, or equipping it with a squirrel-proof conical baffle.

In some parks, such as Kew Gardens in London, these are very tame, but normally they are quite timid and are best photographed using a long telephoto lens. They are often attracted to picnic areas and outdoor restaurants, and can be photographed perched in nearby hedges and shrubs as they watch for the chance to pick up scraps.

Squirrels excepted, most wild mammals are nocturnal and elusive, so they are hard to photograph in parks where access is limited to daylight hours and it is rarely possible to use purpose-made hides. In large parks, however, deer can often be approached by car. A car makes an excellent hide, and a half-lowered window can be fitted with a bracket to support a camera with a long telephoto lens. Start as early as possible when the animals are active, and the morning light and lack of people may help to create some magical images.

Wild roe deer are becoming more common in suburban areas, and frequently come near buildings to feed. They are very shy, though, and a long telephoto lens will help to get the best photographs.

WILDLIFE WATCH

How can I learn more about wildlife photography?

- Most local authorities run evening courses in wildlife photography. They provide training on how to take good pictures, and offer plenty of advice on equipment. There may also be opportunities to buy second-hand specialist equipment.
- The Field Studies Council arranges nature photography courses around the country. The Council's telephone numbers are 01743 852100 or 0845 3454071, or write to the Field Studies Council Head Office, Montford Bridge, Preston Montford, Shrewsbury SY4 1HW. Alternatively, visit www.field-studies-council.org.
- Local natural history societies normally offer their members opportunities to attend talks, exhibitions and presentations by wildlife photographers, who are usually only too happy to talk about their work.
- The Royal Photographic Society can provide information about local photography groups. The Society has a dedicated nature photography group – telephone 0115 928 1050 or write to the Nature Group Secretary, Ravensdale Drive, Wollaton, Nottingham NG8 2SL, or visit the Royal Photographic Society website at www.rps.org.

A year in the life of Rutland Water

Situated in the heart of England, Rutland Water is one of the most important wildfowl sanctuaries in Europe, renowned for the sheer number and variety of waterbirds that visit its lagoons.

Rutland Water is among the top bird-watching sites in Britain. More than 250 species of birds have been recorded there since 1975. Its shallow lagoons and gently shelving banks attract large concentrations of wildfowl throughout the year. The large numbers are a sign of the reservoir's value for migrant wildfowl in particular, and in 1971 it was designated a Wetland of International Importance. It has statutory protection as a Special Protection Area (SPA) and is a Site of Special Scientific Interest (SSSI).

Open to the public all year round, Rutland Water is a delightful place to walk to feel closer to nature and is well worth a visit in any season. In early summer, however, it is quite possible to see more than a hundred different bird species in a single day.

Rutland Water is huge, with a shoreline 45km (28 miles) long. The western end is of most interest for birds. A 14km (9 mile) strip of land, encompassing 180 hectares (450 acres) and a variety of habitats, is protected by the Leicestershire and Rutland Wildlife Trust as two nature reserves – the Egleton and the Lyndon Reserves. The Egleton encompasses three large lagoons that act as a magnet for coots, swans and ducks. The dykes bordering the lagoons offer shelter and food, while the muddy margins attract a variety of waders throughout the year.

Approach of summer

As March gives way to April the thickets and woodlands surrounding the reservoir come alive with birdsong. Wrens, blackbirds, robins, chaffinches and a host of other small songbirds give voice from the hedgerows, aided and abetted by the first of the summer migrants, including chiffchaffs, broadcasting their repetitive two-note song. Willow warblers are abundant by mid-April, blackcaps sing with rich warbling notes from the dense scrub, and the first cuckoos are heard.

At the end of April, terns appear at the water. Most of these are common terns that have returned to breed on their purpose-built shingle

RETURN OF THE OSPREY

Migrant ospreys on passage to Africa often appear at Rutland Water in August. The reservoir makes an excellent hunting ground for these birds, inspiring an attempt to reintroduce the osprey to England as a breeding species. Until recently, all of Britain's breeding pairs nested in Scotland but in 1996 chicks from Scotland were brought to Rutland, artificially reared and then released, as part of a five-year relocation programme. In 2001 ospreys started breeding there successfully – the first time that the species had bred in England for 154 years. It is hoped that youngsters raised at Rutland will return to breed once they have matured.

Ospreys are at their most spectacular in summer, when the young birds are honing their fishing techniques. By September all the birds are on the wing to west Africa.

Throughout the summer, flocks of lapwing feed around the edges of the lagoons, exploding into the air if they feel threatened by a hunting sparrowhawk or peregrine.

islands and floating platforms. However, in poor weather, migrating black terns are forced to lose height and may arrive to sit out the rain until they can continue their journey to their breeding grounds in northern and eastern Europe.

As they hawk for flies over the water, the terns may be joined by migrant little gulls. These beautiful birds are masters of the air and a joy to watch as they feed. On the shoreline ringed plovers, dunlin and perhaps a few black-tailed godwits feed voraciously before continuing their journey north.

Breeding time

By May, most of the summer migrants that breed at Rutland Water have returned and are busy establishing territories. Whitethroats that have wintered in Africa emit their scratchy song from low scrub, often flying up in the air and parachuting down in display. Around the water's edge, resident birds that started breeding in March and April are well on their way to rearing a family. Great crested grebes sit on their floating nests among tangled vegetation, and mallards tend their clutches in secluded sites, attempting to avoid the notice of hungry foxes.

Along the margins, migrant waders probe the mud for food. These may include curlew sandpipers, knot and sanderlings – all species that are scarce inland but annual at Rutland. In the field, parties of yellow wagtails feed among the low vegetation before departing in noisy flocks.

By mid-June, the first returning autumn migrants appear. These are generally waders, one of which will be the spotted redshank, stopping off on its long flight

TREE SPARROW

By the end of May, most birds around the reservoir are busy rearing a family. Close to the bird-watching centre on the Egleton Reserve, tens of pairs of tree sparrows feed their young. The breeding colony here is one of Rutland's many success stories.

Across Britain, the tree sparrow has declined by 90 per cent over the past 30 years. This is thought to be mainly a result of changes in farming practice. However, thanks to a year-round feeding programme and the provision of nestboxes at Rutland, the tree sparrows are thriving, making it one of the best places in the country to see them.

The tree sparrow is a hole nester, and the many nestboxes that are provided for these birds at Rutland Water encourage large numbers to breed.

▲ By 1900 the ruff had vanished from Britain as a regular breeder, but it is now returning in small numbers. In winter small flocks of ruffs feed around the lake.

▼ A broad strip of land around the western end of the reservoir is maintained as two nature reserves, which may attract up to 23,500 waterfowl in a single day.

Many great crested grebes breed at Rutland Water. Their floating platforms of weed may be spotted anchored to the vegetation around the lagoons.

from its Scandinavian breeding grounds to its winter quarters further south. It is among the earliest autumn migrants because of its odd breeding behaviour. The female leaves the male to incubate and rear the family, so any spotted redshanks seen in June are likely to be female. This is also a good month to watch hobbies, as they visit the reservoir on warm summer evenings to catch dragonflies, their favourite prey.

In July wildfowl numbers begin to build as the birds start to fly south to escape the cold as summer comes to an end in their northern breeding grounds. They find plenty to eat at Rutland. Goldeneyes feed on zebra mussels, while coots and wigeon nibble at aquatic vegetation and graze the grassy banks. At their peak, the wigeon can number more than 4500 birds, and the air is full of the distinctive whistling calls of the colourful males.

Many waders, including passage migrants, drop in to feed on the muddy margins of the reservoir, and thousands of ducks arrive at this time to moult on the reserve, which offers a safe refuge from predators at a vulnerable time of their year. Shovelers, gadwall and tufted duck, the males of which are familiar in their striking breeding plumage, gather in rafts out on the lagoons looking uncharacteristically drab. By the time they have moulted into their usual finery, more wildfowl have begun to arrive.

August is one of the most exciting months, with different migrants appearing daily,

▲ The impressive emperor dragonfly, with its bright blue abdomen, is one of more than 15 dragonfly species that have been recorded at Rutland.

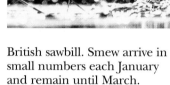

► Common terns catching fish for their young can be watched from lakeside hides during June and July. Rutland Water is famous for the number of migrant terns that stop off there.

including the spectacular osprey. By September, wildfowl are flooding in and coot numbers may exceed 3000.

In late October, winter visitors such as bramblings visit the feeding stations and join up with large, busy flocks of chaffinches to feed among the leaf litter in the adjoining woodlands.

Sawbills and swans

In early November the first goosanders appear. These elegant wildfowl belong to the sawbill family, named for the saw-like serrations on their bills. The birds use these to grip fish, which they catch by diving underwater. The closely related red-breasted merganser is also an annual visitor. Basically a sea duck, it appears in small numbers at Rutland, mostly in winter and spring. The third member of the trio is the smew, the smallest British sawbill. Smew arrive in small numbers each January and remain until March.

Rutland attracts a multitude of other wildfowl that are normally rare inland. The common scoter, an abundant sea duck, is recorded each winter, as are species of geese and swan not usually associated with this part of the country. Bewick's and whooper swans may drop in during winter, and wintering pink-footed geese or migrant white-fronted geese may join the resident flocks of greylag geese, feral snow geese and Canada geese. Small groups of Egyptian geese, which breed at Rutland, are often seen grazing in the fields in spring.

Other visitors

Slavonian and occasionally red-necked grebes, scarce visitors to Britain, may be spotted feeding in deeper water, hidden among their more numerous cousins, the great crested grebes. Black-necked grebes may appear in spring, often in their smart breeding plumage, or turn up in autumn. Divers, which are usually restricted to the coast in winter, also come to Rutland. Red-throated and

▲ The unmistakable oystercatcher is one of many species of wader that can be seen at Rutland Water. They arrive from late February or early March and numbers build up during spring with one or more pairs breeding each year.

◄ Garganey are summer visitors to Britain and a few of these little ducks breed at Rutland Water. This one is a handsome drake.

Places to visit at Rutland Water

Whether you are an experienced birdwatcher or a beginner, Rutland Water is well worth a visit. There are few other places in inland Britain where it is possible to see 100 bird species in a single day in early summer. Such numbers are evidence of its habitat diversity and success at attracting birds.

Rutland is a site of international importance for the gadwall. Introduced to Britain in about 1850, this duck is now established on the reservoir as a regular breeding species.

At the western end of Rutland Water are two nature reserves run by the Leicestershire and Rutland Wildlife Trust on behalf of Anglian Water. A day permit costs £4 and there are various concessions. Trust members can buy an annual permit at a reduced rate.

1 **Egleton Reserve** is the best site to visit if you have limited time. Fourteen hides overlook three large lagoons and two western arms of the reservoir. The Anglian Water Bird Watching Centre is located at this reserve, from which permits should be obtained. Open daily from 9 a.m. to 5 p.m. except Christmas Day and Boxing Day.

2 **Lyndon Reserve** has eight bird-watching hides overlooking the water, and a nature trail, leading through woodland, scrub and open fields, that allows a full exploration of the reserve. From May until the end of October the reserve is open at weekends and from Tuesday to Friday, between 10 a.m. and 4 p.m. Large numbers of wildfowl are also present from November to April and the reserve opens at weekends. A visitor centre houses various interpretive displays, which demonstrate the history and wildlife importance of the reservoir.

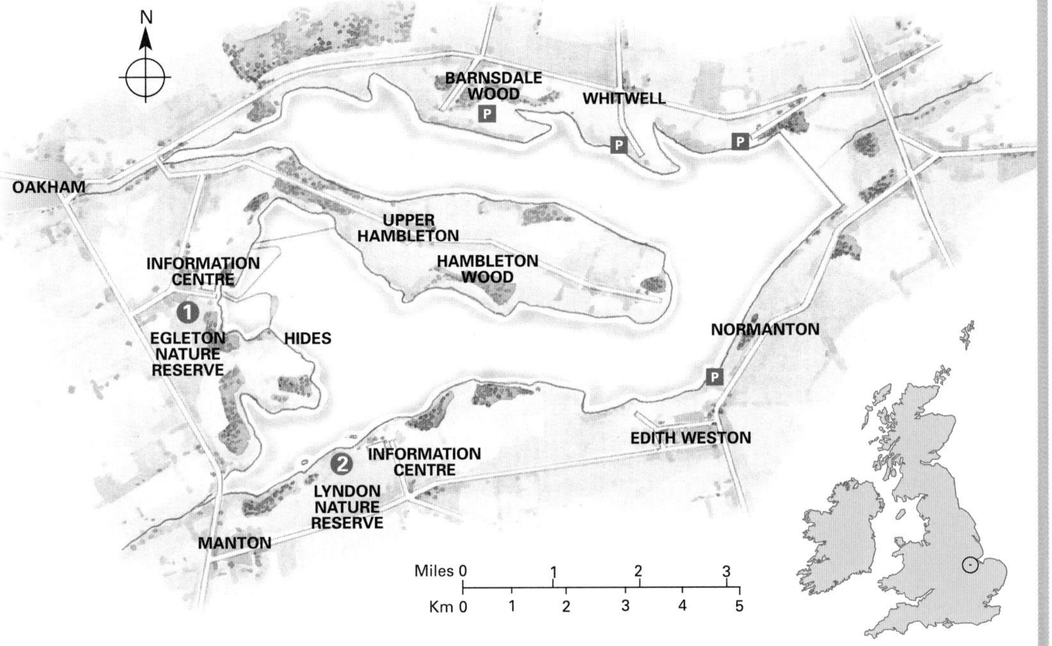

great northern divers are almost annual, and the occasional black-throated diver may arrive, too.

Busy winter

In autumn and winter over 20,000 waterbirds of up to 28 species may be present at any time. As winter loosens its grip and birds start to prepare for breeding, the large lapwing flocks that have been feeding around the margins of the reservoir since summer begin to disperse, although small numbers stay to breed. The few wintering ruff that have fed around the lagoons depart for the north, the last of the smew depart, and flocks of fieldfares cackle overhead as they head off towards Scandinavia to breed.

Islands begin to appear in the lagoons during long dry periods. The wildfowl are counted every month whatever the weather.

WILDLIFE WATCH

What can I do at Rutland Water?

- In August the Egleton Reserve hosts the annual British Birdwatching Fair, the major bird and wildlife event of the year in Britain.
- Special guided tours can be booked to watch badgers at Egleton, where a hide has been constructed, overlooking a badger sett.
- For further information about activities, as well as details of the Leicestershire and Rutland Wildlife Trust, contact the Anglian Water Bird Watching Centre at the Egleton Reserve, Oakham, Rutland LE15 8BT (telephone 01572 770651) or visit the website at www.rutlandwater.org.uk

Animals and plants in focus

Garden watch

- The house mouse
- Watching hedgehogs
- The long-eared bat
- The song thrush
- The wren
- The house sparrow
- The earthworm
- Recognising garden bees
- Aphids
- Garden wall plants

The house mouse

House mice arrived in Britain from Asia more than 2000 years ago. Their remarkable resilience coupled with an ability to feed on almost anything has enabled them to colonise virtually every type of human construction.

The house mouse is an uninvited guest in many homes and public buildings, and during the night tiny scampering feet may be heard as it searches for food.

These days, most of the mice that turn up in suburban houses and garden sheds are actually wood mice or yellow-necked mice. Genuine house mice have become quite scarce in many places, yet early in the 20th century millions of them could be found all over the British Isles.

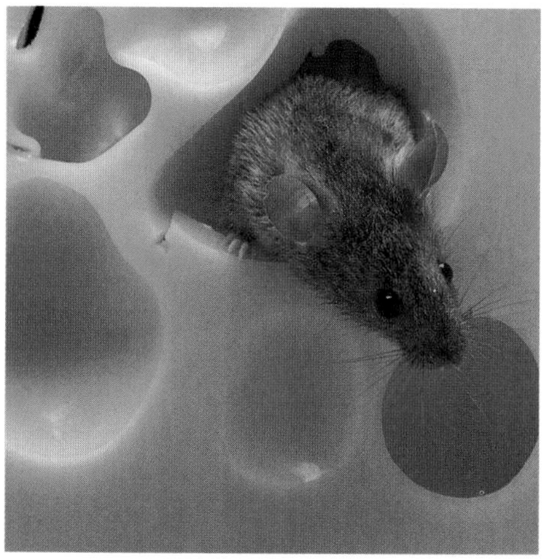

Despite their reputed fascination with cheese, house mice are not fussy eaters. Their acute sense of smell not only enables them to search out all types of food but also alerts them to territorial markings.

In fact, house mice have been present in Britain since at least the Iron Age and in Ireland for several hundred years. The species was so successful that at one time it had a worldwide distribution greater than that of any other mammal apart from humans. These small rodents even managed to colonise offshore islands, where they still thrive in the absence of competition from other small mammals, although in some cases they depend on scavenging around human habitation to survive. For example, the house mice on St Kilda, the outermost of the Outer Hebrides, died out soon after the majority of the human population moved away.

House mice can climb, jump and swim well and, in the past, keeping them out of buildings was almost impossible. Trapping them individually was ineffective because house mice breed rapidly all year round, so from a small initial population numbers build up very fast. They can eat almost anything from grain and fruit to pet food, tobacco, candles, plastic, match heads, soap, aluminium traps and even electric cables. In 1981, house mice caused the closure of the Cambridge to London railway line for three hours by chewing through a 650-volt power cable.

A house mouse does not eat much food – about 4g (under ⅛oz) in a day – but in the process it nibbles at a lot more.

DID YOU KNOW?

House mice normally squeak, but there are many stories about singing mice that made canary-like trilling noises and used to be kept as vocal pets. So-called 'waltzing mice' are a special breed that have defective ears. Their sense of balance is affected so that they spend their time continually chasing round in circles. They do not live long. Most house mice are grey-brown, but more unusual varieties include black, white, yellowish, spotted and even hairless.

HOUSE MOUSE FACT FILE

Extremely alert and fast-moving, house mice are nonetheless easy to identify, with a greyish belly, greasy fur and a pinkish brown, scaly tail. Few houses were without these small rodents 50 years ago, but today they are scarcer.

● NAMES
Common name: house mouse
Scientific name: *Mus domesticus* (formerly known as *Mus musculus*)

● HABITAT
Normally around farms, food stores, old buildings; relatively uncommon in modern houses; sometimes in hedgerows, especially in remote areas and on islands

● DISTRIBUTION
Found throughout Britain and Ireland, including many islands

● STATUS
Around 5 million individuals in Britain; less common than 50 years ago

● SIZE
Length, head and body 75–100mm (3–4in); tail 70–90mm (2¾–3½in); ear 11–16mm (½–¾in); weight, adults usually about 15g (½oz)

● KEY FEATURES
Usually grey-brown with a slightly paler belly; fur greasy; face pointed, ears and eyes large; tail mostly hairless, scaly, with distinct rings

● HABITS
Normally nocturnal, very active; can be quite aggressive, males frequently fight

● VOICE
Loud squeak when alarmed or annoyed

● FOOD
Almost anything from grain and meat to insects and bars of soap; preference for grain and fruit

● BREEDING
Litters of 5–8 young, born at monthly intervals; gestation period usually 19–20 days; breeds all year indoors, spring to autumn outdoors

● NEST
An untidy mess of any available material, such as shredded paper, scraps of wool or cloth

● YOUNG
Resemble adult, but more grey than brown

● SIGNS
Tiny droppings, often black (although colour varies with diet); smelly patches of urine; greasy stains around entrance holes in woodwork

House mice leave large numbers of tiny droppings at favoured sites. These are often found together with urine pillars – accumulations of droppings, dirt, grease and urine up to 4cm (1½in) high.

Distribution map key

Present

Not present

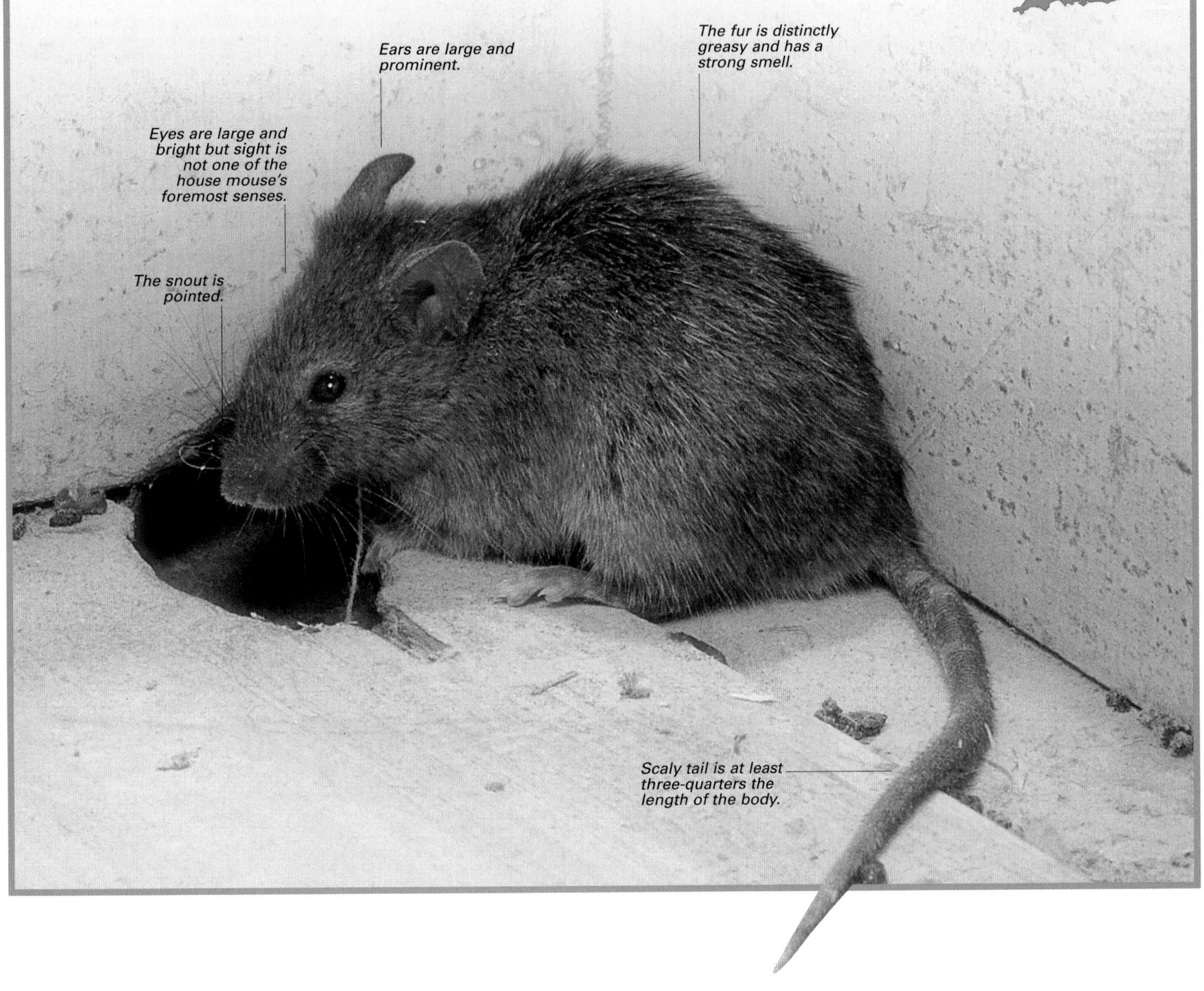
Ears are large and prominent.
The fur is distinctly greasy and has a strong smell.
Eyes are large and bright but sight is not one of the house mouse's foremost senses.
The snout is pointed.
Scaly tail is at least three-quarters the length of the body.

Unlike most wild mammals, reproduction in house mice is not controlled by seasonal changes in day length. Living indoors, sheltered from the weather, they are able to breed all year round.

Aggressive behaviour is uncommon in small family groups of mice. However, as their population densities increase, disputes become more frequent. Subordinate mice surrender food to dominant individuals.

Like other rodents, house mice gnaw sacks and packets, making holes through which food is lost. They also urinate to mark their territory, tainting yet more stored food, everywhere from household larders to large grain stores. Their droppings – 50 or more per mouse per day – can easily get mixed in with grain and cannot easily be separated from it. In addition, house mice have very greasy, smelly fur that gives off an odour that humans find unpleasant.

Mouse control

The damage house mice were causing to food production and storage became a very serious matter during World War II, and new mouse and rat poisons were developed to deal with the problem, saving huge amounts of food from being wasted. People were encouraged to store food in mouse-proof containers, make larder doors fit properly and block up holes and mouse 'highways' linking one house to the next. Nowadays, mice are resistant to some poisons and others have been made in their place. Thanks to better constructed houses and a more hygiene-conscious population, the house mouse is very much in retreat in domestic settings.

On farms a significant change took place with the introduction of combine harvesters. Corn used to be reaped in late summer and stacked in ricks, where it remained for several months. For house mice, the ricks offered shelter and warmth and a ready supply of food. On threshing days, thousands of mice were turfed out as the ricks were dismantled, but by then they had eaten

Scavengers at the table

The house mouse is a compulsive explorer. It does not take long for this highly active scavenger to locate a new source of food, such as an abandoned breakfast table, before the opportunity passes.

A house mouse is led to some buttered toast by its sensitive sense of smell. It licks at the fat-rich spread…

…before turning its attention to the crusts of toast.

The mouse then searches the dish below the cereal bowl for splashes of milk.

An adventurous house mouse may join a colony in a hedgerow and live and breed there during the summer, but come the winter the mice must retreat indoors or die.

or spoiled more than 10 per cent of the grain. Later in the season, the mice would begin again, nibbling sacks and ruining the stored grain. Combine harvesters enable corn to be cut and threshed simultaneously as the machine trundles around the farmer's fields. The grain is then stored in huge rodent-proof silos, so house mice do not have much chance to feed on it. As a consequence, their populations have plummeted in farmland areas.

The house mouse does not often survive in fields or woodlands because other mice and voles, which are much better adapted to these habitats, monopolise the food and the best nesting sites. However, the house mouse has adapted to living in the open countryside, in hedgerows, for example, and even on salt marshes.

TOUGH AND ADAPTABLE

House mice often do well in old factories and other institutional buildings, where it is difficult to find and seal all the holes to prevent them from gaining access to food remains from canteens or dustbins. They do not require much food to survive. Moreover, since house mice originally came from semi-deserts in south-west Asia, they drink little. This enables them to survive indoors in environments that would defeat many other species.

▲ Where potential sites are limited or population density is high, house mice nest communally, such as here in a wall cavity. These gaps also offer convenient paths for the mice to travel along.

► A rarely used tool drawer provides a good place to make a home. Any material that is soft and easily shredded, such as grass, paper, clothing or cardboard, will be built into a substantial nest.

Mice can live in modern offices, where they may cause trouble by nesting inside computers and gnawing at cables or other parts. They are so adaptable that they can also survive in meat cold stores, where they gnaw sacking to create nests in which to keep warm and consume the food provided in the form of frozen meat. Some mice have been known to spend their entire lives inside meat carcasses in freezer storage units at the docks. Such colonies live in perpetual darkness and cope with temperatures of -10°C (14°F).

House mice may nest in armchairs or piles of junk, among bed springs or even inside stuffed animals in museums. The nests are made out of shredded cloth and paper, which can be a serious nuisance if the paper happens to be from valuable books or important letters. Similarly, the cloth may be curtains, clothes, carpets or handkerchiefs. A piano makes a good place to nest, with sheet music at hand for its construction. Any mice populations that are discovered are swiftly destroyed.

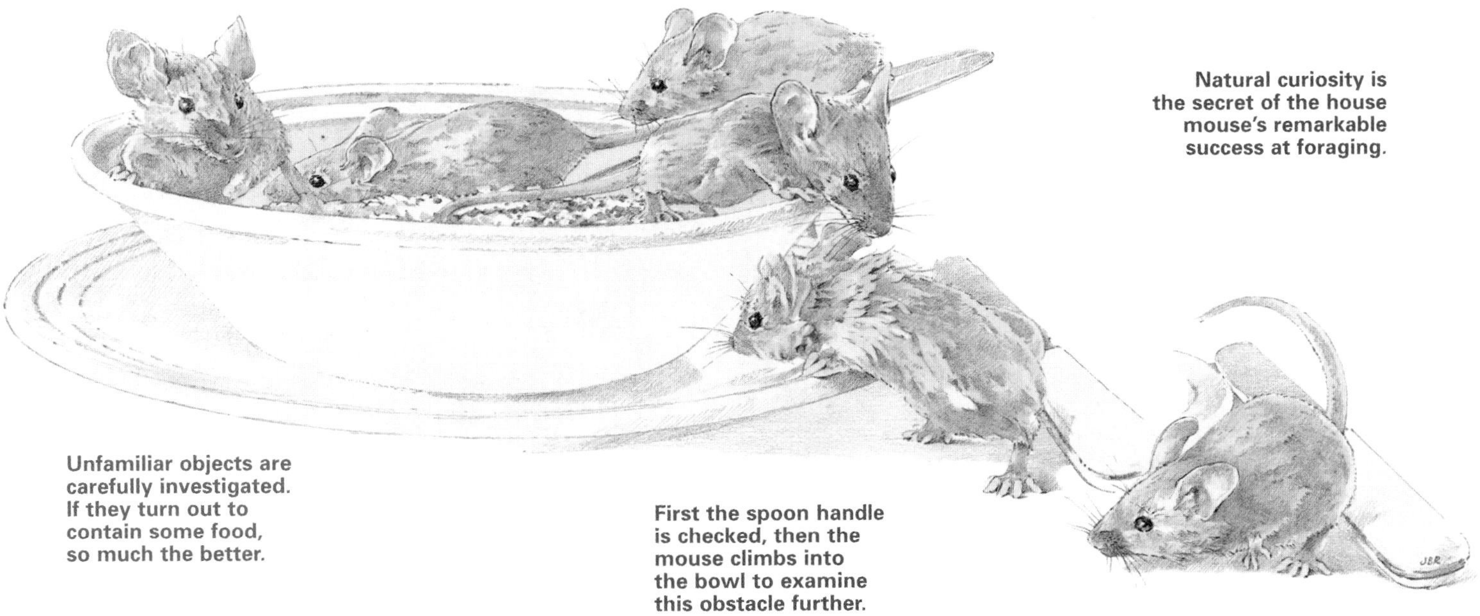

Natural curiosity is the secret of the house mouse's remarkable success at foraging.

Unfamiliar objects are carefully investigated. If they turn out to contain some food, so much the better.

First the spoon handle is checked, then the mouse climbs into the bowl to examine this obstacle further.

MICE ON THE UNDERGROUND

Thriving populations of house mice exist on the London Underground. Here they have access to an extraordinary variety of food, ranging from discarded chips, sandwiches and sweets to cigarette ends. Moisture seeping through the walls provides water if it is needed. The mice construct nests out of shredded paper and human hair – more than 1 million people use the Underground each day, and if every one loses just a single hair daily, that provides plenty of bedding.

The mice do not do much harm but their nests can clog points and switching gear, creating a fire hazard or safety problem. Travellers awaiting trains may find the mice intriguing. The animals dart silently at high speed from one dark corner to another, leaving people uncertain of whether they saw something move. Often, though, mainly during quieter periods and after the last train has gone, the mice feed in full view.

The London Underground's tracks provide shelter for mice and also trap a regular supply of food. The mice are not alarmed by the rumble of the trains, scampering to safety at the last moment.

House mice are born naked and helpless and are suckled for about three weeks. Females can breed from as young as six weeks of age.

Rapid breeding

House mice mature at around six to 12 weeks old. Females then breed regularly, producing five or six litters per year in urban populations. (Formerly, there were up to 10 litters a year in hayricks.) Each litter consists of five to eight young, which take just three weeks to become independent. Their mother is then free to breed again.

Male mice can breed for up to 18 months, but females are more quickly worn out and generally do not breed after they are a year old. Nevertheless, during her lifetime a female can produce an average of 40 young, sometimes many more.

Populations of house mice living indoors tend to contain a much higher proportion of older animals than those living outdoors. This is probably due to their relative safety from predators. Indoors, house mice may live to be two years old, but out in the wild these and other small rodents are lucky to survive for more than a few months. House mice living outdoors have an average life expectancy of around 100 days, with cats, owls and rats being their main enemies. Harsh frosts also kill many, especially younger animals. Again, indoors, these threats are much reduced.

In mammals, high population densities usually result in a lowering of the reproductive rate, but house mice do not seem to conform to this effect of overcrowding. However, normal territorial behaviour breaks down and some animals may move away, although this is hard to do when the colony is living in an isolated building, for instance.

▼ It is very hard to keep a house mouse out as it can squeeze through the tiniest holes, its small frame compressing easily. Mice can also jump and climb well, infiltrating even difficult-to-reach holes.

Compact territories

Unlike other mice, house mice do not normally stray widely. Even when they inhabit hedges or open country their entire life may take place within an area of just 100 sq m (about 1100 sq ft). In barns and chicken sheds, a house mouse may wander over no more than 5 sq m (55 sq ft), perhaps with occasional forays beyond. As a result, house mouse populations often seem to be made up of tight-knit, inbred family groups.

Some individuals, perhaps more adventurous than the rest, do scatter, sometimes moving a few hundred metres away or occasionally as much as 1km (half a mile). About one in five house mice breeds away from where it was born, with males and females being equally likely to move on. This means that over three-quarters of house mice spend their lives in one place.

Communication

The sense of sight is relatively unimportant to house mice, and many live in dark, confined spaces where vision would be of little use. Their sense of hearing is acute and is the main means of detecting danger. Smell is vitally important and house mice regularly leave scent markers, in urine and smeared on to fixed objects, for other mice to sniff and interpret. Dominant mice, especially males, urinate often but subordinates are more restrained and do not leave scent

◀ House mice scramble up electrical wires or cables with ease. They are notorious for chewing the insulation on flexes; this is to wear down their sharp front teeth, which would otherwise grow too long.

marks so often. The mice can recognise each other at a distance by smell alone. Breeding in females is much affected by the scent of other mice in the vicinity and may, in some cases, be suppressed altogether as a result.

If mice do not recognise each other when they meet, their immediate reaction is normally to leap apart. If they meet again, the dominant animal may hold its ground and wait for the other mouse to retreat. Dominance is often disputed, however, so fights are frequent. Squabbling mice squeak loudly and attempt to bite each other. Territorial males are particularly aggressive and may be seriously wounded as a result of frequent fighting. Female mice are more placid and produce a scent in their urine that is believed to inhibit aggression in other mice.

WILDLIFE WATCH

Where can I see house mice?

- If house mice become a problem in buildings, the owners usually catch them with traps or pay pest-control officers to dispose of them. Thus there are few places where sightings of the species are guaranteed, except perhaps railway stations, including the London Underground.
- Farm buildings, particularly poultry sheds, are often good places to look for mice. However, they are wary and not normally active in daylight. A lot can be learned about house mice by watching domestic mice kept as pets, which are descended from wild mice.

If the nest is disturbed, a female mouse will carry her offspring to safety elsewhere. This is easy while they are only a few days old, but may be impossible if they are heavier.

Although it may seem unappetising, a bar of soap can provide a meal for a house mouse. It contains useful nutriment in the form of modified lipids or fats.

House mice thrive under floorboards, feeding on crumbs that fall through the gaps. In the majority of cases, the householder may be unaware of their presence.

Watching hedgehogs

Most of the wild mammals that visit gardens are elusive, but hedgehogs are an exception. Their prickly defences make them unusually bold and they may often be spotted as they forage for food on summer evenings.

Hedgehogs are often common in suburban residential areas with plenty of gardens. They typically follow a set route through several adjacent gardens, leaving evidence of their visits in the form of scattered droppings. These are usually almost black, about the size of a little finger, and studded with shiny black beetle fragments that glisten with purple and green iridescence. On dewy nights hedgehogs may scrape their low-slung bellies through the damp grass, leaving clear trails that are often visible early the next morning.

Foraging hedgehogs pursue an erratic course through a garden, poking their noses into places where earthworms and beetles may be hiding, and snuffling in the vegetation and leaf litter. They can be quite noisy, and on a still night may even be heard from inside the house, tempting the residents out for a look.

Bold visitors

Hedgehogs are so well protected by their spines that they have little to fear from most predators, so they behave much more boldly than other wild mammals. They may even tolerate torchlight, although it is best to cover the torch lens with a red filter made from transparent red plastic. Humans can see quite well in red light but hedgehogs cannot, so they will not be unduly disturbed by a red torch being shone at them. They are much more likely to be frightened by any sudden noise. They have very sensitive hearing, and the click of a torch being switched on is likely to alarm them much more than a sudden beam of light.

A startled hedgehog normally 'freezes' and raises the spines on its head and neck, pulling them forwards over its face. It often remains motionless in this bristling state for many minutes, so it is best to back away until the animal relaxes and becomes active again.

Feeding tactics

It is often possible to watch hedgehogs as they feed. They find beetles easy to catch, crunching them up with enthusiasm. They also enjoy earthworms, but these can be hard to haul from the earth in one piece. When a hedgehog locates a worm, it seizes it, pulls it tight and then holds still. After a while the worm relaxes to adjust its grip on the soil. At this crucial moment the hedgehog pulls again, dragging the worm a short way out

▲ Hedgehogs prefer gardens with plenty of cover. When hunting for food they often seek out areas that are likely to harbour slugs, and sometimes noisily turn over stones in rockeries to find their prey.

▼ In July a mother hedgehog may bring her young to look for food in the garden. The adults in such family parties are always females because male hedgehogs take no part in raising their young.

▲ **Hedgehogs are inquisitive and are not discouraged by strange scents. They often explore garden sheds and other storage areas in the hope of finding either food or a daytime refuge.**

of the ground. If the worm gets a grip, the hedgehog pauses to avoid breaking it in two. After two or three attempts, the hedgehog finally whips the worm from the soil and eats it.

Noisy courtship

If more than one hedgehog visits the garden, it is worth watching them closely to see how they behave towards each other. Sometimes one is dominant over the others, and it is not always a male.

In early summer, however, males can become very assertive as they court the females, and this activity can sometimes be watched in the garden. The male circles the female while both animals snort and puff loudly, and the noise often attracts other males. The rivals may then fight by butting each other, colliding and recoiling like shunting trains. Eventually one male gives up and runs off, leaving the victor to mate with the female.

NIGHT PATROL

A round trip

In the course of a night, a hedgehog travels an average distance of a kilometre (half a mile) in an area where food is plentiful. It moves slowly and methodically along a familiar route, pausing to investigate every nook and cranny that may contain a meal.

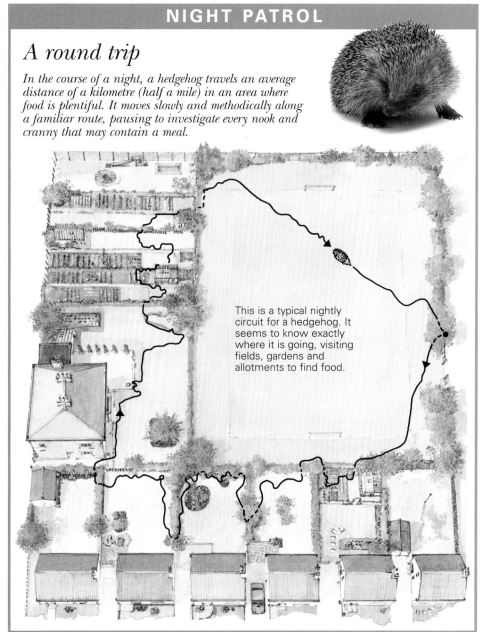

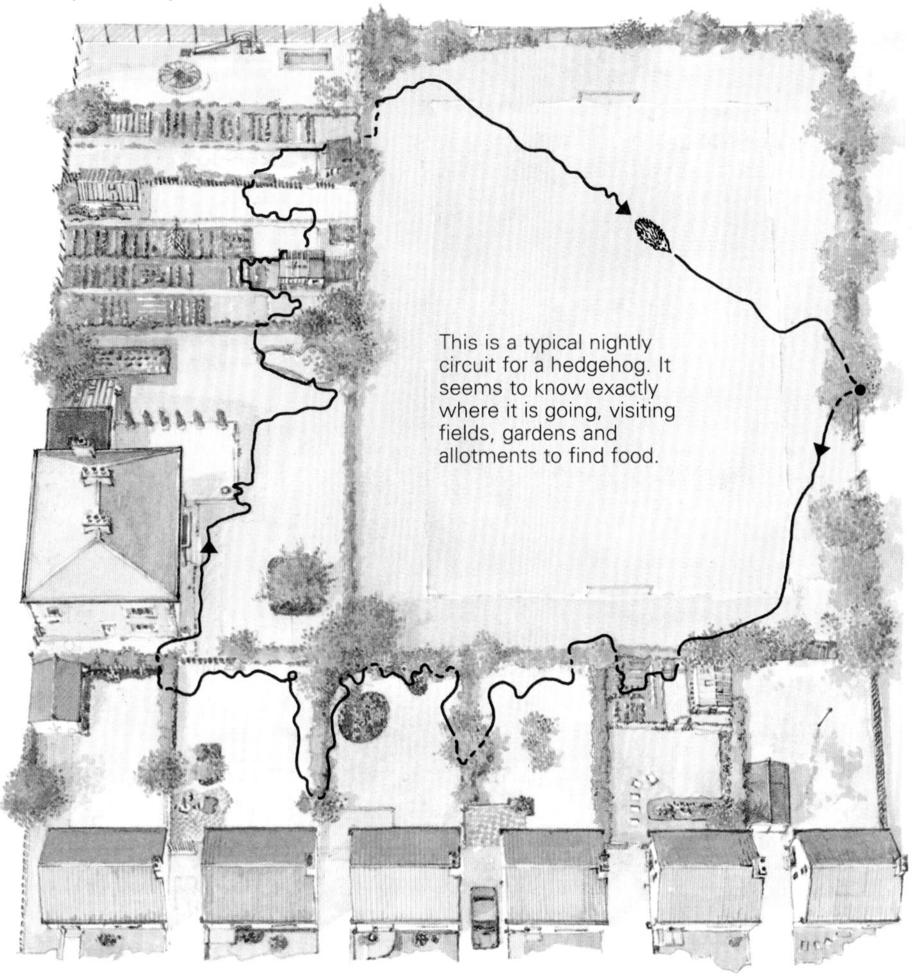
This is a typical nightly circuit for a hedgehog. It seems to know exactly where it is going, visiting fields, gardens and allotments to find food.

WILDLIFE WATCH

How can I encourage hedgehogs to my garden?

- Put out food for hedgehogs, any time between May and October. Try cat or dog food, crumbled and moistened dog biscuits, or maybe bread soaked in milk diluted with water.
- Don't be too tidy! Heaps of leaves and brushwood, undisturbed patches behind log piles and beneath shrubs, a bramble bush somewhere out of the way or even a sheet of board leaning against the shed may make an ideal refuge for a hedgehog.
- Try building a potential hedgehog home. It needs to be in a secluded corner, with a rough wire frame to hold the nest together and plenty of dry leaves and grass for the hedgehog to build its hibernation nest.

A young hedgehog's jaws are armed with sharp teeth that make short work of its invertebrate prey. As the animal gets older its teeth become blunter, mainly through eating gritty earthworms.

The long-eared bat

With ears almost as long as its body, the long-eared bat appears ungainly, yet it is amazingly agile when in pursuit of prey. A frequent resident of suburbia, it often roosts in attics or bat boxes, and thrives on close association with humans.

As its name suggests, extremely long ears are undoubtedly this bat's most striking feature. It is Britain's second most abundant bat species, after the pipistrelle, and since it lives near to, and even inside, human habitation, is a fairly common sight.

Before sleeping and during hibernation it folds its ears down and tucks them safely away under its wings to prevent them drying out or getting frostbitten. When moving around on the ground or when roosting, the long-eared bat keeps its ears curled up like a ram's horns. A series of creases along the back edge of each ear allows the ear to collapse and lie back over the bat's shoulder. When the bat is about to fly and during flight itself, tiny muscles, aided by blood pressure, enable the ears to extend fully. Tiny stiffening rods of cartilage at the front edges help to keep the ears firm and prevent them from flapping during flight.

Slow-motion flight

The long-eared bat flies with its ears pointing stiffly to the front and the resulting wind resistance makes flying quite hard work. The bat expends 21 times as much energy in flight as it does when resting. It expends even more energy in rapid flight but, when necessary, long-eareds are able to fly much more slowly than other bats.

The flight of the long-eared bat is special in other ways, too. It can manoeuvre easily in a space just 1m (3ft) or so in diameter. Being nimble enough to fly around in small spaces means that long-eared bats are the most common species of bat to be found indoors, especially when windows are left open in hot weather. They are entirely harmless and do not bite or even squeak in protest when handled properly. A trapped long-eared bat can be helped out of the window, held gently and carefully in a towel or handkerchief.

Thanks to its broad wings, the long-eared bat can even hover, flapping its wings vigorously in order to keep its body virtually stationary in mid-air. This skill enables it to pick caterpillars and spiders off branches, twigs or the surface of leaves, and these invertebrates form a considerable part of its diet.

The long-eared bat is able to twist and turn in flight in small spaces. Here, time-lapse photography has been used to show a long-eared bat's movements as it chases an insect.

LONG-EARED BAT FACT FILE

Instantly recognisable due to its strikingly long ears, which are particularly obvious in flight, the long-eared bat is one of the last bats to become active each evening. It emerges soon after sunset, leaving its roost to feed in parks, gardens and woodland clearings.

● NAMES
Common names: long-eared bat, brown long-eared bat, common long-eared bat, whispering bat
Scientific name: *Plecotus auritus*

● HABITAT
Open woodlands, parks and gardens; often lives in house attics, especially in the north

● DISTRIBUTION
Throughout Britain and Ireland, including some larger islands

● STATUS
Relatively common; perhaps more than 200,000 individuals

● SIZE
Length, head and body 37–53mm (1½–2¼in), tail 34–55mm (1⅜–2¼in), ear 30–41mm (1¼–1⅝in); wingspan 24–28cm (10–11in); weight 5–12g (about ¼–½oz)

● KEY FEATURES
Fur long, wispy, light brown, paler below, often yellowish on neck; base of hairs dark brown; ears huge, almost as long as body, meet at base; nose and eye area light brown or pinkish; wings and ear membranes brown

● HABITS
Nocturnal; generally stays close to roost; hibernates October/November–March

● VOICE
Occasional squeaks; echolocation calls very quiet – even electronic bat detectors pick up sound within only 1–2m (3–6ft)

● FOOD
Mainly moths, also spiders and caterpillars, taken in flight or gleaned from foliage; larger prey taken to perch to be eaten

● BREEDING
Single young born in nursery roost in June, sometimes into July; twins rare

● NEST
No nest, but roosts in bat boxes, bird nestboxes, attics, even bedrooms; hibernates in cool places such as cracks in walls of caves, mines, cellars and old buildings

● YOUNG
Like adult, but grey with dark face; young fly at 4–6 weeks and breed in 1–3 years

● SIGNS
Droppings about 1cm (½in) long, similar to other bat droppings, crumble into dust made up of tiny insect fragments; droppings often found in long lines beneath roof beams and other linear roost sites; piles of moths' wings often accumulate under feeding perches in porches or garden sheds

Long-eared bats have superb control in tight spaces. They can fly among the branches of trees and even, as here, inside a house.

Distribution map key

Present all year round

Not present

PROTECTED!

Long-eared bats are fully protected by the Wildlife and Countryside Act 1981. It is illegal to catch or disturb them, or to interfere with the places where they breed or hibernate.

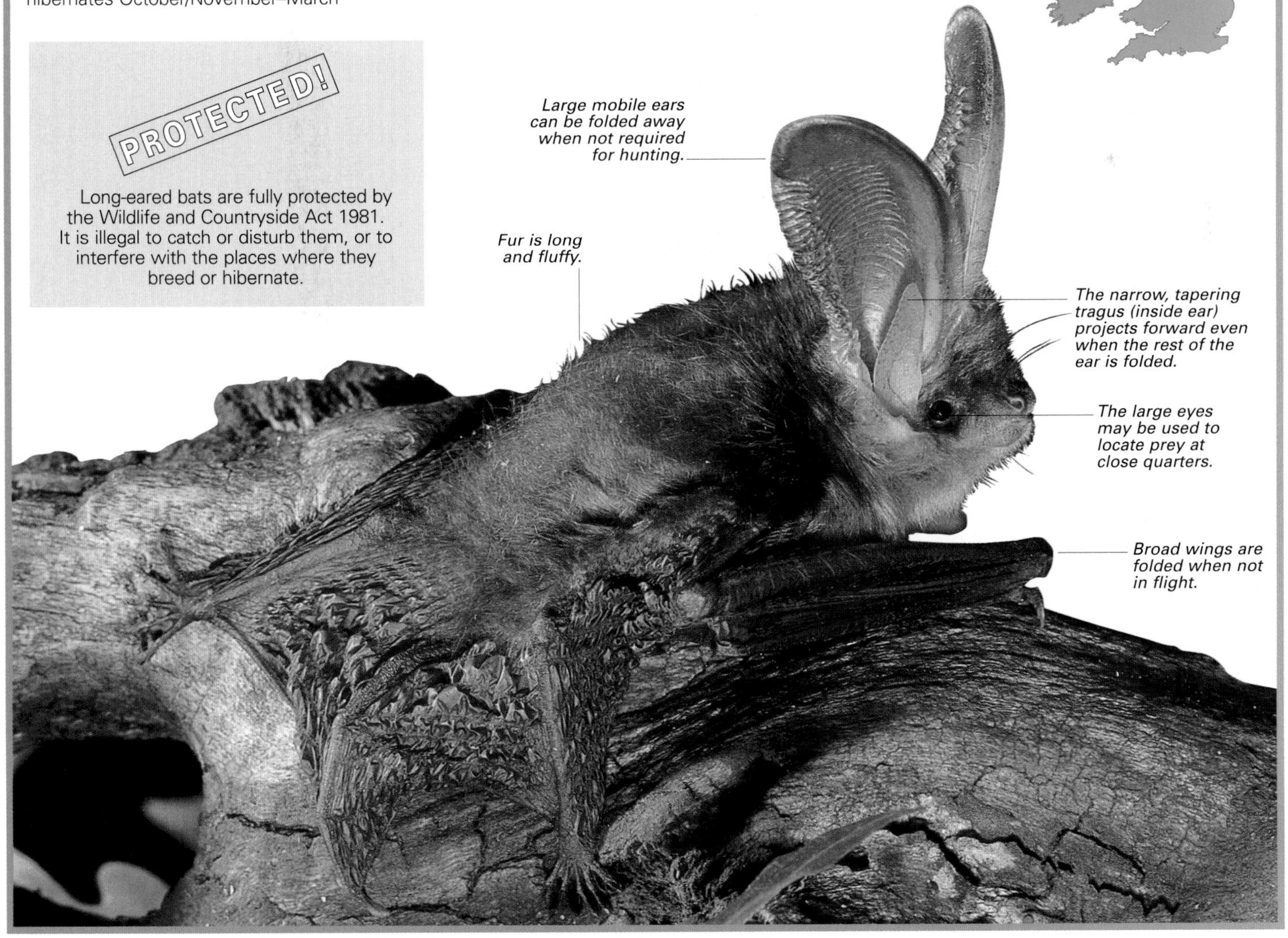
Large mobile ears can be folded away when not required for hunting.
Fur is long and fluffy.
The narrow, tapering tragus (inside ear) projects forward even when the rest of the ear is folded.
The large eyes may be used to locate prey at close quarters.
Broad wings are folded when not in flight.

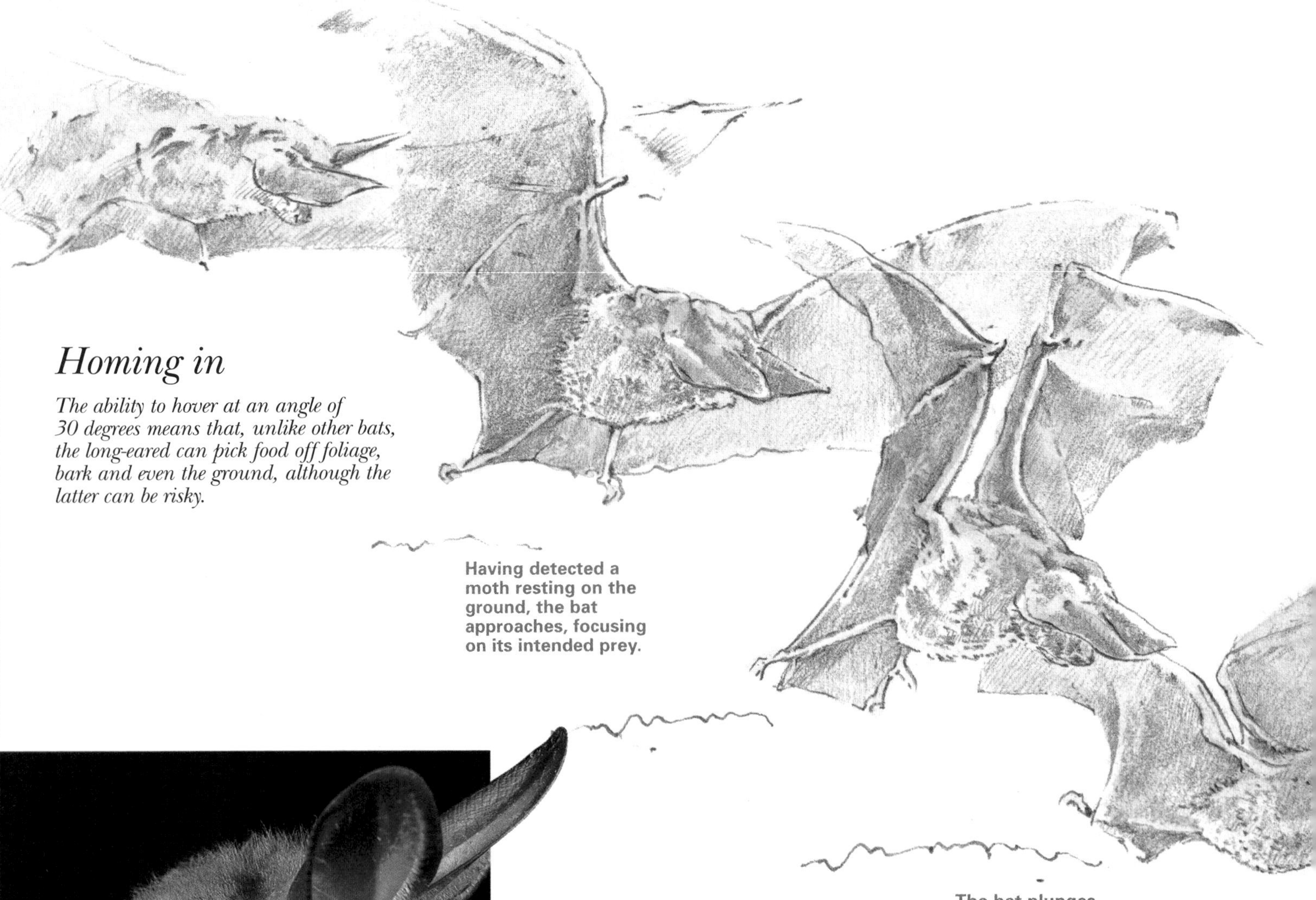

Homing in

The ability to hover at an angle of 30 degrees means that, unlike other bats, the long-eared can pick food off foliage, bark and even the ground, although the latter can be risky.

Having detected a moth resting on the ground, the bat approaches, focusing on its intended prey.

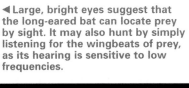

The bat plunges downward, controlling its speed with wings spread wide.

◀ Large, bright eyes suggest that the long-eared bat can locate prey by sight. It may also hunt by simply listening for the wingbeats of prey, as its hearing is sensitive to low frequencies.

Other species of bat occasionally snatch insects as they flash past, but can neither hover nor fly slowly enough to make it a habit.

The long-eared bat's tiny feet and claws enable it to hang from surprisingly smooth surfaces and the eyes, larger than those of other bats, are probably used to find food at close quarters. Most bats do not use their eyes much.

Another useful skill displayed by the long-eared bat is the ability to take off from the ground. Bats that lack its broad wings must crawl to a vertical surface and then climb up it a few metres before launching themselves into the air.

Hunting technique

The long-eared bat's method of hunting – known as gleaning – is not simply a question of manoeuvrability, however.

A long-eared bat can pluck insects from the foliage and branches of trees and shrubs, which requires aerobatic flight to match the pinpoint accuracy of its echolocation.

Bats detect their prey by echolocation, sending out loud squeaks that are too high-pitched for humans to hear. They listen for the echoes that bounce back off obstacles and potential food items, such as insects or spiders. A flying moth is clearly distinct from the surrounding air and therefore easy to pick out by its echo. A spider on a leaf, on the other hand, can be very difficult to detect by echoes alone because the sound waves bounce back from all the surrounding surfaces. The nearer the prey is to a complex object, such as a tree or bush, the louder and more confusing the echoes become for the bat.

For most bats, the many echoes from foliage merge into a deafening muddle but this is not so for the long-eared bat, which uses a very quiet and precise echolocation system. Its huge, highly sensitive ears are specially tuned to detect faint echoes from prey settled on leaf surfaces in the dark. Long-eareds are often called 'whispering bats' because their voice is so faint that even sensitive bat detectors cannot pick it up from more than a couple of metres away. This gives the long-eareds an advantage over noisier bats when hunting moths because the moths are less likely to be aware of their approach.

Like all of Britain's bats, long-eared bats possess an impressive array of sharp teeth. These make short work of the soft-bodied larval stages of moths and beetles.

Attic roosts

Each April, female long-eared bats gather to await the birth of their young and, unusually, the nursery roost often has males present, too. Attics provide snug places in which to rear the offspring. A house roof frequently gets very warm, even on overcast days – attic temperatures may exceed 40°C (104°F), especially under dark slates. This helps the adults to keep warm but is particularly important for the babies, which have no fur for the first two or three weeks of life. In periods of unseasonally cool weather they lose body heat easily and may soon die. In cooler parts of Britain, living in a warm attic can make all the difference between the young surviving or dying of cold.

The long-eared bat is one of just five species of bat that is found throughout Britain and in northern areas, especially in Scotland, the availability of suitable

To maintain control, the bat uses its tail and wings as a brake, effectively parachuting to the ground.

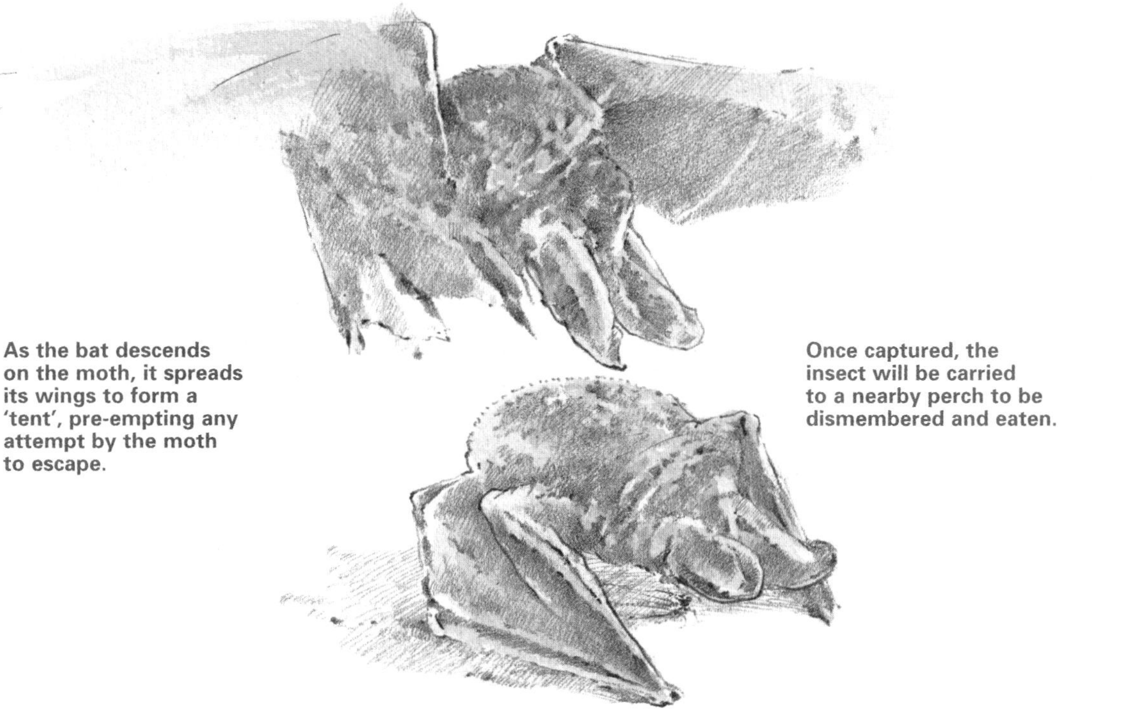

As the bat descends on the moth, it spreads its wings to form a 'tent', pre-empting any attempt by the moth to escape.

Once captured, the insect will be carried to a nearby perch to be dismembered and eaten.

Even on warm summer nights, a long-eared bat spends time hanging from the foliage of a tree between bouts of active hunting, consuming and digesting prey.

GREY LONG-EARED BAT

A second species of long-eared bat is one of the rarest of all British mammals. The grey long-eared bat so closely resembles its plentiful brown relative that the pair are very hard to distinguish except by measurement of the teeth, thumb and tragus (the fleshy prong inside the ear).

Grey long-eareds have a dark grey base to the body hairs, whereas in the common species the base of the fur is brown. Grey long-eared bats mainly live in Dorset, Hampshire and the Isle of Wight. They bite vigorously, while common long-eared bats are usually completely docile when handled.

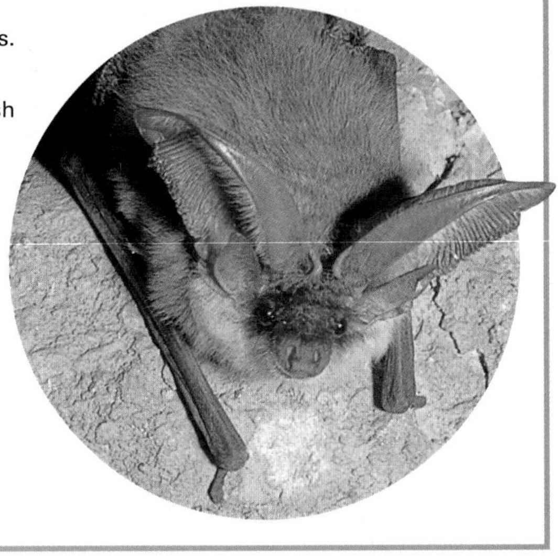

The grey long-eared bat favours similar wooded habitats to its more abundant brown-furred relative.

house roof spaces may be the most important factor in determining where they live. Favoured houses tend to be old rather than new, and close to woodland where the bats can feed.

If no suitable roof space can be found, the bats will live in woodland in tree holes. Forestry plantations provide plenty of insect food but the trees are generally too young to have holes in which bats can roost safely and so the long-eareds will quickly occupy any available bat boxes that may have been specially erected.

The bats cope with cold weather by clustering together. In addition, they can save energy by allowing their body temperature to drop for a few hours each day. This reduces the amount of heat lost to the surroundings. Since bats use a lot of energy hunting, such energy-saving behaviour is essential.

Home-loving animals

Wherever they choose to live, these bats do not travel very far – usually less than 500m (1600ft) from their daytime roost. Long-eared bats do not like to fly out in the open, preferring closed surroundings among trees and houses. If they do need to travel from one area to another, they tend to follow lines of trees or other prominent landscape features.

Occasionally, long-eared bats have been found on ships and oil rigs far out at sea but these individuals have probably been blown off course by strong winds. Very few – and only males – ever go to live in another roost, and even then they will not travel any more than 5km (3 miles) to do so.

It follows that almost all of the animals in a colony are closely related. Studies using DNA testing have revealed that most of the babies are fathered by the same few males. During the winter, long-eared bats hibernate alone – although other members of the colony may sleep nearby – but tend to return to the same roost each spring, living together in groups that can include up to 50 bats in summer.

However, most colonies consist of between 10 and 20 bats. The colony members can recognise each other, probably by smell. Female long-eareds are able to identify their own baby

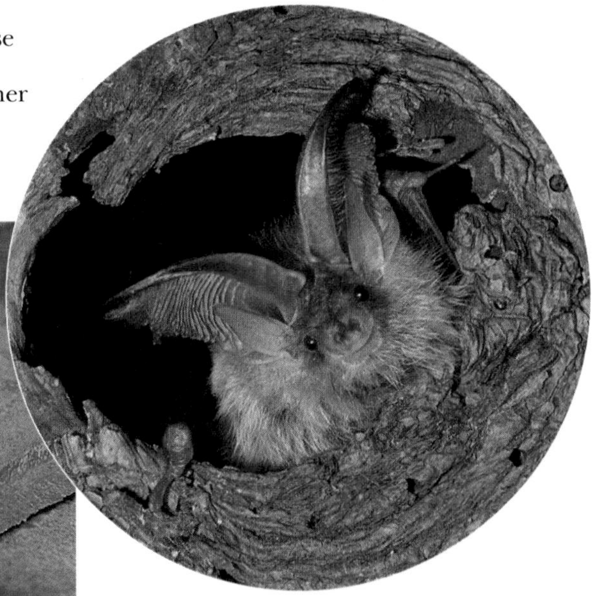

▲ Principally a species of wooded areas, the long-eared bat often establishes its summer nurseries in a hole in a tree trunk or thick branch. However, its winter roosts are only occasionally sited in trees.

◀ In summer, nursery colonies of females and their offspring, together with a few males, often cluster in attics in groups that may number up to 50 bats. Each female produces just one baby a year.

among a cluster of youngsters in the roost, in spite of the darkness and mass of bodies. The young usually huddle together for warmth and are not easy to approach separately. A female returning from a foraging trip listens for the calls of her baby before finding it amid the group and checking its identity by scent.

A female produces just one baby a year and provides milk for her own offspring only. She will not feed any others. Bats do not easily abandon their young, going to great lengths to retrieve them should they fall from the roost or wander away from the main cluster.

Survival rates for long-eared bats are high – around 80 per cent of females and 60 per cent of males live to the following year. In some years, however, particularly when there is a poor summer or long winter, fewer bats will survive. The average life expectancy for long-eared bats is about 16 years but some individuals have lived for more than 20 years. This is a long time for such small animals, although typical of bats in general.

CAT ATTACKS

Long-eared bats have few natural predators, but domestic cats manage to catch a surprising number of bats near their roost sites and in gardens. Some cats may actually get into an attic to attack the bats as they roost, although most seem to sit on walls and window-sills, swatting the bats as they flit by. The bats brought down in this way are rarely eaten, probably because their strong scent glands make them distasteful. Nevertheless, some cats have been known to kill dozens of bats. Such losses could have a severe impact on small colonies.

The domestic cat poses a real threat to several of Britain's native mammals, including low-flying bats such as the long-eared.

Hibernation

In autumn, long-eared bats increase their weight by up to 40 per cent by laying down fat reserves. They tend to hibernate quite late and may still be active in November. Even though they spend the rest of the year keeping warm, long-eareds seek out cool, damp but frost-free places in which to spend the winter, often underground in caves, mines and cellars. They select cooler places than many other bats because they are more easily awoken and nudged into energy-sapping activity, which they try to avoid. They may roost close to the entrance of a cave or mine, where it is cooler than deeper underground.

Large, hollow trees are alternative hibernation sites, particularly in early or late winter. Long-eareds tend to switch roosts in response to changes in air temperature. Studies have shown that long-eared bats prefer to hibernate at temperatures below 8°C (46°F), usually around 6°C (43°F) or less, although if it gets really cold, the bats wake up and move to a less chilly place, usually within the same underground space.

During warm spells, the bats may wake up and fly out to search for insect prey. For most of the winter, however, they are sustained by the fat reserves accumulated in autumn. As these reserves are used up, the bats sometimes lose more than 20 per cent of their total body weight. In some years, when the winter is prolonged, the bats run out of fat. This particularly applies to young born the previous year because they will have spent more of their precious energy in growing, leaving less to store as fat. So in years when spring is late, many young bats will die.

WILDLIFE WATCH

How can I see long-eared bats?

- The best place to watch long-eared bats is below their roost in a house roof or when they are feeding around a tree in a street that has lighting or in a garden or park. At dusk or under artificial lighting, their big ears are clearly visible.
- On warm summer evenings, bats will occasionally feed in the vicinity of outside lights to which moths and other insects have been attracted.
- Long-eared bats are affected by the preservative chemicals used to protect roof timbers from wood-boring insects. Try to use environmentally friendly products that are not harmful to bats.

In order to locate an insect among the swaying stems of meadow grasses, this long-eared bat has to make repeated passes over the potential meal. It will sometimes hover in order to pinpoint its prey.

The song thrush

A pile of broken snail shells indicates the presence of this popular bird, especially in dry weather. It may be seen tugging worms out of lawns or perched on high, pouring out its rich song in countless gardens and parks.

The song thrush lives up to its name, energetically delivering a succession of repeated musical phrases from a high perch such as a treetop. It can be heard from the early morning until dusk throughout much of the year.

A familiar visitor to many gardens and parks, the song thrush is often seen on lawns and in flowerbeds. It has a habit of sweeping aside dead leaves and other ground litter with its bill in its search for earthworms, beetles, snails and other invertebrates. However, this bird is best known for its beautiful song, which consists of up to a hundred or so different, frequently repeated loud phrases. The song thrush's scientific name, *philomelos,* comes from the Greek *philo,* meaning 'beloved', and *melos,* meaning 'song'.

Common names abound for the song thrush – 'throstle' is one and 'mavis' is still used in Scotland. Many people simply refer to it as the thrush but this is imprecise as there are six species of thrush that can be seen regularly in Britain and Ireland: the song thrush, mistle thrush, redwing, fieldfare, blackbird and ring ouzel. However, only three of these – the song thrush, mistle thrush and blackbird – are resident all year.

Identifying thrushes

At first glance, three members of the thrush family look very alike: the song thrush, mistle thrush and redwing. They are all mainly brown with a paler, copiously spotted breast and have a similar shape and stature.

The mistle thrush is Britain's largest thrush. Its upperparts are greyer than the song thrush's, which are a rich shade of brown, and it has more rounded, blacker spots on its breast and telltale white outer tail feathers. Slightly smaller than the song thrush is the redwing, a winter visitor with which it is often confused. The best way to tell a redwing from a song thrush is to look for the redwing's whitish eyestripe and the red flash on its flanks and underwing. The song thrush has no eyestripe and the flash under its wing is a muted orange.

There is a clear pecking order between the different thrush species when a number of them are feeding together, which they often do in winter, when frozen soil makes invertebrates hard to find. Then they may all supplement their diets with berries or fallen apples.

SONG THRUSH FACT FILE

This medium-sized thrush is warm brown above with a pale, boldly spotted breast. Its long legs and upright gait give it an alert look. Most often seen feeding in leaf litter or grassy areas, the song thrush is also easy to spot on its prominent song posts.

● NAMES
Common name: song thrush
Scientific name: *Turdus philomelos*

● DISTRIBUTION
Throughout Britain and Ireland

● STATUS
Population declining in recent years; possibly fewer than 1 million pairs in Britain and Ireland, compared to 2.5 million 30 years ago

● SIZE
Length 23cm (9in); weight 70–90g (2½–3¼oz)

● KEY FEATURES
Uniform, warm brown upperparts; underparts pale with golden-brown wash, breast marked with small, elongated spots that fade on belly; orange-buff underwings that show well in flight

● VOICE
Song is a loud, penetrating series of simple phrases, some melodious, others harsh, each repeated several times, sometimes including mimicry of other birds; common flight call *'tsip'*; alarm call *'tchuck-tchuck'*

● FOOD
Wide range of invertebrates, especially snails, earthworms and caterpillars; berries and other fruit in winter

● BREEDING
March–July, peak breeding season April–May; earliest nests may be built in February; often 2 or 3 broods per year, very productive pairs in the south can raise 4 broods

● NEST
Neat structure of twigs, grass and moss, lined with thick coating of mud, dung or wood pulp; concealed in tree, bush or climbing plant, generally at head height or above

● EGGS
Smooth and slightly glossy, bright pale blue with sparse dark speckles and spots; clutch of 3–5; early clutches in March and late ones in June usually smaller; incubation 10–17 days, mainly by female

● YOUNG
Fledge at 14–16 days, earlier if disturbed; independent after a few days

The nest is loose towards the edges, but more compact inside and thickly lined with smoothed mud, dung or wood pulp.

Face is indistinctly marked with a pale eye ring and throat.
The upperparts are rich brown, with a golden wash to the sides of the breast and flanks.
Dark spots with an arrowhead shape speckle the pale underparts, some forming streaks.
The legs are quite long and pale pink.
Over 11,000 ringed song thrushes have been recovered, yielding the information that, on average, they move just 1km (½ mile) from home.

Distribution map key

Present all year round

Present during summer months

SONG THRUSH CALENDAR

JANUARY • FEBRUARY

Song thrushes start to sing and carve out their territories early in the new year. Many pairs will have formed before the end of February and, in a warm spring, nest building may begin.

MARCH • APRIL

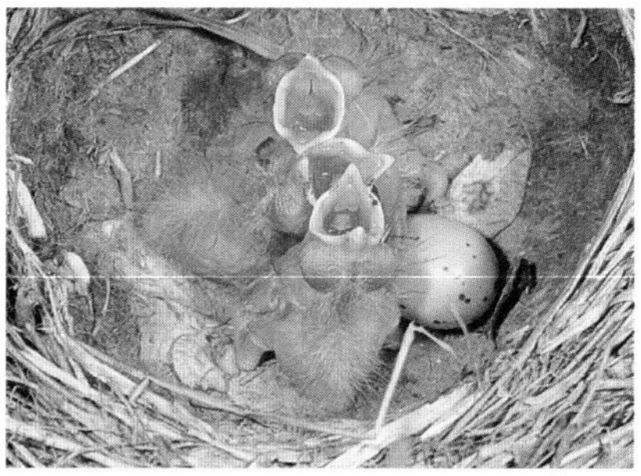

Egg-laying begins in March. The eggs are incubated, mainly by the female, for around two weeks. The first brood of youngsters will have fledged by the end of April.

MAY • JUNE

Adult thrushes continue breeding, and the increasing numbers of independent juveniles, such as those pictured, take advantage of the glut of food available throughout the summer months.

JULY • AUGUST

Breeding stops in July, especially if the summer is hot. Song thrushes are regular visitors to gardens at this time, and their ability to feed on snails gives them an advantage over other songbirds.

SEPTEMBER • OCTOBER

In autumn, northern populations of song thrushes move south to lower ground, and some fly to the Continent. Resident birds flock to feast on berries to fatten up for winter.

NOVEMBER • DECEMBER

The song thrush suffers in cold winters, but birds on the way south from Scandinavia boost numbers temporarily. Some birds from Holland and Belgium winter in southern Britain.

Hammering open snails

In prolonged dry weather, snails may still be found when most normal food sources are scarce. Despite their hard shells, song thrushes are able to feed on them. Curiously, other species of thrush have not managed to acquire this useful skill.

The song thrush swings the snail into the air and then smashes it down onto a hard surface or convenient rock, known as an anvil.

The thrush may have to beat the snail on the stone repeatedly to crack off part of the tough shell, or smash it into fragments.

Firmly grasping the lip of the shell or the snail's soft body, the song thrush sets about removing the animal from its protective shell.

The growing young are fed by both parents on a protein-rich diet of invertebrates, especially earthworms. These contain plenty of water and have few hard parts, so therefore are easily digested.

A great deal of energy is expended by the song thrush when smashing snail shells. The sound of a thrush battering shells to open them can be audible at considerable distances.

The order of precedence in mixed flocks of thrushes – often enforced by threat displays and other posturing – is usually dictated by size. Mistle thrushes are dominant, followed by fieldfares, slightly smaller winter visitors from northern Europe. Then come blackbirds, with song thrushes next and redwings last. A mistle thrush may well be twice as heavy as a redwing, while a song thrush averages only two-thirds of its weight, so it is not surprising that the stocky mistle thrush prevails. The different species may often be seen vying with each other over berry-laden bushes in parks and gardens. Ring ouzels are scarce summer visitors and so never feature in these squabbling groups.

Song thrush territories

The song thrush lives wherever grass and trees or shrubs are found in close proximity, providing a plentiful supply of invertebrate food. Suburban gardens and city parks may support good numbers, while woodland edges, farms, hedgerows and bushy commons are also favoured.

Territories vary in size, depending on the availability of food and nesting sites. Typically, the territory of a pair of song thrushes covers two hectares (five acres) although as many as three or four pairs may inhabit just one hectare of land (one or two pairs per acre).

When times are hard and invertebrate food is scarce, during summer drought or wintry weather for example, the song thrush concentrates on finding snails. Its ability to feed on these molluscs is unique among songbirds and gives the song thrush a source of food denied to other birds of parks and gardens. The snail shells are opened by smashing them on a large stone or brick or a paving slab along a garden path. A song thrush will return to the same spot again and again to

Once the shell is cracked open, the snail is flicked free. The thrush may wipe it on the grass to remove fragments of shell before eating it. If it is too large for the thrush to eat whole, the bird keeps thrashing it upon the ground, tearing off bite-sized pieces with each blow.

The song thrush can often be seen searching lawns for worms, tilting its head to one side to look or listen for any movement in the grass. Once located, a worm is seized and pulled from the soil.

THE MISTLE THRUSH

The mistle thrush is the larger relative of the song thrush. Apart from size, it is easily recognised by its even bolder, more upright stance, stronger, rounder spots, rattling alarm calls and different song. Simple and far-carrying, the mistle thrush's song is rather like a blackbird's but less richly melodious and much louder. One simple phrase is repeated over and over. The mistle thrush is sometimes called the storm cock as it is often the only bird singing on cold, blustery winter days.

In spring and summer, the mistle thrush feeds mainly on insects and various other invertebrates, but in autumn and winter it is particularly fond of the sticky berries of mistletoe. It also eats holly, hawthorn, rowan and yew berries. The mistle thrush breeds widely across Britain and Ireland, in woodland edges and open country with scattered trees and bushes. It is also found on farmland where the mosaic of fields is bordered by hedgerows and trees. In common with the song thrush, the mistle thrush prefers tall trees as song posts.

Mistle thrushes indulge in a type of behaviour known as resource guarding. This begins in early autumn when an individual – or occasionally a pair – starts to defend a berry-bearing tree or bush, such as holly or cotoneaster, from all other birds. The objective is to preserve some berries until spring, so that the mistle thrush can eat its fill and be in good shape for the start of the breeding season.

The main problem occurs during harsh weather. Dozens or even hundreds of birds, including both resident and migrant winter thrushes, may try to steal berries from the mistle thrush 'owner', making it impossible to defend the tree or bush.

The aggressive nature of the mistle thrush can also be observed during the breeding season when pairs vigorously defend their nest against predators, such as sparrowhawks and magpies. Unless a marauding magpie is threatening their nest directly, most small birds keep a low profile when such predators are spotted. However, mistle thrushes boldly attempt to challenge them. Perhaps surprisingly, the predators usually leave. This is good news for other local birds because a sparrowhawk has little chance of catching a small bird, or a magpie of locating a well-concealed nest, when a pair of large thrushes is dive-bombing them.

► The mistle thrush is a powerful flyer. It closes its wings after each flap, pressing them to its sides. This produces a long, elliptical silhouette and an undulating flight path. The underwings, visible on the upbeat, are white.

▼ From October, mistle thrushes defend a concentrated food source such as a well-laden pyracantha shrub or holly. Each bird remains near its tree throughout the winter and if lucky will preserve a supply of berries until the breeding season begins.

▲ The brood of three to five speckled mistle thrush chicks stay in the nest for around 14 days. During this time the young are fed by the male, especially if its mate already has another brood.

The female song thrush spends a lot of time gathering grass, twigs and moss to construct the nest, and also collects mud, dung or wood pulp to form the inner lining.

despatch snails, leaving a conspicuous heap of broken shells. It is believed that this behaviour is largely innate, or instinctive, which would explain why no other thrush has acquired the necessary skills. The snails that the song thrush eats most often are the medium-sized striped ones of the genus *Cepaea*.

Population decline

Until about 1940, song thrushes outnumbered blackbirds in Britain, but in recent years the balance has been reversed. Today, song thrushes are still declining in numbers. Between 1972 and 1996, the Common Bird Census recorded that song thrushes had decreased by 66 per cent on farmland and by 33 per cent in woodland. The downward trend is similar in gardens and parks.

Further research has shown that there is an annual fluctuation in the size of the song thrush population and up to about 20 years ago this was mostly determined by the severity of winters. However, in more recent years the decline has apparently been due to an increase in first-year mortality. Song thrushes seem to lose out to the larger, more aggressive resident blackbirds when they compete for a single food source during the winter.

A widely held concern is that some pesticides used in gardens and on farmland to combat slugs and snails directly poison thrushes and other birds, as well as hedgehogs and small mammals. Another factor that may be involved in the song thrush's recent decline is climate change. In very dry summers the ground may be too

▲ A song thrush chick still has some downy feathers after leaving the safety of the nest. The young birds tend to split up and usually hide among surrounding vegetation.

▶ Even after the fledglings leave the nest, the parent birds continue to respond to an offspring begging for several days, feeding it worms and grubs.

hard for the birds to extract earthworms and they may not be able to find enough snails to sustain themselves and their offspring – earthworms and snails form a major part of the song thrush's diet during the breeding season. Likewise, especially cold winters, with ice or deep snow, prevent the birds from finding food in the soil.

On the move

Most song thrush populations are resident in the same area of Britain or Ireland throughout the year. However, those that breed in the north often move south or south-west for the winter. This strategy is known as partial migration.

The movements of song thrushes and the numbers involved are largely dictated by the onset of cold weather. If very severe weather strikes, even some of the birds living in the south, which do not normally migrate, will head for warmer conditions, flying off to France, Portugal, Spain and even North Africa.

Almost all song thrushes from Scandinavia, Germany and eastern Europe are full migrants, as they are unable to withstand the cold winters that occur in those parts of the world. Some of them winter in Britain while others, known as passage migrants, stop off along the east coast during their journey south as far as the Mediterranean and North Africa.

In the past, song thrushes were among many species of bird regularly attracted to the rotating lights of lighthouses. The migrating birds would try to follow the moving lights and end up hopelessly lost. New technology using electronics to make the lights flash on and off rather than rotate has saved the lives of millions of birds every year.

Although the larger mistle thrush has more of a reputation for aggression, the song thrush will readily defend valuable food sources. Here, a song thrush protects a bowl of mealworms from a juvenile starling.

WILDLIFE WATCH

How can I see song thrushes?

- It is quite easy to see song thrushes by going for a walk in the local park. Take a pair of binoculars for a closer view. In order to encourage song thrushes into the garden, avoid using chemicals to control invertebrates. Even if the chemicals are not directly harmful to birds, the absence of slugs, snails and worms will mean that thrushes have much less food.
- Song thrushes are remarkably easy to observe on the Isles of Scilly, off Cornwall, where they seem to be indifferent to human observers to the point of being tame. They can often be approached when feeding, to within a few metres.
- In particularly cold weather, especially when snow is on the ground, put out apples or other fruit to attract song thrushes. Crush it underfoot to help the birds feed.

The wren

Often the loudest, shrillest song to be heard in the garden is produced by one of the tiniest birds – the wren. This fine songster uses its voice to attract mates and maintain its territory.

The wren spends most of its time deep in scrub or dense vegetation, close to ground level. Its agility enables it to capture many kinds of invertebrates, while its slender bill is ideal for gleaning prey from awkward nooks and crannies.

The wren is the shortest bird in the British Isles but not the smallest. With its squat, rotund body, it weighs twice as much as the slightly longer goldcrest, which is more slender and delicately built.

From February to July, the explosive song of the male wren is a common sound as he goes about the business of building several domed nests and attracting a mate. The female chooses one of the nests and lines it with feathers. She usually lays two clutches of five to eight eggs each year, although the male may father several more families as he may have more than one mate.

Following several mild winters in a row, the wren population may build up to such an extent that it becomes the most common breeding bird in Britain and Ireland, with as many as 10 million breeding territories. These include gardens and parks, woodland, hedgerows, well-vegetated moorland and remote sea cliffs, and are most numerous in places with thick ground cover.

Maintaining territories

Song is the wren's main way of signalling territory ownership. A male wren's powerful, rich, warbling notes, which generally end in a trill, are amazingly loud and far-carrying. Neighbouring wrens recognise the voice of the resident songster, which tells them that the same bird is present. An intruder's call will be spotted immediately, the presence of a 'stranger' provoking agitated activity among neighbours who fear that some of their territory might be taken from them.

DID YOU KNOW?

Wrens are distinguished by the scientific name *Troglodytes troglodytes,* from the Latinised Greek word for 'cave-dweller', and wrens can be found nesting in caves from the coast to high mountain areas. For non-cave dwelling birds, the name reflects their preference for nesting in dark, cave-like places, and their habit of creeping through 'tunnels' of vegetation while hunting for food.

WREN FACT FILE

An unmistakable bird, the wren is a tiny, restless species that from a distance appears to be no more than a compact ball of brown feathers. At close range, it is easier to appreciate the wren's cocked tail, subtly marked plumage and furtive movements.

● NAMES
Common name: wren, northern wren, European wren
Scientific name: *Troglodytes troglodytes*

● DISTRIBUTION
Throughout Britain and Ireland wherever there is cover for feeding and shelter

● STATUS
There may be 10 million breeding territories after a series of mild winters, making this the most common bird in Britain and Ireland

● SIZE
Length 9–10cm (3½–4in); weight 8–12g (¼–½oz)

● KEY FEATURES
Long bill; body short and rotund with characteristically cocked tail; plumage rich brown, striped and spotted with flecks of lighter colour

● HABITS
Scuttles around in dense vegetation, usually close to ground level

● VOICE
Song very distinctive and loud for such a small bird; male sings all year; each male has several different phrases in its repertoire, usually distinguished by loud ringing trill at end; local dialects

● FOOD
Insects, spiders, other invertebrates; picked from vegetation and ground; tiny fish and tadpoles sometimes plucked from water

● BREEDING
In warm springs, first eggs laid before end of March; most first clutches in April, second in June; replacements laid up to early August

● NEST
Ball of material in hole in bank, wall or climbing plants growing on tree, in rocky crevice or nestbox; male usually builds 5 to 8 'cock' nests; female chooses one and adds lining

● EGGS
Pale, glossy white, with reddish-brown markings at broad end; clutch size generally 5–7; female alone incubates for about 16 days

● YOUNG
Brooded almost continuously for first few days; male may help if monogamous pairing but often has other broods elsewhere; fledge at 14–19 days; fed by both parents (or female alone if male has more than one mate) for another 9–18 days

Each year most female wrens produce two broods of about six young, filling the tiny nest that is often squeezed into a rock crevice. Like adults, the young have slim bills and disproportionately large feet.

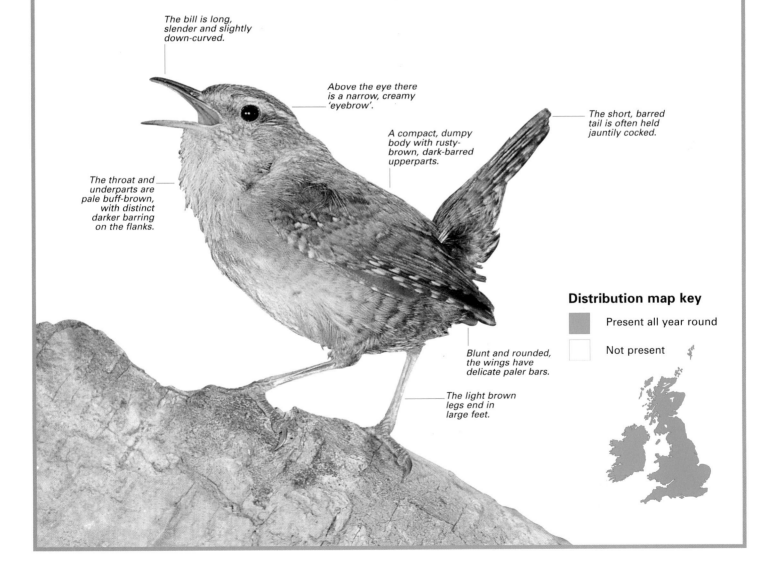

The bill is long, slender and slightly down-curved.
Above the eye there is a narrow, creamy 'eyebrow'.
The short, barred tail is often held jauntily cocked.
A compact, dumpy body with rusty-brown, dark-barred upperparts.
The throat and underparts are pale buff-brown, with distinct darker barring on the flanks.
Blunt and rounded, the wings have delicate paler bars.
The light brown legs end in large feet.

Distribution map key

Present all year round

Not present

◀ Dense lichen and climbing plants, such as ivy, on the trunks of trees usually indicate a profitable foraging site for wrens to seek invertebrates and their grubs.

▼ The wren's song is extremely loud for such a small bird. When it sings from an open perch, the amount of energy required to maintain its vigorous and complicated tune can sometimes be seen, the bird's diminutive frame trembling with the effort.

Territory is so important because each bird depends upon the knowledge it acquires about its own area for survival.

In the wooded hills of southern England, such as the Chilterns, there may be two or three breeding pairs per hectare (about one pair per acre) in the summer. However, the woods are bleak and cold in the winter and summer visitors are nowhere to be seen. Unlike almost all warblers, for instance, which leave for the warmer climate of Africa, wrens just move nearer to the ground, favouring areas of tangled, wet vegetation, such as reedbeds. Since water retains heat better than air, the microclimate of such locations is slightly warmer than elsewhere, and insect prey remains active for longer. The birds usually return to the same wintering spots in subsequent years. This is a successful arrangement because the areas are too wet for wrens to breed, so damp-loving warbler species do not experience competition for their summer territories on their return in the spring.

In sedentary populations, male wrens are territorial for most of the year, relaxing their defences once they have a thriving nestful of chicks and during the winter. Territories are maintained both by sight and sound, and altercations between rivals tend to be extremely rapid. A quick display on a mutual boundary, reinforced by hard, rattling '*tic-tic-tic*' calls, usually serves to establish the border without wasting any valuable feeding time.

Winter survival

Like all small birds, the wren faces the problem of how to keep warm when its surroundings are cold. It loses heat rapidly because of its tiny size and is

Scuttling about

Wrens are often very difficult to locate since they tend to feed low down, well below eye level. They are usually seen only briefly as they flit and hop among the tangle of stalks, stems and foliage in semidarkness.

A wren patrols its territory, watching for the slightest movement of prey. Every now and again it dives into a crevice to pluck out a morsel of food.

Short, rounded wings give good manoeuvrability. This is invaluable as the bird chases small insects through thickets and bushes.

unable to lay down a thick enough layer of fat to provide insulation against the cold, let alone accumulate reserves for use as energy.

In spite of this, the wren is readily able to live in cold conditions, even with a blanket of snow covering its favourite bramble and thorn thickets, provided that enough food is available. Its first line of defence against heat loss is an efficient layer of feathers. The wren has roughly the same number of feathers as many much larger birds. When fluffed out against the cold, these provide an effective insulating barrier that traps warm air next to the body.

The shortage of daylight at the coldest time of the year presents another real problem for the wren and other small birds that hunt by sight. At the very time when the wren is most in need of fuel, there is least time to find it. Furthermore, the ground-living invertebrates that make up most of the bird's diet are likely to be lethargic, if not completely static, hidden away from the cold. This makes them hard for the wren to find.

Wrens have a distinctly mouse-like gait when scuttling around in the vegetation. While the light holds, they move deftly through dense shrubbery, searching for tiny food items. These nimble birds snatch spiders, beetles and other insects, plucking them from the surface of leaves, or plunging their bills into earth, leaf litter, crevices in tree bark or cracks between bricks to tweak out their prey.

During especially harsh winter weather, wrens may be forced to abandon their territorial behaviour and roost communally to survive.

SHORT-TERM MATES

Wrens seldom form long-lasting pair bonds. On the mainland, in good habitats such as woods, about half of all male wrens court a succession of females. In spring, they build a series of nests in their territory. These ball-shaped nests – known as cock nests – resemble those made by mice. They are usually domed and formed of leaves, moss and grass.

These structures are an attempt to entice a female into pairing with their constructor. Once the female has chosen the best nest for laying, she will add a lining of feathers and hair. While the female is incubating her clutch, the male may fly off to court other females and try to tempt them with one of his other nests. This means that some males may have from two to four mates nesting within their territory, leaving each one after mating to court the next one. These males are kept busy by their multiple courtings and have little if anything to do with the rearing of their chicks. Few of the females will nest with the same male for their second brood of the year.

Wrens may nest over a period of three months, and some cock nests frequently remain unlined and unused for several weeks. Eventually a female may line an old cock nest for her second or third brood.

▲ The female often assumes full responsibility for feeding the young. A nutritious diet of invertebrates, such as spiders, ensures the young grow quickly and are ready to fledge within three weeks.

◀ The male builds nests that are usually camouflaged to blend into a recess in a tree, ivy, a wall or bank. Once padded with feathers and moss, each nest forms a snug nursery for the young.

Relatively long, strong legs and feet enable the wren to stretch and poke its way into confined spaces in rock outcrops and walls.

On extremely cold nights they may roost in tight-packed groups. Commonly used sites for communal roosting include wide cracks in tree bark, nestboxes, old house martin nests and under the eaves of buildings. The total amount of heat lost from a group of wrens inside a nestbox or other site is much less than that lost from the same number of birds roosting individually. There are several records of 30, 40 or 50 wrens – and even on one occasion more than 60 wrens – roosting in a single nestbox. More usually, such winter roosts contain up to ten birds.

This emergency strategy does not always work and every now and then the wren population will be devastated by a severe winter. A few days of cold weather may cause some problems, but usually even several spells of frosty weather can be endured. However, a prolonged spell of very cold weather or even a short

Warmth gained from the sun's rays is useful for a small, highly active bird such as the wren. Splaying its wings and crouching on the sun-warmed earth enables the wren to increase its surface area, absorbing as much heat as possible after the cool of night.

Looking and listening

Perched on a twig, the wren is ever-alert to its surroundings. Its sharp eyes detect prey, while it listens for calls and songs that might indicate what its neighbours and potential rivals are doing.

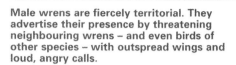

Male wrens are fiercely territorial. They advertise their presence by threatening neighbouring wrens – and even birds of other species – with outspread wings and loud, angry calls.

WREN CALENDAR

JANUARY • MARCH

Wrens are most at risk from cold weather early in the year. As spring approaches, males burst into song and establish themselves in a breeding territory.

APRIL • JUNE

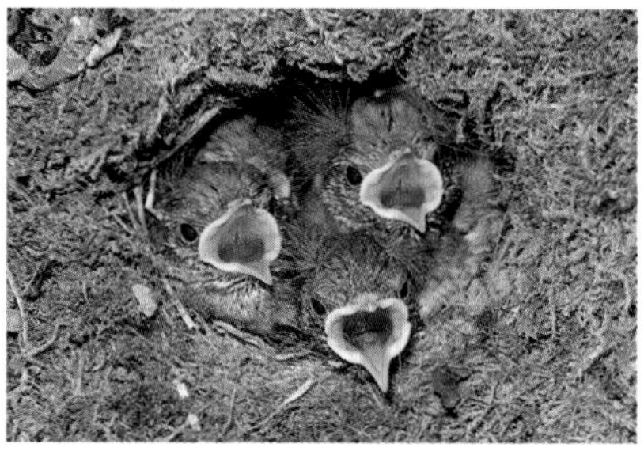

Males build several nests with which to tempt potential mates. The young are well camouflaged, revealing their orange mouths only when begging for food.

JULY • SEPTEMBER

Wrens become increasingly easy to see as juveniles explore possible breeding areas in the vicinity and young from the second and third broods hatch and fledge.

OCTOBER • DECEMBER

Many upland wrens move to sheltered valleys. If the weather turns really cold, large communal roosts may build up, the birds huddling together for warmth.

period – just a few days – of glazed ice conditions can result in vast losses. Ice often seals the surfaces that wrens would normally be able to investigate for food. These conditions usually succeed partly thawed hoar frost or periods of freezing fog when the weather gets even colder. The wrens need as much food as possible merely to maintain their body heat in the cold conditions, and denied this vital resource many will perish. In bad years, the loss of wrens may result in the breeding population during the next season falling by up to 80 per cent.

Replenishing numbers

Such devastation would seem to endanger the continued existence of any bird, even one as common as the wren. However, the breeding potential of these tiny birds is exceptional. A wren pair producing two or occasionally three broods a year, each comprising a clutch of five or six, can easily rear 12 youngsters to independence. In addition, the cold weather will not only have affected wrens. Other small birds, such as goldcrests and long-tailed tits, will suffer depleted populations too, so competition for food will be significantly reduced. As a result, more of the birds will survive the next winter. Normal population levels will be restored within four or five years and wrens will occupy all the available territories once again.

The wren found in mainland Britain is very widespread throughout most of Europe and across the middle of Asia. The same species is also found in North America from Newfoundland to Alaska, where it is called the winter wren. In North America and in South and Central America, it has more than 70 relatives in the wren family.

Closer to home, some of the Scottish islands are home to a number of different subspecies of wren. Living in caves, on the seashore and among tangled bracken, these populations are mainly sedentary, since winter weather is often warmer on the islands than on the mainland, being influenced by the relative warmth of the sea.

Some of the island wrens have been isolated for generations. On the islands of the Inner Hebrides and Orkney the wrens are very similar to those on the mainland. However, on remoter islands, more distinct subspecies have evolved. The unique wren population on the extremely isolated Outer Hebridean island of St Kilda is known as *Troglodytes troglodytes hirtensis*; on other Outer Hebridean islands the wrens are *T. t. hebridensis*; on Fair Isle there is *T. t. fridariensis*; the Shetland subspecies is *T. t. zetlandicus*; and the Faeroes have *T. t. borealis*.

These birds have different proportions from the mainland wrens. In particular, they have progressively longer bills, tails, wings and feet the further north they live. Their plumage also differs. For example, wrens from St Kilda and Fair Isle are greyer above. Those from the Outer Hebrides and Shetland are darker and more barred above and paler below.

These island species are thought to behave differently from the mainland birds during the mating season. Whereas mainland wrens are typically polygymous – that is, each male will mate with as many females as possible – the island wrens (and those inhabiting harsh mainland areas where food is difficult to find) are thought to form faithful pairs that bond for the whole year.

▲ The wren's whirring flight is direct and rapid, but not suited to long distances. Its small size and rounded wings give it an almost bee-like appearance in flight.

► In winter, reedbeds and waterside roosts are warmer than other places, and in spring and summer wrens may venture to pond margins in search of food.

Wrens are among many species of British birds that are occasionally tricked into raising young cuckoos. It might be expected that the huge size of the chick would alert its smaller foster parents, but this is not so.

WILDLIFE WATCH

How can I see wrens?

● With such a large population of wrens in Britain, in a wide variety of habitats, it is not too difficult to find this species. Wrens may be territorial throughout the year; their explosive song with the characteristic trill at the end can give away their presence at 100m (110yd) or more.

● Too close an approach may cause a wren to stop singing. It will make short, aggressive *'tchack'* calls of disapproval.

● A favourite garden haunt is the compost heap, or around farms and stables, the muck heap or midden. Here, the heat generated by the rotting organic matter provides a warmer micro-climate that encourages insect life and makes a rewarding foraging site.

The house sparrow

Equally at home in bustling cities or rural villages, the house sparrow draws attention to itself with its chirping, bold behaviour and frequent squabbles.

One of the most familiar of all wild birds, the house sparrow lives in close proximity to people and often becomes very tame. This small songbird has been among the most successful creatures in the world at taking advantage of urban life. Its relationship with humans has developed gradually over many generations and it owes much of its success to this partnership.

The house sparrow is native throughout Europe and North Africa and in parts of Asia, and has been introduced – both accidentally and intentionally – to North and South America, South Africa and Australia, making this one of the world's most widespread birds. City streets, town parks, suburban gardens, country villages and isolated farmhouses are all among its haunts. In fact, its distribution is almost entirely restricted to areas near human habitation, and changes in the urban environment may be one of the reasons for its recent decline in numbers in Britain. The average flock size in gardens has dropped by 30–50 per cent since 1970 and its general distribution has shrunk, too.

The male house sparrow (centre) takes almost full responsibility for the care of the fledglings. Both sexes bring insect food, but the female will be intent on incubating her next clutch of eggs.

Adaptable species

However, the house sparrow is highly adaptable and its previous success was due to its ability to exploit whatever opportunities are available. Roosting and nesting sites are provided in the nooks and crannies of buildings, in the climbing plants that grow over them and in the bushes and shrubs of parks and gardens. Not only does the house sparrow use a variety of nest sites, but it eats a wide range of food and quickly takes advantage of new sources of supply. For instance, over the last 40 years, it has learned to copy the tits that hang acrobatically on birdfeeders in order to get to whatever dietary supplement they may conveniently contain, usually nuts.

Group nesting

House sparrows may nest throughout the year if the weather is mild, but generally breed between May and August. These social birds congregate in small, loose but discrete colonies. A colony typically contains up to one or two dozen breeding pairs. They build their nests very close together, although nest entrances will generally be at least 15cm (6in) apart. Nests are ideally placed in cavities in buildings and are untidy structures of grass and straw lined with feathers. However, if the core area of the colony does not provide enough natural holes, some birds will be forced to build free-standing domed nests in the branches of a tree or in creepers on a wall. They quite often take over the nests of house martins and customise them to fit their stockier body shape. If nestboxes are provided, the birds readily take to them, abandoning open nests.

Each colony has a home range of a few hectares, chosen for its potential to provide nest sites, a safe roosting area and feeding grounds, all of which are essential to the colony. In areas of low breeding density and good food resources, colonies may remain entirely isolated from neighbouring ones, separated by several hundred metres of intervening land. Such colonies have limited contact with each other. However, at higher densities or where food resources are more spread out, such as in urban areas, birds from different colonies mingle.

The house sparrow often lives close to humans and owes its success to its adaptability. An abandoned frying pan makes just as good a place to bathe and drink as a puddle for this bird.

HOUSE SPARROW FACT FILE

Often overlooked in the past due to its subdued colouring, the house sparrow repays closer observation. This small, sociable species has many different calls and displays a wide range of behaviour at its nesting colonies in spring and summer and when feeding in flocks.

● **NAMES**
Common name: house sparrow
Scientific name: *Passer domesticus*

● **HABITAT**
Most areas of human habitation

● **DISTRIBUTION**
Throughout the British Isles except for parts of Scotland; scarcer at altitude but found on offshore islands such as Orkney, Shetland and the Outer Hebrides

● **STATUS**
7–8 million; major ongoing decline began last century

● **SIZE**
Length 14–15cm (5½–6in); weight 25–32g (1–1⅛oz)

● **KEY FEATURES**
Small, robust, thick-set bird; head large, bill heavy and conical; male boldly patterned, warm brown upperparts marked with dark streaks, chestnut nape, grey crown, greyish white cheeks, black eyestripe and bib; female slightly smaller and much duller, pale buff brown with darker streaks, pale buff streak behind each eye, one distinct pale wingbar

● **VOICE**
A wide range of loud chirping and other calls; male has simple chirping song

● **FOOD**
Mainly plant material, especially seeds, buds, shoots and berries; wide range of household scraps; grain and other food on farms; young are fed insects and other invertebrates

● **BREEDING**
Starts early April; pairs raise up to 3 or 4 broods each year; last young fledge in August

● **NEST**
Untidy ball of loosely woven material, free-standing or fitted into available cavity, including nestboxes; nest in colonies

● **EGGS**
White, pale greyish or greenish, smooth, variably speckled grey or black; generally 3–5 eggs per clutch; hatch in 11–14 days

● **YOUNG**
Chicks remain in nest until they fledge at 14–16 days; female becomes less attentive as fledging time approaches, but both parents feed their offspring for a further 11–19 days

The female house sparrow lacks the black bib and grey crown of the male. The female's distinguishing features are a pale stripe behind the eye and a whitish wingbar.

Distribution map key

Present all year round
Not present

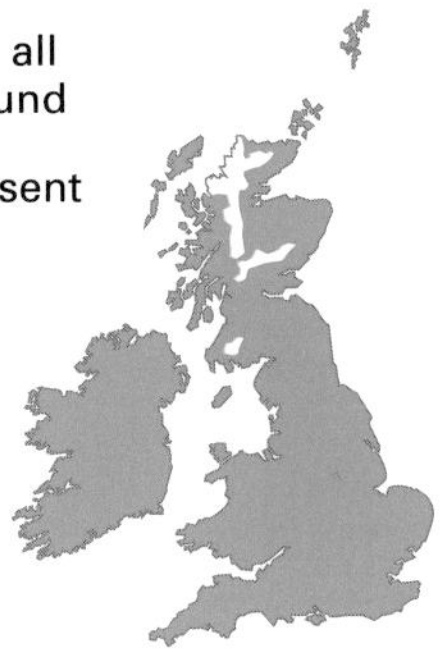

The grey crown occurs in the male only.
The male's grey bill turns black in the breeding season.
In males, the black mask extends into a black bib with an untidy lower edge. This reaches further down the breast in the breeding season.
The underparts are grey in both sexes.

Hyperactive feeders

In spring and summer, flocks of house sparrows scour gardens, parks and hedgerows for seeds, shoots, buds, berries and other plant food. They chatter noisily and almost constantly as they hop and flutter amid the twigs.

Ever on the hunt for food, the house sparrow seeks out morsels in trees, shrubs and bushes.

DUST BATHING

▼ In summer, groups of house sparrows can often be seen wriggling in patches of dust or the topsoil of flowerbeds. The fine sediment helps to remove grease and parasites from their feathers.

Many birds use dust as well as water to clean their feathers. It is not unusual to see a small flock of sparrows flapping about in a shallow, dusty scrape in the ground – and apparently thoroughly enjoying it.

Similar techniques are employed to bathe in dust as for a water bath. The sparrows duck their heads while flapping the dirt on to their backs with their wings, then shiver to work the dust into their plumage. Dust bathing is efficient at removing oily deposits and dirt in the feathers and helps to keep the plumage in good condition. It may also help the birds to rid themselves of small parasites, such as fleas and lice, which lodge among their feathers and suck their blood.

Both sexes collect nesting material, such as grasses, and all available space within the nest will be packed with a soft lining. Normally, the first clutch of three to five pale, speckled eggs is laid in April.

Shared feeding areas are usually within a 500m (⅓ mile) radius of the birds' nesting sites.

Feeding flocks

Once they reach independence, juvenile house sparrows form small flocks to forage. During the summer, these flocks combine to form larger aggregations at suitable feeding sites, and may also be joined by young birds from several neighbouring colonies. The flocks increase in size as more young fledge and they are inflated further by an influx of adults that have finished breeding and are preparing to begin their annual moult. Once this is completed the adults return to their breeding colony to reclaim their old nest site – a good site may be used for several years running. The juveniles usually disperse from their natal area between June and August, but rarely wander more than a mile or two away.

Population changes

Sparrows generally do not stray too far from their home sites to feed so a colony's territory must have feeding areas as well as nesting and roosting sites. Even if food is available elsewhere, sparrows tend to stay close to home, and this may partly explain the continuing decline in house sparrow populations.

The loss of a main breeding or roosting site, however, perhaps due to the demolition of an old building or the felling of an ancient, ivy-covered tree, is enough to disrupt the birds' lives completely. It can cause a whole colony to abandon its territory, the birds either moving as a group or splitting up and scattering to try to join other local colonies. If adult sparrows join other groups and the resources available to those colonies become restricted, the less experienced, juvenile birds in those groups will be excluded. They will be left with less food and inferior roosting sites, and face a difficult fight for survival.

Breeding habits

Within each colony there is a definite pecking order, defining each bird's position in relation to the other members of the group. For the males, social status is reinforced by the size of the black bib on the throat and breast, which effectively serves as a status badge.

Breeding is determined by status. Although mates remain together, they can hardly be described as faithful pairs. Males often maintain two or more additional females in nearby nests, while females may solicit matings from males

At least one bird in the group keeps an eye out for danger, whether it be a sparrowhawk in the air or a cat on the ground.

The parent birds bring back beakfuls of invertebrates for their growing young. Although adult house sparrows are usually vegetarian, a more nutritious diet is important for the fast-growing chicks, especially in the first few weeks.

other than their partners. Females may also lay eggs in nests belonging to other pairs. Such activity is commonplace. Recent DNA-testing techniques have demonstrated that in most nests many of the chicks raised each year will have been fathered by neighbouring cock birds as opposed to the resident male.

Courtship displays

Male house sparrows choose a nest site with an eye to attracting a mate and they advertise the nest to the best of their ability. Sitting at the entrance, each male chirrups away, proclaiming the nest's ownership. When a potential mate approaches, the male adopts a posture with his black bib thrust forward and wings spread wide to show off the bright white wingbars. The tail is held raised and fanned. If a female house sparrow pays any attention to this display, the male becomes increasingly excited. He hops around her, stiffly bowing up and down, and when the male is particularly agitated, he shivers his wings.

If the cock sparrow is lucky the female may stay and they will establish a pair bond. If the female sparrow is not interested, she will threaten the displaying male and fly off. A chase may ensue, which soon attracts an excited band of other males. On landing, the female may

HOUSE SPARROW CALENDAR

JANUARY • FEBRUARY

Large flocks of sparrows may visit gardens where food is supplied regularly. Peanuts are a rich source of fat and help the birds to endure the months of hardship.

MARCH • APRIL

Males select a nest site, singing loudly to proclaim their ownership and displaying whenever a potential mate comes near. Pairs are formed soon afterwards.

MAY • JUNE

The first young fledge in May and the adults continue to raise successive broods for several months. The young sparrows flock together as soon as their parents stop looking after them.

JULY • AUGUST

By August, the breeding season winds down and both adults and juveniles undergo a complete moult. The feathers are lost in strict rotation so that the birds are never flightless.

SEPTEMBER • OCTOBER

Until recently, huge flocks of sparrows congregated on stubble fields for spilt grain and weed seeds. Today, farming is more efficient and there is less waste grain for sparrows to eat.

NOVEMBER • DECEMBER

In winter, harsh weather can cause problems for the house sparrow, since a blanket of snow may cover its food supply. Many populations rely on people to provide food.

THE TREE SPARROW

The tree sparrow, *Passer montanus*, is the smaller country cousin of the house sparrow. It can be distinguished by its trimmer shape, its rich chestnut crown and nape, and white cheek patches. These almost form a white collar that contrasts with the crown and the small, black bib, which marks only the throat and not the breast as in the house sparrow. The cheeks are marked by a distinct black spot below and behind the eye. The call is similar to that of the house sparrow, but more of a '*tchip*', being shorter, sharper and higher-pitched than the latter's '*chirrup*'. The flight call is a hoarse '*teck teck*', which usually sets off a chattering chorus from the rest of the flock.

The tree sparrow is a bird of fields and open woodland rather than towns and gardens. It prefers to nest in holes in trees, but farm buildings are sometimes used. Free-standing nests are flattened spheres with a side entrance leading to a cup packed full of moss, wool, feathers and hair. Part of the male's display involves the conspicuous addition of nest material to the nest hole. The birds sometimes decorate their nests with fresh leaves, the scent of which may act as an insect repellent. Alternatively, four or five pairs may nest together in the base of an abandoned heron's or carrion crow's nest.

► Tree sparrows use nestboxes where they can oust the original occupants, such as blue tits. The tree sparrow's smaller size enables it to exploit holes that a house sparrow cannot squeeze into.

The first clutch of two to seven (usually four to six) pale eggs, heavily blotched with brown, is normally laid at the end of April or in early May. The young hatch after 11 to 13 days, fledging after just 15 to 20 days. The interval between one brood fledging and the next eggs being laid is frequently less than five days, and three broods may be reared by the end of the season in August.

Despite this impressive rate of breeding, healthy, thriving populations may disappear suddenly. Nestbox sites with dozens of breeding birds, built up over eight or ten years, are deserted without warning. However, much more worrying is the population decline of over 90 per cent that has been recorded nationally over the last 25 years. The cause of the decline is attributed to the intensification of agriculture. Tree sparrows are affected by both declining weed seed stocks in winter and the insufficient supply of insect food for their chicks in summer.

▲ The tree sparrow is a sociable species and outside the breeding season large flocks build up at feeding sites. Tree sparrows often form mixed flocks with house sparrows, finches and buntings.

◄ The tree sparrow is much more shy and retiring than its urban relative. Its favourite habitat is lightly wooded farmland, which provides both trees for nesting and access to cultivated fields and farmyards for feeding.

House sparrows are pugnacious birds and disputes over food or territory can lead to violence. Their claws are their main weapons so fights often take place on the ground, with the rivals rolling in dirt.

be encircled by her boisterous suitors and subjected to their attentions. They attempt to peck at her cloaca and force her to copulate. However, such matings are to no avail unless the female is already paired and has a nest in which to lay the resulting eggs.

As the breeding season progresses, the male's advertisement calls and song displays gradually die down, but he is reinvigorated when the brood comes to maturity. This is thought to be a necessary stimulus for the female to nest again and produce another clutch with the male.

Since male sparrows are very quick to take advantage of any available female, it is not surprising that hybrids between the house sparrow and its close relative the slimmer tree sparrow occasionally occur. Hybrids are likely to be the product of casual matings rather than of established pairs because each species has an inherent preference for the females of its own kind. These brief couplings are rarely part of a lasting pairing.

Varied diet

House sparrows are mainly herbivorous, eating seeds, buds and berries. One food preference is for the nutritious nectar of the yellow crocus – sparrows snip off the flowers in spring. However, urban house sparrows in particular are not fussy eaters. Some probably eat little natural food at all, subsisting on scraps and handouts from humans. Sparrows rapidly become confident when they find good, regular sources of food, and will even feed from a person's hand. Despite being an occasional nuisance, house sparrows

◀ Once fledged, young sparrows sit quietly where their parents left them until they return. When a parent reappears, the young birds start begging, crouching low and quivering their wings.

▶ House sparrows prefer to nest in small crevices, but where their nests are free-standing, such as in a hedgerow, they are domed structures of loosely woven grass and straw, lined with a thick bed of feathers and other soft material.

normally manage to live off items discarded by humans without people even realising it. Foodstuffs provided for chickens and other livestock, including oats dropped from horses' nosebags and undigested cereals in their dung, make an easy meal for sparrows and other birds.

In late summer and autumn, house sparrows flock to nearby ripening grain fields, although the birds are less common on farmland now than in the past. Stackyards where the grain was kept used to be good places for sparrows, but these yards have disappeared with the advent of the combine harvester. Instead, the birds must rely upon locating grain spilt from trailers and lorries as it is being transported round the bends and over the bumps of country lanes.

Threats to sparrows

House sparrows have given their name to one avian predator, the sparrowhawk. These birds of prey are now more common in towns and cities as well as in rural areas, so urban sparrow populations are at risk. Male sparrowhawks, which are smaller than females, hunt smaller birds as well, but both sexes prey on sparrows. Sparrowhawks hunt their prey by gliding low over the ground, skimming the hedges and rooftops. Adult sparrows are difficult to take by surprise in this way, but the less wary juveniles are easier to catch.

Sparrows are also killed by domestic cats. Patches of white feathers on a sparrow are often a sign that it has had a narrow escape, since flesh wounds may damage the pigment-producing cells around feather follicles.

House sparrows collide with windows quite frequently, which can be fatal but most times they escape unharmed. In a minority of cases, the hard, horny bill breaks. While broken bills can grow back, the new growth often fails to match up with the other mandible and bizarrely overgrown beaks result. If both mandibles are damaged, they may grow into a 'crossbill'. Birds that have suffered such an injury may appear to be incapable of feeding normally, but this is not so. Ornithologists catching such birds report that they are often as heavy as birds with perfectly formed bills, although they occasionally have many more parasites than would be normal due to the bill deformity preventing effective preening.

Hanging precariously from aquatic vegetation, a male house sparrow drinks from a pond. Even quite small ornamental ponds in parks and gardens provide the perfect place for sparrows to drink and clean their plumage.

WILDLIFE WATCH

Where can I see house sparrows?

- Nowadays, watching house sparrows may not be a case of simply looking in the garden. The British Trust for Ornithology estimates that there are 10 million fewer house sparrows in the UK than there were 25 years ago, and that there has been a 50 per cent overall decline in the suburban garden population. Rural gardens have the most house sparrows.
- House sparrows are birds of habit. A local group of sparrows tends to use the same roosting and nest sites, and the birds forage in the same area year after year. Ideal places include areas where food or animal feed is produced. Farms where livestock is kept or where the grain is stored on site are better than purely arable farms, where the crop is moved out as soon as it is harvested.
- In towns, docklands and tourist areas are good for house sparrows. In the docks, they rely on spilt grain for food and in tourist areas plenty of fast food is usually dropped by visitors. The birds can be a nuisance at outdoor cafés. Apart from the question of hygiene, the birds may even try to steal food before it is eaten. Many establishments have stopped putting out bowls of sugar as sparrows have been known to eat it.
- In spring, watch out for males showing off at the entrances to their nest sites as they try to impress females. Their excitement is compounded by the efforts of their neighbours, and mass hysteria can run through a colony. This has the effect of making well-positioned nest sites extremely desirable to potential female mates.

The earthworm

Earthworms literally eat their way through the soil, churning it up and helping to maintain its fertility. Every single grain of topsoil in a garden is likely to have passed through an earthworm's body many times.

Earthworms exist in enormous numbers, especially in soils with plenty of organic matter. Population estimates peak at 7.5 million worms per hectare (3 million per acre) in old grasslands and orchards. They are less numerous in gardens, but there may be up to 25,000 worms in a well-established garden of 0.1 hectare (¼ acre). Gardeners probably dig up at least one worm with every forkful of soil. Worm tunnels play a vital role in aerating and draining the soil, and helping plant roots to grow.

There are 26 native earthworm species in the British Isles, but only about ten of these regularly occur in gardens. Although they differ in length and the number of segments, they all look much alike. They are generally pink, but often tinged with red, brown, blue or green.

Earthworms belong to the group of animals known as annelids, the bodies of which consist of numerous rings or segments. There is no real head, although the front end is more pointed than the rear. Part of the way along the body, a mature worm has a slightly swollen region, called the saddle or clitellum, which is involved in egg-laying.

Swallowing soil

Most earthworms live in the top 30cm (12in) of soil, but some can be found 1m (3ft) or more below the surface, especially in prolonged cold or dry weather. Worms tunnel partly by forcing their way between particles of earth, but mainly by swallowing soil as they go. They digest rotting plant roots and other organic matter in the soil and often augment their diet by pulling dead leaves into their burrows.

An earthworm requires great muscular power to thrust its snout forward through the soil. Tiny bristles called chaetae on the underside of the body dig into the tunnel walls and anchor the body, while the front end is pushed forward.

An earthworm makes ideal prey for many animals. Its protein-rich body has no protection from the sharp bills of birds such as this song thrush. However, worms that manage to avoid predators can live for over ten years.

The mature worm has a saddle-like bulge, known as the clitellum, part way along its length. The outer skin of this slips off after mating, collecting eggs and sperm and then forming a protective cocoon around the eggs.

▲ The common earthworm lives in a permanent burrow up to 1m (3ft) deep. Earthworms are usually active throughout the year, but they become dormant in very cold or dry weather.

BODY REGENERATION

The popular myth that if an earthworm is cut in half it will grow into two worms is false. Indeed, such victims of the gardener's spade usually die. However, if they lose only a short section from the rear end, they are able to regenerate the lost segments quite easily. Some species can even regenerate lost front ends.

Moles often store worms in autumn and winter, preventing them from escaping by biting off their heads. The worms do not die and should a mole fail to return they gradually regenerate their snouts and move away to safety.

This earthworm is regenerating its front end. A series of segmental nerve centres take over the job of coordinating the body until the worm's tiny 'brain' can regrow.

► As they travel along, two worm species in the genus *Allolobophora* regularly throw soil on to the surface in the form of coiled worm casts. The tunnels allow water and air to pass downwards through the soil.

Undigested soil passing out of the worm's rear end is deposited as worm casts, usually in the upper part of the burrow just below the surface. The naturalist Charles Darwin estimated that worms could bring about 25 tonnes of soil to the surface of each hectare (10 tonnes per acre) every year – more recent studies suggest that in places this could be 60 tonnes per hectare (24 tonnes per acre).

Fertilising the soil

Earthworm excavations perform a very valuable rotovating operation, returning mineral-rich soil to the upper layers where plant roots can use it. The soil of worm casts contains a mixture of organic and inorganic matter and, being in little 'packets', this improves the texture of the soil as well as its fertility.

As earthworms swallow soil from under stones, leaving it on top and around the sides, the stones are effectively buried. None are to be found near the surface of an old lawn – all have sunk to lower levels due mainly to tunnelling of worms.

Most earthworms are hermaphroditic, that is, each individual has both male and female sexual organs. Nevertheless, they still need to pair up. Several species mate on the surface on warm, damp nights. With their rear ends securely anchored to the upper walls of their burrows, ready for a quick retreat if danger threatens, the worms explore the surrounding area. When two worms meet, they bind their front ends together with slime.

Facing in opposite directions, they exchange sperm, often taking several hours to complete the process, and each worm is soon ready to lay its eggs. A collar of skin becomes detached from the saddle and the worm wriggles backwards out of it. As it does so, it squirts its eggs into the collar, together with sperm received from the other worm. Once the collar is free of the body, its two ends close up to form a fluid-filled, pea-sized cocoon containing one or more eggs. The eggs take from several weeks up to five months to hatch, depending on the species; the worms need another year or more to mature.

WILDLIFE WATCH

How can I watch earthworms?

- Worms may be seen on the surface at night, but the easiest way to watch them is to keep some in a wormery, which can be bought or home made. Fix two sheets of glass above and below a length of hosepipe bent into a U-shape, or a wooden frame. Sticky tape will keep the glass in place. Fill the shape with layers of moist soil, sand and grass cuttings. Add a few worms and cover the wormery with a cloth.

  The worms will make some of their tunnels next to the glass and if you lift the cloth every now and then you will be able to watch the worms moving along them. Look for casts on or near the surface and notice how the soil layers soon become thoroughly mixed.

Common earthworms mate on the surface at night or in the early morning, usually after damp weather. They lie head to tail with their sexual organs close together, clasping each other with hooked hairs that line their bellies.

Recognising garden bees

The gentle humming of bees flitting from flower to flower is a familiar sound on summer days as honeybees and bumblebees are joined by many other bee species in regular garden visits.

Throughout the summer, at least ten bee species may frequent the garden at any one time. They vary greatly in size from relative giants, such as bumblebees, to creatures not much bigger than worker ants. These tiny bees probably escape the notice of all but the most keen-eyed observers.

Bees fall into two groups – social and solitary. Social bees, comprising the honeybee and the various bumblebees, have a single queen that lays the eggs after mating and is helped by numerous workers in a hive. The workers are all sterile females.

Solitary bee species have males and females and no workers. The female does all the nest building, food gathering and egg laying on her own. She makes a small nest in the earth or in decaying vegetation, or even in crumbling mortar, in which she lays a few eggs. After stocking the nest with food for the eventual larvae, she repeats the process until all her eggs are laid, after which she dies.

Many bees that visit gardens are equally attracted to weeds and cultivated plants. A corner left to grow wild provides plenty of nectar and pollen for these insects.

WILDLIFE WATCH

Where can I find garden bees?

● During the day, bees can be seen foraging for nectar and pollen on flowers in the garden. Both male and female bees take nectar as food for themselves, while female workers also forage to feed the developing larvae in the nest.

● Male solitary bees may be seen sitting on leaves in the vicinity of flowers on which females of their species are foraging. This increases their chances of finding a suitable mate.

● Look out for little heaps of soil with a hole down the centre, resembling miniature volcanoes, especially in short grass on the lawn. These will be the nests of one or other species of mining bee.

● Neat circles or ovals cut out of the leaves of roses or other plants in the garden almost certainly indicate the activities of one or more of the leaf-cutting bee species.

● One garden plant that is particularly favoured by bees is the lamb's ear or woolly-leaved woundwort, *Stachys byzantina* (or *Stachys lanata*). Close examination of its leaves during the summer will often reveal that large areas of hairs have been shaved off. This is unmistakable evidence of wool carder bee activity.

● The large flowers of foxgloves, snapdragons and nasturtiums are favourite foraging sites for bumblebees. These bees may also be seen flying in and out of old mouse holes or to and from heaps of moss, in which they build their nests.

● Gardens and parks attract bumblebees, many of which are declining in the wild due to intensive farming practices. For this reason, gardens and parks are important to the survival of several species.

Busy bees

From the first warmth of the day until the cool of evening, social worker bees and solitary bees are never still. The workers of the hive bee, for example, may undertake around 10 million nectar-collecting trips to make just 500g (1lb) of honey.

Not only do the bees collect nectar, they also gather pollen, which contains the protein that is essential for the growth of bee larvae, or grubs. Female solitary bees also collect nesting materials. For instance, leaf-cutter bees neatly trim pieces of leaf for their nests, wool carders gather hairs from downy leaves, and mason bees collect balls of mud.

EASY GUIDE TO SPOTTING GARDEN BEES

WHAT ARE BEES?

- Bees belong to a group of insects called the Hymenoptera, which includes wasps, sawflies and ants. Around 270 different species of solitary bees live in Britain. Social bees comprise 25 species of bumblebees, including six cuckoo bees, and just one honeybee.
- Most of the bees found in gardens are female solitary bees or worker hive bees, visiting flowers to collect pollen and nectar and nesting material.
- Male bees are less often seen than female solitary bees, worker hive bees and even the bumblebee queens.

HOW CAN I IDENTIFY BEES?

- Garden bees may be confused with a number of hoverflies that mimic them. Hoverflies also have membranous wings but unlike bees, which have two pairs of wings joined, such flies have only a single pair of wings.
- Female solitary bees and worker bees have long tongues for collecting nectar and 'baskets' of feathery hairs, either on the legs or beneath the abdomen, for collecting and carrying pollen.

Distribution map key

Present | Not present

This uncovered nest of the small garden bumblebee shows the wax brood cells and attendant workers.

HONEYBEE OR HIVE BEE *Apis mellifera*

Generally the best-known of all the bees, the honeybee has a dark brown abdomen with pale orange stripes. The workers collect pollen in 'baskets' on their hind legs and, when full, these are very noticeable. As well as collecting pollen, each worker uses its sucking mouthparts to collect nectar, which it takes back to the hive where in due course it is converted into honey.

The worker honeybee's long tongue makes it a major, if short-lived, pollinator of deep-throated blooms. Workers rarely live more than a few weeks in summer.

- SIZE
  12–15mm (½–⅝in)
- NEST
  Cells in combs made of wax; most garden honeybees are from hives; wild colonies usually nest in hollow trees
- DISTRIBUTION
  Throughout Britain and Ireland
- SEASON
  Spring to autumn and warm days in winter

RED MASON BEE *Osmia rufa*

The common name of this solitary bee refers to the fact that its abdomen is clothed in long reddish hairs, although the thorax is black. Unlike most other solitary bee species, the male is regularly encountered because he will often seek out a foraging female and make a loud buzzing noise as he tries to induce her to mate.

A female red mason bee carries a pellet of mud in her jaws. The 'horns' on the front of the head, below the antennae, are used to tamp down the mud with which she builds the nest.

- SIZE
  12–14mm (½–⅝in)
- NEST
  Cells made of mud in gaps between bricks or stones, or in holes in woodwork
- DISTRIBUTION
  Most common in southern England
- SEASON
  April–July

TAWNY MINING BEE *Andrena fulva*

An early spring solitary bee, the tawny mining bee is covered in a dense pelt of bright orange hairs. Females feed at the flowers of soft fruit bushes, such as gooseberries, and play an important part in their pollination. Small mounds of earth on lawns are most likely to have been made by this bee, nesting in the soil. Females secrete a waterproof coating to line the nest.

All mining bees, of which there are 65 species, look similar to honeybees but are slightly smaller. The bright orange colour shows that this one is a female.

- SIZE
  12–14mm (½–⅝in)
- NEST
  Elliptical cells at end of underground burrow, usually in short turf
- DISTRIBUTION
  Abundant from Yorkshire to the south coast; very rare in Ireland
- SEASON
  March–May

EARLY MINING BEE *Andrena haemorrhoa*

The early mining bee's thorax is covered in a dense layer of orange-brown hairs and its abdomen is black with an orange tip. Large colonies of this solitary species are common and their presence is often given away by numerous female cuckoo bees (identifiable by their brown and yellow stripes), waiting to lay their eggs in the mining bees' nests, which are coated with a waterproof lining.

Dandelions are are a favourite foodplant of the early mining bee, which is also a common visitor to plum blossom, blackthorn and sallow (a willow).

- **SIZE**
  9–11mm (⅜–½in)
- **NEST**
  Elliptical cells at end of underground burrow, usually in longish grass
- **DISTRIBUTION**
  Throughout Britain as far north as central Highlands; also in Ireland
- **SEASON**
  Spring – one of the earliest bees

COMMON DIGGER BEE *Anthophora plumipes*

This solitary bee closely resembles a small bumblebee, except it has the ability to hover in flight – often apparently examining the observer – accompanied by a loud buzzing of its wings. Females are all black, while the brown-and-black males, which emerge before the females, are seen just as often. This species readily enters greenhouses or conservatories to feed on the flowers of house plants.

A male common digger bee is pictured feeding from a garden wallflower. This bee is also known as the plume-legged bee.

- **SIZE**
  11–17mm (½–¾in)
- **NEST**
  An underground burrow in a bank or holes in soft mortar, lined with a waterproof coating secreted by female
- **DISTRIBUTION**
  Southern half of Britain
- **SEASON**
  Spring to early summer

LARGE GARDEN LEAF-CUTTER BEE *Megachile willughbiella*

A solitary black bee with varying amounts of pale brown hair on the thorax and abdomen, the large garden leaf-cutter bee is likely to be seen cutting leaves for its nest, or flying off with a section of leaf. The female first removes large, oval-shaped sections to construct the main part of the nest-cell, and then cuts smaller, perfect circles with which to cap the cell once the eggs are laid and it is full of pollen and nectar.

This female large garden leaf-cutter bee is combing sweet-pea pollen into the basket beneath her abdomen.

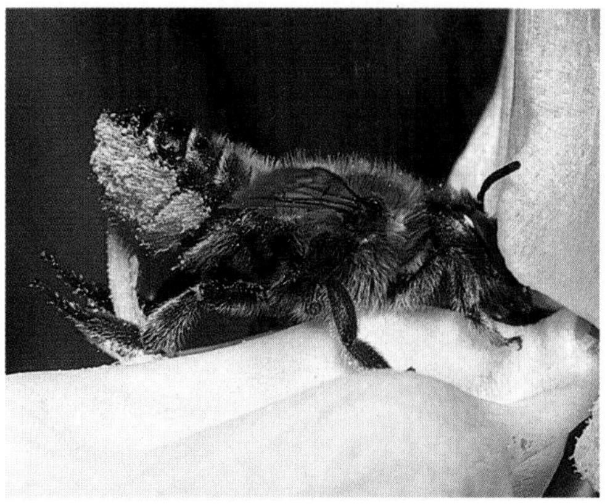

- **SIZE**
  10–12mm (⅜–½in)
- **NEST**
  Cells in holes in the ground or hollow stems, lined with pieces of leaf
- **DISTRIBUTION**
  Most abundant and widespread in southern England
- **SEASON**
  May–August

PATCHWORK LEAF-CUTTER BEE *Megachile centuncularis*

Very similar in appearance to the large garden leaf-cutter bee, a female patchwork leaf-cutter may be heard at work before she is spotted, for the sound she makes as she clips through a rose leaf with her sharp jaws is clearly audible. Like the female large garden leaf-cutter bee, this solitary bee has a 'basket' of dense hairs on the underside of her abdomen with which she collects pollen.

This bee takes pollen from wild flowers, such as thistles, and benefits from the creation of wilderness areas in gardens.

- **SIZE**
  9–11mm (⅜–½in)
- **NEST**
  Cells in holes in the ground or hollow stems, lined with pieces of leaf
- **DISTRIBUTION**
  Most common in southern England; overall the commonest leaf-cutter bee
- **SEASON**
  May–August

WOOL CARDER BEE *Anthidium manicatum*

Named after its practice of pulling hairs from verbascum, among other plants, this solitary bee uses the fluff to line its nest. Males set up territories around foraging sites and accost females as they arrive to feed, mating with as many as possible. The sturdy males – which are larger than the females – may accidentally kill bees of other species when defending their territories from what they perceive to be intruding males of their own kind.

A female wool carder bee shears hairs from the surface of a cultivated woundwort plant.

- **SIZE**
  8–15mm (⅜–⅝in)
- **NEST**
  Cells lined with hairs cut from surface of leaves; in any available hole or gap
- **DISTRIBUTION**
  Occurs widely below a line from mid-Wales to the Wash; extremely rare in north; none in Ireland
- **SEASON**
  May–August

SMALL GARDEN BUMBLEBEE *Bombus hortorum*

A fairly large, long-haired, yellow-and-black bee, with white hairs clothing the end of its abdomen. As with all bumblebees, the queens and workers have long tongues, allowing them to feed on long-tubed flowers. They also have pollen 'baskets' on the hind legs. In a good year, with high temperatures and plenty of food, colonies may contain up to 100 workers.

The queen of the species emerges from hibernation in early April, coinciding with the flowering of the primrose, a favoured food source.

- **SIZE**
  Up to 25mm (1in)
- **NEST**
  Cells made of wax; among plant roots or in dry grass or moss, just above or below ground
- **DISTRIBUTION**
  Throughout most of Britain, including outer islands; less common in Ireland
- **SEASON**
  March–September

WHITE-TAILED BUMBLEBEE *Bombus lucorum*

Very similar in size and appearance to the small garden bumblebee, this social bee differs in having a single yellow band at the front of the thorax, and a yellow band in the centre, rather than at the front, of the abdomen. In common with other bumblebees, the queens eat voraciously in late summer and early autumn in order to build up fat supplies to last through the winter hibernation.

Chrysanthemum flowers are popular with the white-tailed bumblebee. The obvious two-banded pattern distinguishes it from the small garden bumblebee.

- **SIZE**
  Up to 25mm (1in)
- **NEST**
  Cells made of wax; in the ground in a ready-made hole such as a mouse burrow
- **DISTRIBUTION**
  Most of Britain and in parts of Ireland
- **SEASON**
  February–September

BUFF-TAILED BUMBLEBEE *Bombus terrestris*

Larger than all other British bees, and broader bodied, the buff-tailed bumblebee's size helps to distinguish it from the white-tailed bumblebee. Also, it is tawny where the latter is yellow, and it has a fawn rather than a white tail. In a good year, this social species may produce a large colony with as many as 400 workers.

A queen buff-tailed bumblebee feeds on a cultivated guelder rose. The bees feed on wild flowers, too, and may be encountered in locations other than gardens and parks.

- **SIZE**
  Up to 28mm (1⅛in)
- **NEST**
  Cells made of wax; in the ground in a mouse burrow or in a hedge bank
- **DISTRIBUTION**
  Scarce in Ireland and very scarce in northern Scotland
- **SEASON**
  March–August

EARLY BUMBLEBEE *Bombus pratorum*

Similar in appearance to the buff-tailed bumblebee, the social early bumblebee is smaller, with the tawny band in the centre rather than at the front of the abdomen. Also, it has an orange, not fawn, tail. In a good year, with plenty of flowers, the workers are large, approaching the queen in size. In a poor year, they will be very much smaller, attaining perhaps only half her size.

An early bumblebee takes nectar from a comfrey flower through a hole previously cut in the flower tube by a buff-tailed or white-tailed bumblebee.

SIZE
Up to 22mm (⅞in)

NEST
Cells made of wax; under dry grass on the ground but also in old birds' nests and nestboxes

DISTRIBUTION
Scarce in far northern Scotland and Ireland

SEASON
Early spring to midsummer

COMMON CARDER BUMBLEBEE *Bombus pascuorum*

The thorax of the common carder bumblebee is covered in orange fur while the abdomen is lightly clothed in tawny hairs. These hairs may be sparse, especially in older workers of this social species, which may give the bee a slightly ragged look. It is the smallest of the garden bumblebees and one of the last to be seen in autumn.

Common carder bumblebees are often attracted to wild areas of the garden where species such as thistles provide them with nectar and pollen.

SIZE
Up to 15mm (⅝in)

NEST
Cells made of wax; on the ground or in old birds' nests

DISTRIBUTION
Most of mainland Britain and in parts of Ireland

SEASON
April–November

RED-TAILED BUMBLEBEE *Bombus lapidarius*

Large and predominantly black in colour, the red-tailed bumblebee has dense reddish orange fur on the final third of its abdomen, making it readily distinguishable from other social species. The males have a striking yellow collar on the thorax. One favourite flower of this bumblebee is wild thyme, so planting thyme in a herb bed may well attract the bees to the garden.

A male red-tailed bumblebee feeds on bramble. Queens and workers are very similar to males in appearance but both lack the collar of yellow hairs.

SIZE
Up to 27mm (1in)

NEST
Cells made of wax; in a ready-made hole and often under stones

DISTRIBUTION
Rare in northern Scotland

SEASON
April–August

VESTAL CUCKOO BUMBLEBEE *Psithyrus vestalis*

Due to the relative lack of hairs, cuckoo bumblebees appear shinier than their host bumblebees, in whose nests they lay their eggs. The vestal cuckoo does, however, have a band of tawny hairs at the front of the thorax and white and yellow patches of hair at the end of the abdomen. All the offspring grow into queens or males. Cuckoo bumblebees rely on their host's workers to raise their young.

The vestal cuckoo bumblebee has a short tongue, so must feed at plants with shallow flowers, such as thyme.

SIZE
Up to 27mm (1in)

NEST
Uses nests of buff-tailed bumblebees

DISTRIBUTION
Widespread only in southern and eastern England

SEASON
April–August

Aphids

Few animals can match the phenomenal reproductive capacity of aphids, which form enormous populations in summer. Found among almost all plant life, these little insects provide food for a host of other creatures.

Almost all wild and cultivated plants, from flowers and shrubs to vegetables, cereal crops and trees, are host to aphids. These tiny, sap-sucking bugs are commonly known as greenfly or blackfly. Another of their many names is plant lice. Gardeners sometimes refer to serious infestations of aphids as 'blight', a term that is also used for a variety of unrelated plant diseases.

Most aphids are about 2–5mm (1⁄16–1⁄4in) long and more or less pear-shaped, with a small head and long antennae. The sucking mouthparts are in the form of a piercing, needle-like beak and are concealed beneath the body when not in use. There is usually a pair of horns called cornicles at the rear of the body. These produce a sticky, waxy substance in defence against birds and other predators. Aphids may be winged or wingless – they possess wings at certain times of year and lack them at other stages of their life cycle.

Aphids feed on leaves, shoots, roots and, sometimes, flowers and fruits. More than 500 species of aphid inhabit the British Isles and many of them are pests of agricultural crops, orchard trees and garden plants.

Damage to plants

The removal of sap by an aphid does not in itself harm a plant. However, aphids are often present in very large numbers. It has been estimated that there may be as many as five billion of these insects per hectare (about two billion per acre). Such high densities of aphids weaken the plants on which they are feeding, causing severe distortion of their shape and premature leaf fall. For example, this frequently happens when apple trees are infested with the rosy apple aphid, *Dysaphis plantaginea*, in the spring.

The most severe damage is inflicted not by the aphids themselves but by the disease-causing micro-organisms that they carry. When aphids are feeding, these micro-organisms are pumped into the plants with their saliva. Aphids carry the

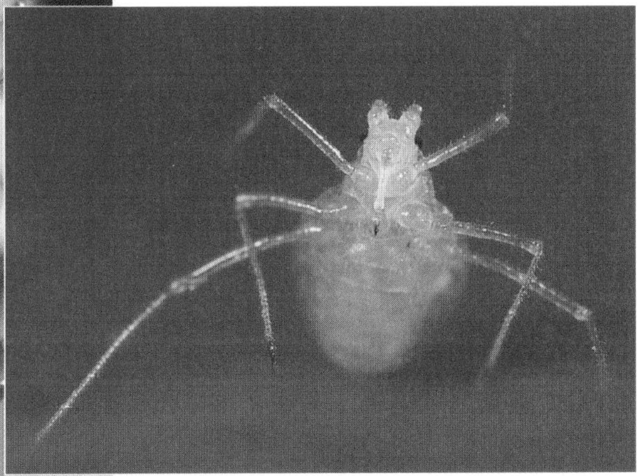

▲ The squat, pear-shaped body and small head typical of aphids can clearly be seen in this close-up photograph of a rose aphid. Despite this aphid's name, it occasionally feeds on plants other than roses.

◄ Rose aphids make their first appearance in April or early May. In just a few weeks, their numbers will have reached such densities that entire plants can be covered. Most aphids seen at this time of year are wingless forms.

▲ **Black bean aphids, or blackfly, often infest broad beans but also thrive on wild plants, such as dock. The aphids congregate on fresh, young shoots where the sap is richest in nutrients.**

► **Aphids have prodigious reproductive powers, and during the spring and early summer females give birth to live young. The tiny offspring emerge fully formed from their mother's body.**

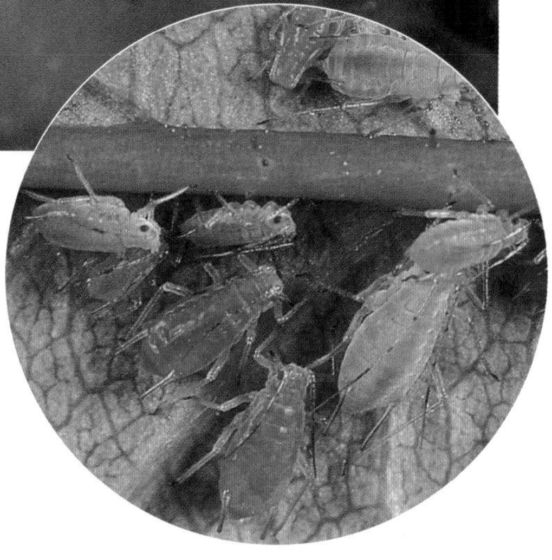

► **Rose aphids are often green in colour – hence their common name, greenfly – but they also come in pink and yellowish forms. Whatever the body colour, this species has black 'horns' at the rear end of the body.**

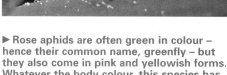

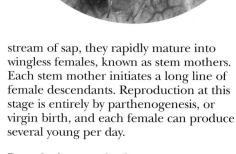

viruses responsible for sugar beet yellows, potato leaf roll and many other serious diseases of farm and garden plants.

Two-host aphids

Many aphids have complex life histories with both sexual stages and asexual stages, and they often attack different host plants at different times of year. The black bean aphid or blackfly, *Aphis fabae*, is a good example of a 'two-host aphid'. They pass the winter as shiny black eggs, which are quite large for such a small insect. The eggs can be found easily by examining the bare twigs of spindle, *Euonymus*, and guelder rose, *Viburnum*. They can also be found in gardens on mock orange, *Philadelphus*. These three shrubs are known as the primary hosts of the black bean aphid.

The eggs hatch as the sap starts to rise in spring and the young, called nymphs, push their beaks into the opening buds to feed. Nourished by a continuous stream of sap, they rapidly mature into wingless females, known as stem mothers. Each stem mother initiates a long line of female descendants. Reproduction at this stage is entirely by parthenogenesis, or virgin birth, and each female can produce several young per day.

Population explosion

A young aphid already contains its own embryos at birth. Within two weeks it gives birth to its offspring, which is why aphid populations can build up so quickly. The first few broods are all wingless like their parents and they form dense clusters on young shoots and leaves. As aphid numbers increase, winged individuals begin to appear. These are called spring migrants and they fly off in search of other plants. Instead of shrubs, they seek herbaceous plants such as docks, nasturtiums and poppies, and crops such as sugar beet and broad beans. These plants are the black bean aphid's secondary hosts.

The population growth continues on the secondary hosts, where the aphids feed on leaves, tender shoots and flowers. Again, the first-born broods are usually all wingless, with winged forms appearing

PROTECTED BY ANTS

Ants are very partial to the sweet honeydew excreted by aphids. As well as lapping it up from the leaves of plants on which aphids have been feeding, many ant species obtain fresh supplies by stroking the aphids with their antennae. This process induces the aphids to produce honeydew and is known as milking. In return for the 'milk', the ants protect the aphids. The mere presence of the ants deters some aphid predators and parasites. One study of an English birch wood showed that trees in areas with wood ant nests had up to 80 times more aphids than trees without ant nests nearby.

Some ants herd the aphids like cows. Yellow meadow ants feed mainly in the soil, where they milk aphids that are attached to roots. They collect the aphids and transfer them to roots running through their nests, where they can be easily tended and guarded.

► **Were it not for the sugar-rich honeydew they produce, which earns them the protection of ants, the vulnerable aphids would soon become a meal for their shepherds.**

▲ The proportion of winged forms in aphid populations increases during late spring and summer. Aphids that can fly disperse to other plants to start new colonies, often travelling long distances.

► In lowland areas, almost every plant is attacked by at least one aphid species. Even plants such as yarrow, which has highly aromatic leaves that deter large grazing animals, cannot ward off aphids.

as the population density increases. Poor food quality or simply a shortage of food may trigger the development of winged aphids, but the main factor seems to be crowding. The closer together nymphs are, the more likely they are to develop wings. The winged nymphs spread the infestation from plant to plant. They can drift on the wind for miles, so aphids are able to spread over a wide area.

Thus far in the black bean aphid's life cycle, all the insects have been produced by virgin birth. However, as autumn approaches, changes in the length of daylight and perhaps in the quality of plant sap trigger a change to this strategy. Winged females fly back to spindle bushes and other woody hosts where they give birth to the year's final brood of wingless aphids and this generation cannot reproduce without mating.

Meanwhile, the males necessary for sexual reproduction are being produced in the dwindling aphid colonies on the herbaceous plants. Fully winged, they fly to shrubs to mate with the sexual female aphids there. After mating, the females lay the eggs that will overwinter and begin the life cycle all over again. Although each female lays only about six eggs, the total number produced is huge. Despite being a source of food for blue tits and other birds in winter, plenty survive.

Several other common aphids have two host plants during their life cycle. The peach-potato aphid, *Myzus persicae*, is one of the most abundant. This pale green aphid uses peach trees as its primary host, causing the leaves to curl up in spring. The summer generations then use a wide range of herbaceous plants, including potatoes, cabbages and other crops.

The most familiar species of greenfly in gardens is the rose aphid, *Macrosiphum rosae.* It smothers rose buds and shoots in spring and then flies off to teasels and scabious plants for the summer. The rose-grain aphid, *Metopolophium dirhodum*, is shiny green and infests rose buds in spring before flying off to attack cereal crops in summer. In some years, it reaches plague proportions, with millions leaving the ripening cereals in July and August to fly back to their woody hosts. At this time, these aphids get in people's hair, clog up machinery and fill spiders' webs.

Most European aphids spend winter in the egg stage, almost always on woody plants – the primary hosts. However, not all aphids return to their woody hosts in autumn. They may survive mild winters on their secondary hosts, continuing to reproduce asexually throughout the winter, albeit more slowly than in summer.

Single-host aphids

Some aphids have only one type of host plant. For example, the sycamore aphid, *Drepanosiphum platanoides*, and lime aphid, *Eucallipterus tiliae*, spend their entire lives on trees or shrubs. The cabbage aphid,

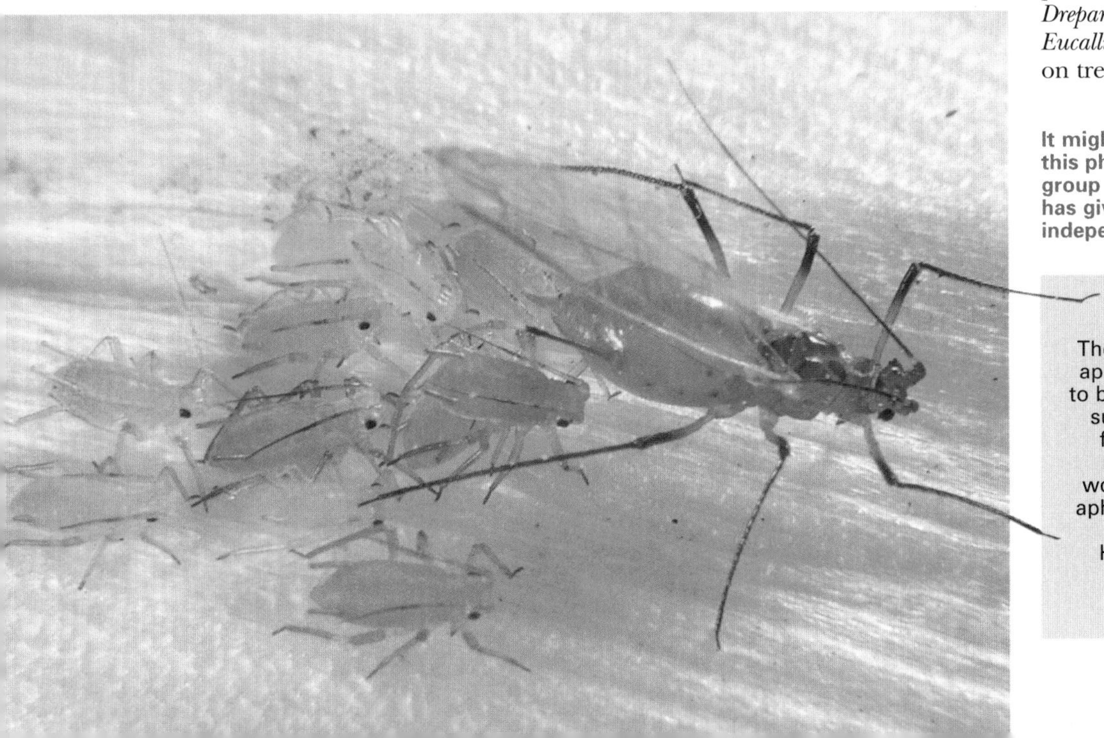

It might appear as if the adult aphid in this photograph is caring for a family group of nymphs, but once a female aphid has given birth, its offspring are all totally independent.

DID YOU KNOW?

The main advantage of virgin birth to aphids is that it enables them rapidly to build up vast populations during the summer. In summer every aphid is female and capable of producing numerous offspring. In theory, it would take just 100 days for a single aphid to give rise to 10 million tonnes of aphids if they all survived. However, countless predators eat aphids and help to prevent populations growing so large.

APHID DEFENCES

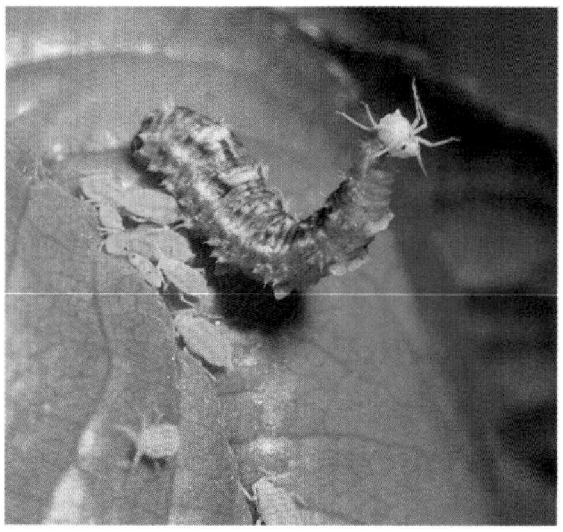

Aphids have many predators, including birds, ladybirds, lacewings, hoverfly larvae and various bugs. They are also attacked by small parasites. The aphids have a variety of defences and are not as helpless as they might seem. When threatened, their cornicles release waxy fluids that gum up the jaws of would-be predators. The odour of the wax also warns neighbouring aphids to move away from the source of danger. Aphids can kick out quite vigorously with their long back legs when ladybirds or other predators approach. These thrashing movements stimulate neighbouring aphids to start kicking, and the seething mass of legs certainly deters a number of small predatory animals.

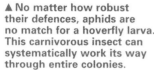

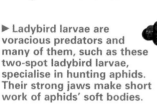

▲ No matter how robust their defences, aphids are no match for a hoverfly larva. This carnivorous insect can systematically work its way through entire colonies.

► Ladybird larvae are voracious predators and many of them, such as these two-spot ladybird larvae, specialise in hunting aphids. Their strong jaws make short work of aphids' soft bodies.

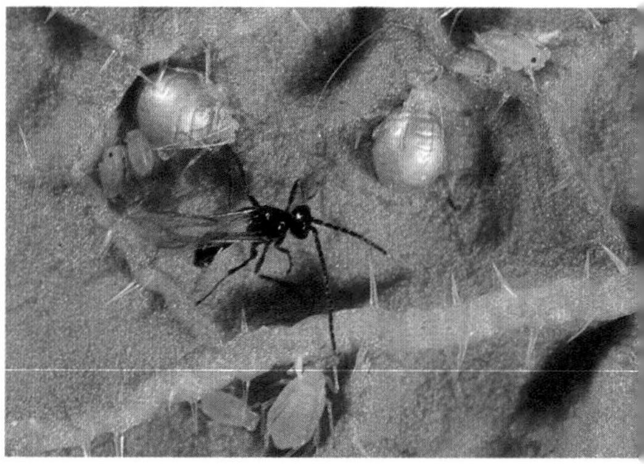

This parasitic wasp, *Aphidius metricariae*, has just emerged from the lifeless husk of an aphid inside which it lived as a larva. The wasp will now go in search of other aphids on which to lay its eggs.

Brevicoryne brassicae, is one of many species to complete its life cycle on herbaceous plants. It is a serious pest in gardens, where colonies of mealy grey aphids smother the leaves of various brassicas.

The woolly aphid, *Eriosoma lanigerum*, is a North American insect that is now widely established on apple trees in Britain. Its body is purplish brown, but the species is named for its covering of fluffy white wax threads. Each colony of aphids acquires the appearance of cotton wool. These woolly colonies develop on young twigs or around fresh wounds in bark, and they are most conspicuous in the summer. Eggs are rarely produced in Britain and the insects rely almost entirely on asexual reproduction. The nymphs survive the winter in bark crevices or, more rarely, feeding on the tree's roots.

Many aphids inhabit abnormal plant growths called galls that develop when their feeding activities cause excessive growth of the host plant's tissues. Familiar galls caused by aphids include purse and spiral galls on poplar leaf stalks, pouches on elm leaves and pineapple galls on spruce. Pineapple galls resemble young cones, but are actually formed from the swollen bases of young needles, which swell when the aphids start to feed. All aphids excrete a sticky waste product, known as honeydew. Those that live in galls cover this liquid with wax so that it does not stick to them inside the gall.

Sugary honeydew

Plant sap contains a lot of sugar but little protein. To obtain enough body-building proteins, aphids have to take in far more sugar than they need. Most of it goes straight through them and is released as droplets of honeydew. These coat the leaves of plants, and the sticky residue is often noticeable on cars parked under trees, especially limes and sycamores.

Ants and many other insects feed on the aphids' sweet honeydew. The speckled wood and several other butterflies obtain most of their food from it in midsummer. Far more honeydew is produced than is consumed, however, and much of it is colonised by sooty mould fungi that turn leaves black in late summer.

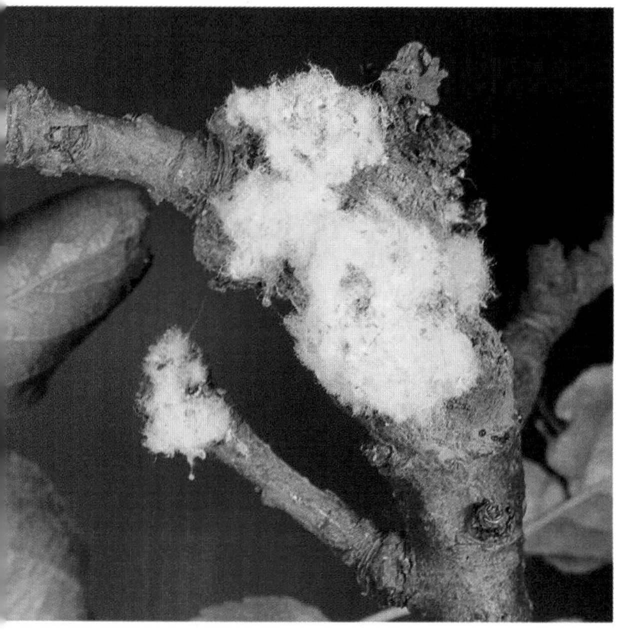

▲ Plant galls, such as these swollen pouches on the surface of an elm leaf, provide food and shelter for many aphids. The galls swell up as the leaf unfurls and may be green, yellow or red in colour.

◄ Woolly aphid colonies become covered in waxy fluff produced by the insects. This is a form of defence against predators and may prevent the aphids from drying out. Woolly aphids are easiest to find on apple trees.

WILDLIFE WATCH

Where can I see aphids?

- To find aphids, look no further than the garden. Almost all plants seem prone to attack at some time in the growing season. Roses and cultivated vegetables often support some of the heaviest infestations.
- Aphid infestations seldom threaten the life of a plant but they do affect its vigour. For gardeners anxious about too many aphids, spraying them with soapy water is a good way to remove them. It is best not to use pesticides because aphids are important as food for other animals.
- The best defence against aphids is to destroy old cabbages and other unwanted plants as soon as they are finished with in late summer and autumn. This will destroy the aphid eggs they harbour and reduce the risk to new crops in spring.

Garden wall plants

An old wall makes an attractive feature in any garden and provides a home for a wealth of plants. The plant life, in turn, offers welcome food and shelter for butterflies, birds and small mammals.

Wall flowers

Numerous flowering plants colonise garden walls, their lightweight seeds having been blown into the walls' crevices. Larger seeds may be dropped by birds, while oily seeds are often transported by ants. The seeds then take root in cushions of moss or directly in crumbling mortar, which larger plants may contribute to by loosening the bricks or stones.

Yellow corydalis, which has much-divided leaves like those of the wall-rue fern, is one of many plants that prefer a wall's vertical surfaces to the top or ledges. Other familiar flowers that are commonly to be found sprouting from old walls include foxgloves and rosebay willowherb.

► Ivy-leaved toadflax sprawls profusely over vertical and horizontal wall surfaces, its mauve and yellow flowers peeping out from the shiny leaves throughout the summer.

▲ Bright orangey yellow patches of the lichen *Xanthoria parietina* encrust old stone walls. They are most common near the sea.

◄ In places where the mortar is beginning to decay, garden walls are colonised by plants more often associated with cliffs, rocky hillsides and river banks.

Colourful lichens

Lichens are usually the first organisms to colonise garden walls. A lichen is a combination of a fungus and an alga and it can grow on bare brick, stone or concrete. The alga exchanges some of the food it makes for mineral salts absorbed from the wall's surface by the fungus. Many wall lichens are brightly coloured. For example, *Xanthoria aureola* is one of several golden species. Some lichens form slow-growing, circular patches that can live for hundreds of years. By measuring their diameter, it is possible to estimate the age of the wall.

WILDLIFE WATCH

How can I grow wall plants?

- Check native species that support many forms of wildlife and plant ones that grow best in your area. The Royal Horticultural Society's *Plant Finder* provides useful information on where to buy plants. Ask a local wildlife trust or urban wildlife group for their advice if necessary.

- Lack of water is the main problem for plants that are rooted in walls. It will help if the wall is shaded from direct sunlight.

Wall ferns

Ferns take root in the mortar of shady walls across the country, although they are most prolific in the wetter climate of western Britain, because many species require abundant moisture at certain stages of their life cycle.

Three species of fern are particularly associated with walls. Maidenhair spleenwort forms rosettes of bright green fronds, each with a blackish midrib and numerous oblong lobes. The rusty-back fern is recognised by the scaly brown undersides of its fronds. The fronds often curl up in dry weather, but revive after rainfall. Wall-rue does not look like a fern at all, but examination of its much-divided fronds reveals slender rows of spore capsules, characteristic of ferns, on the underside.

◀ Maidenhair spleenwort is one of several ferns that grow well on shady walls, especially in the west of Britain and Ireland.

Garden escapes

Oxford ragwort was brought to Britain from the mountains of central and southern Europe and has been producing wonderful displays of golden flowers on many walls and waysides since escaping from the Oxford Botanic Garden in 1794. It spread furthest along railways, the plumed seeds being swept along in the vortex of air created by the trains.

Many other plants to be found growing wild on garden walls are versions of cultivated varieties, including the wallflower and red valerian, which is now common throughout most of Britain. Its attractive deep pink flowers are visited by pollinating butterflies.

▶ Wallflowers are native to the Greek islands of the Aegean but have been popular garden plants here for so long that escapes can be found in most parts of Britain and Ireland.

◀ The spore capsules of *Tortula* mosses dry out in the breeze and explode, casting tiny spores into the air.

Mossy cushions

Several mosses form neat little cushions on the tops of walls and especially on ledges. The bright green *Tortula muralis* is one of the most abundant species, carrying slender, upright orange spore capsules on orange stems in the spring.

Greyish green cushions of *Grimmia pulvinata* commonly grow with *Tortula*, while *Bryum capillare* forms more extensive mats. Its drooping, pear-shaped spore capsules are bright green when young, but become chestnut coloured as they mature.

SCRAMBLING IVY

Ivy is an evergreen, woody climber that grows on many established walls throughout the British Isles. It generally climbs up from the ground with the aid of thousands of tiny roots that spring from the stems and take hold in the slightest of irregularities on the bricks or stones. Many gardeners cut it back ruthlessly, because it can cause damage to a wall if it becomes excessively heavy.

Nevertheless, this vigorous plant plays a vital role for a variety of wildlife. The flower buds feed the caterpillars of the holly blue butterfly and, when the buds open, the nectar-filled flowers feed numerous insects and are pollinated by flies and wasps. The berries are eaten by birds in spring, and the foliage provides shelter for insects, birds and small mammals all year round.

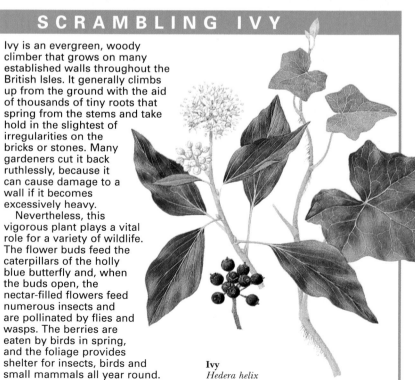

Ivy
Hedera helix

Park watch

- The grey squirrel
- The muntjac deer
- The pied wagtail
- The swift
- Recognising damselflies
- The ladybird
- Recognising snails
- Black garden ants
- Large umbellifers

The grey squirrel

Within 100 years of its arrival from North America, the grey squirrel has become a common sight in parks and woodland, sitting on tree stumps and branches to feed or running up and down tree trunks with ease.

A native of the hardwood forests of the eastern United States, the grey squirrel was deliberately introduced to Britain during the 19th and early 20th centuries. These days the introduction of foreign species is carefully controlled, but a century or so ago interest focused on adding more species to the resident fauna. Being less specialised in diet and habitat than the native red squirrel, the grey squirrel was able to thrive, displacing its once widespread smaller cousin.

Conquering colonisers

Between 1930 and 1945, grey squirrels spread like wildfire across the Midlands and over most of southern England, despite efforts to control them. For a while there was an official government 'bounty' paid for every grey squirrel killed, but still the species prospered, living in woods, hedgerows and on farmland. Intelligent and adaptable, these squirrels invaded towns as well as countryside, delighting many visitors to parks with their acrobatic antics and bold character.

The spread of grey squirrels into Wales, Cornwall, East Anglia and other regions was slowed by wide expanses of treeless countryside – squirrels rarely stray far from trees – but they are now well established in all these regions. In England, by the 1960s only a few areas in the north remained uncolonised. Populations in Scotland are increasing although greys are still less numerous there than reds. Today two-and-a-half million grey squirrels are to be found in Britain, 80 per cent of them in England. They have also reached Ireland, where they can be seen in central and northern parts of the country.

Squirrels are unusual among British mammals in that they are active during daylight. Unlike other animals they also sit up to feed, manipulating food in their paws. This appealing behaviour adds to their attractiveness and grey squirrels are popular animals – at least among people who are not trying to protect the red squirrel or earn a living by growing trees.

Foresters dislike squirrels because they gnaw tree bark. The gnawing often occurs in patches just above a convenient side branch where the squirrel can sit. It strips off sections of bark with its sharp teeth, eats the juicy parts underneath and then drops the waste to the ground below.

Grey squirrels feed heartily during summer and autumn. Their success in finding food at this time crucially affects their survival over winter and breeding success the following year.

GREY SQUIRREL FACT FILE

These squirrels often become quite tame in parks, where they are easy to see at close quarters. Their hind legs are surprisingly long and very powerful, enabling them to make bounding leaps.

● NAMES
Common name: grey squirrel
Scientific name: *Sciurus carolinensis*

● HABITAT
Deciduous woodland, parks, gardens, hedgerows; urban areas with trees

● DISTRIBUTION
Throughout most of England and Wales; central Scotland; parts of Ireland

● STATUS
An estimated 2.5 million individuals in Britain; unknown but increasing number in Ireland

● SIZE
Length 24–28cm (9½–11in), tail 19–24cm (7½–9½in); weight 400–600g (14–21oz), pregnant female heavier

● KEY FEATURES
Grey fur on neck, back and tail; underside creamy white; flanks and feet sometimes reddish in summer; tail has a white fringe (each hair is banded brown and black with a white tip)

● HABITS
Active in daylight, on ground and up trees

● VOICE
Loud '*churrrrr*' or slow '*chuk-chuk-chuk*' when annoyed

● FOOD
Buds, flowers, fruits, nuts, fungi, tree bark; occasional birds' eggs and nestlings

As well as building nests, grey squirrels use tree holes, which they enlarge and line with bedding material. Old dens are often renovated and reused.

● BREEDING
Mating chases in late winter; 1 or 2 litters of 1–6 young (usually 3, occasionally 7) produced February–July; in the south of England, young may be born as early as January and as late as September

● NEST
Called a drey, about the size of a football; made of twigs with leaves still attached; built in trees and tall bushes

● YOUNG
Born naked and blind; fur grows in 2–3 weeks, eyes open in 4 weeks; independent in 2½–4 months; resemble adult but tail less bushy

Distribution map key

Present

Not present

LISTED SPECIES

The grey squirrel is not legally protected but is listed on Schedule 9 of the Wildlife and Countryside Act. This means that any squirrels that are captured (or taken into care because they are injured, for instance) may not be re-released into the wild. It is also illegal to keep grey squirrels in captivity without a licence.

A grey squirrel's ears are rounded and never have tufts.

In summer, grey squirrels are often orange-brown on their back, flanks, legs and head.

Unlike many mammals, squirrels grasp food between their front paws when feeding.

A grey squirrel's tail is used not only for balance but also for signalling to other squirrels. With its tail flat on the ground, this squirrel is feeling relaxed.

In hot weather a grey squirrel sometimes drinks from a pond or stream. Squirrels are generally wary of water because they are not good swimmers; their tails are easily waterlogged, making swimming a struggle.

This sort of damage not only disfigures the tree, resulting in significant losses of some hardwoods, but may cause the tree crown to die. Removal of bark also exposes the tree to the danger of fungal infections. The work and investment of several decades can be severely affected in just a few weeks by these marauding mammals.

Squirrels also cause trouble when they get into roof spaces or lofts and gnaw electric wires or stored clothing. Less serious is the squirrel's theft of food left out for birds.

Born acrobats

The squirrel is beautifully adapted to life in the trees, with sharp claws on each of its toes and powerful gripping feet. It is able to hang on to tiny branches in high winds, scamper up smooth bark and defy gravity by running down a tree head-first. It can also hang head downwards by its hind toes. This is made possible by having double-jointed ankles, which allow the hind feet to be turned backwards.

A squirrel's eyes face forwards, allowing accurate judgement of distances. It can leap 6m (20ft) or more and its tail acts as a balancer, flicking from side to side to help the animal avoid falling while it finds a hold with its feet.

In summer, the grey squirrel's coat is much thinner than it is in winter and turns orange-brown along the back, flanks, legs and head. This sometimes causes confusion with the red squirrel and people often suggest (wrongly) that perhaps the two species may interbreed to form hybrids. In fact, grey squirrels can be distinguished from reds, which are a bright chestnut colour, in a number of ways. Firstly, grey squirrels are larger and more heavily built than red squirrels. Secondly, the grey squirrel's tail has a dark core with a white fringe, while the red squirrel's tail is the same chestnut colour throughout. Yet another way to distinguish between the two species is to look at their ears – the red squirrel has long tufts of hair at the tips of its ears, while the grey squirrel does not.

Occasionally, albino grey squirrels occur, especially in the south-east of England. These are pure white with pink eyes. Another distinctive colour variant is found in parts of Bedfordshire and adjacent counties. These squirrels are inky black all over and are referred to as 'melanistic' varieties. They are the descendants of a rare genetic strain that was released in Woburn Park, Bedfordshire during the Victorian era because of the perceived 'novelty value' of the species.

Squirrel homes

Squirrels build nests, called dreys, from twigs bitten off a living tree. Each twig bears some green leaves which, although they become shrivelled, remain attached to the twigs. As a result, the typical squirrel drey has a bushy assortment of leaves visible on the outside. Magpies build similar-sized nests – a little larger than a football – but use dead twigs as building material, so their nests do not have leaves visible on the outside.

The interior of a drey is lined with soft material such as moss or finely shredded bark. The summer drey is often little more than a platform of twigs, often constructed among the thin branches at the top of a tree. In winter, with no leaves on the tree, such a position would be very exposed to the elements, so winter dreys

Leaps and bounds

Although they are adapted for life in the trees, grey squirrels spend a lot of their time searching for food on the ground.

When startled grey squirrels can move at great speed, heading for the nearest tree in a series of bounds.

WILDLIFE WATCH

Where can I see grey squirrels?

- Grey squirrels are common in many parts of the country. The best places to observe them closely are city parks where the animals can become very tame and will often take food from the hand.
- Early in the morning is a good time to see them. The squirrels are hungry and go out foraging before disturbance levels rise during the day.
- Grey squirrels are often attracted to garden bird tables and birdfeeders, where they display considerable agility and ingenuity to reach the food.

In parts of Bedfordshire and Cambridgeshire, glossy black squirrels may be seen. These are a genetic variant of the grey squirrel.

are more robust and built closer to the tree trunk or in substantial tree forks. Outside the breeding season, squirrels may share dreys or visit nests built and used previously by other individuals. They will also take up residence in old woodpecker holes or tree hollows, enlarging the entrance as necessary by gnawing away bark and wood.

▲ Protected by a thickened coat of silvery grey, squirrels are out and about on bright days throughout the winter. They can usually find enough to eat, and can always fall back on reserves hidden away the previous autumn.

◀ Grey squirrels appear to relish the challenge of reaching food meant for birds and the rewards are rich indeed – nuts and seeds usually shelled and ready for eating.

On the ground, a squirrel keeps a sharp lookout for danger. Its erect tail is a sign of alertness and caution.

The squirrel runs with its front legs held out to the sides. It uses the same style when running vertically up a tree, keeping its body close to the trunk.

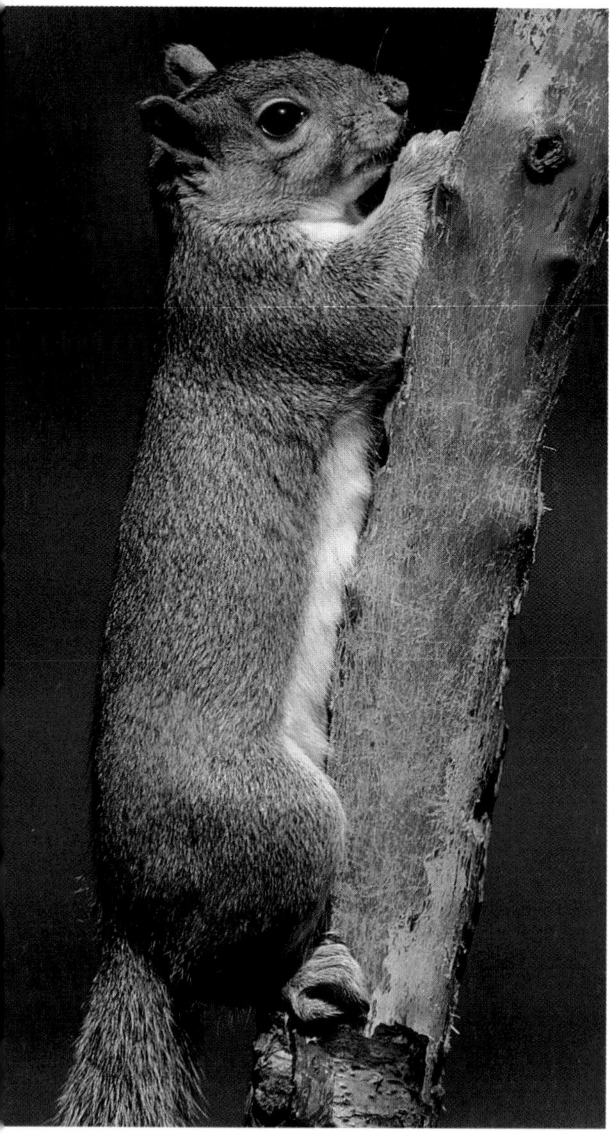

▲ The squirrel uses its powerful jaws and teeth to strip off tree bark so that it can feed on the layers underneath.

Tree-top skills

The feet of the grey squirrel are adapted both for digging and clambering in trees. The long fingers and claws are almost birdlike. The thumb of the front foot is only vestigial.

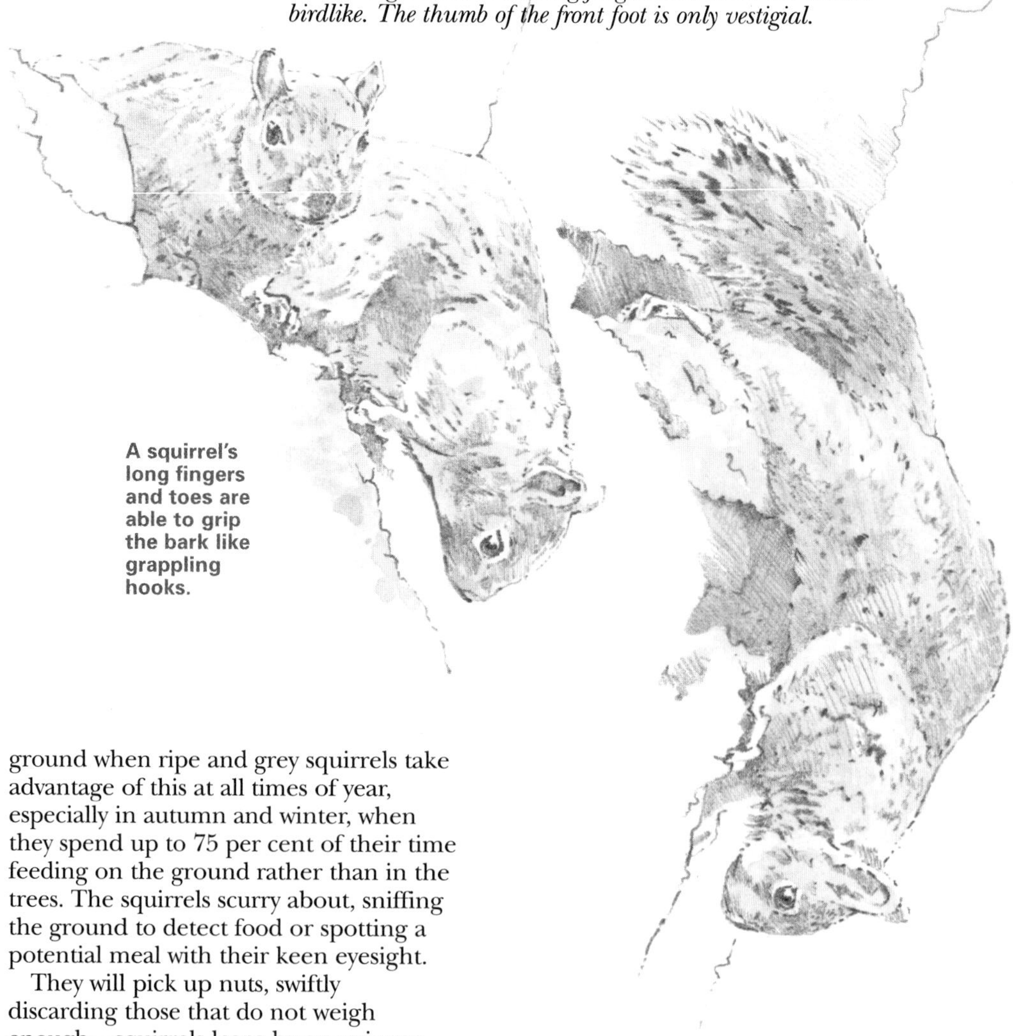

A squirrel's long fingers and toes are able to grip the bark like grappling hooks.

Squirrels do not hibernate but they will often remain inactive in their nests for many days if the weather is cold and wet. On sunny days they will be out seeking food, even in the snow.

In spring, the squirrels feed mainly up in the trees on the buds of developing leaves. They also scamper through the branches, sniffing at flowers to select those that are at the right stage of development, when they are highly nutritious, before biting them off to eat. In summer, they eat increasing quantities of insects, including caterpillars, which are often abundant in the tree canopy. They will also eat birds' eggs, if they find them, but squirrels do not appear to make special efforts to seek out nests and eggs, nor is it likely that these raids have a significant effect on bird numbers.

Later in the year they eat acorns, beech mast and all sorts of seeds and fruits, as well as fungi. Squirrels are especially fond of hazelnuts and bite them off the tree branches while they are still green. However, all sorts of nuts drop to the ground when ripe and grey squirrels take advantage of this at all times of year, especially in autumn and winter, when they spend up to 75 per cent of their time feeding on the ground rather than in the trees. The squirrels scurry about, sniffing the ground to detect food or spotting a potential meal with their keen eyesight.

They will pick up nuts, swiftly discarding those that do not weigh enough – squirrels learn by experience to distinguish between worthless shells, where the nuts have been eaten from the inside by insects, and those that contain a nice solid kernel. Squirrels strip chestnuts and acorns of their outer coverings, whereas hazelnuts have to be gnawed until the squirrel can insert the tips of its incisor teeth and split the nutshell apart. Some smaller nuts may be cracked in the squirrel's jaws. The shells are left in jagged pieces and look quite different from the nuts opened by mice and dormice, which have a neat hole in the shell where the rodents have gnawed them.

In the autumn there is often too much to eat all at once, so squirrels store food, collecting nuts and burying them all over the place. They do not remember where they hide their larders but they do recognise the patches of ground used for this purpose. Later they return and seek out the nuts by smell and by experimental digging. Of course, some nuts are never found and these are able to germinate away from the tree that produced them. So, in providing themselves with their main source of food for the winter, squirrels also help to disperse tree seeds.

While nuts are abundant in autumn, the seeds inside pine cones are present at all times of the year. This is another food source exploited by squirrels. They gnaw the scales off the cones, eat the seeds and discard the cone cores, just as people throw away apple cores. These stripped cone cores, surrounded by the debris of nibbled cone scales, are a characteristic sign of squirrel feeding activity. Stripping a cone takes quite some time, so the squirrels prefer to do it sitting on a prominent branch, tree stump or fencepost from where they can watch for approaching danger.

Early breeding

Food is very important in determining breeding success in squirrels. In a good year, when there is plenty of autumn food, the animals start the winter in good condition and are still quite fat and well fed when the breeding season starts in January. Energetic mating chases are frequent at this time, and females will then have to invest further energy resources, not only in producing young, but also the milk to feed them. All this has to take place before much new food

Thanks to their double-jointed ankles, squirrels can run down a tree, hanging from their hind feet, as fast as they can run up it. If necessary, the squirrel can hang by just one foot, releasing its grip by uncurling its long toes.

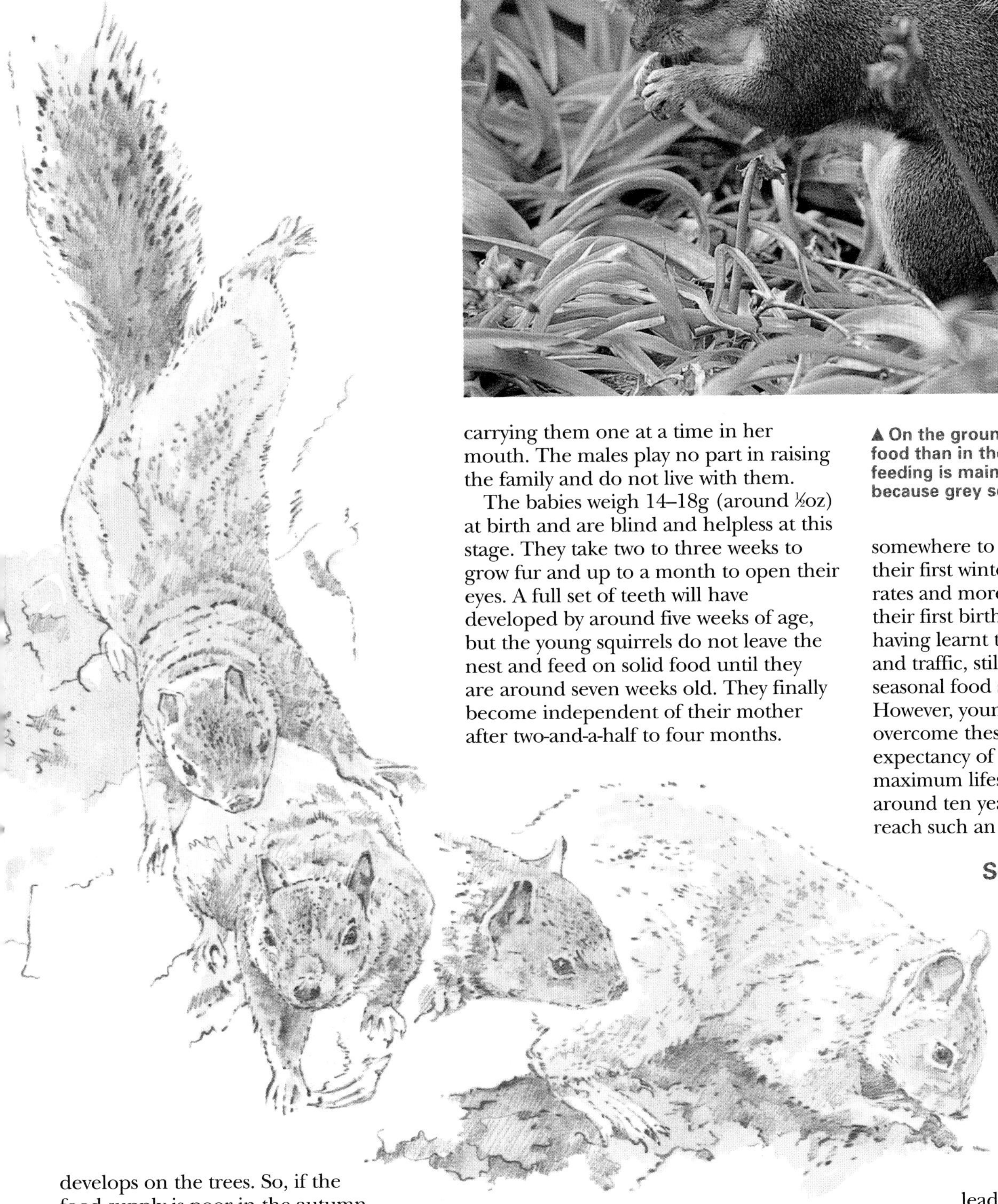

▲ On the ground there is a wider variety of food than in the tree-tops. Even so, ground feeding is mainly done in dry weather because grey squirrels dislike getting wet.

develops on the trees. So, if the food supply is poor in the autumn, fewer young will be raised successfully the following spring. If the winter has been particularly harsh, the female's body will be in poor condition and many of her young will die as a result of her inability to feed them properly.

The young are born from February (or even January in the south) onwards. Up to seven babies may be produced in a single family, but three is more usual. If the mother is disturbed, she will often take her offspring to a safer place, carrying them one at a time in her mouth. The males play no part in raising the family and do not live with them.

The babies weigh 14–18g (around ½oz) at birth and are blind and helpless at this stage. They take two to three weeks to grow fur and up to a month to open their eyes. A full set of teeth will have developed by around five weeks of age, but the young squirrels do not leave the nest and feed on solid food until they are around seven weeks old. They finally become independent of their mother after two-and-a-half to four months. The mother may then have a second litter, born from July onwards. All the juveniles will have left the family before the onset of winter, sometimes travelling more than 3km (2 miles).

Squirrels become mature enough to breed when they are about a year old, but many die long before this. Cats kill unwary baby squirrels, as do cars. Large numbers are run over, especially in late summer when the inexperienced juveniles are dispersing and looking for somewhere to live. Young animals facing their first winter suffer high mortality rates and more than half will die before their first birthday. Those that do survive, having learnt the dangers of predators and traffic, still have the problems of seasonal food shortages to contend with. However, young individuals that overcome these hazards have a life expectancy of several years. The maximum lifespan in the wild is probably around ten years, although very few will reach such an age.

Squirrel territories

Female grey squirrels use an area of 2–10 hectares (5–25 acres) throughout the year but males range more widely, especially in the breeding season when they are looking for mates. Population densities can sometimes be quite high, often more than two per hectare. This can lead to aggressive activity in the breeding season, with scent marking, growling and tail-wagging used as territorial signals to other squirrels. Violent clashes may ensue and, although fighting is unusual, this is probably the main cause of damaged ears that seem to be fairly prevalent among grey squirrels.

However, in winter, peace reigns and the animals often share nests, huddled together to keep warm. Sometimes six or more squirrels may live together in a tree hole at this time of year.

The muntjac deer

Britain's smallest deer, the muntjac is a timid creature, rarely venturing into the open during the day, preferring to remain hidden in the safety of leafy bushes and shrubs.

The tiny Reeves's (or Chinese) muntjac deer was brought to Britain at the end of the 19th century as an interesting addition to the native wildlife. Now, the population comprises more than 40,000 animals, with densities as high as 100 per square kilometre (260 per square mile) in some areas.

Unlike other British deer, which are seasonal breeders, muntjac breed all year round. This means that numbers are increasing rapidly despite the fact that the young are born one at a time. The females, or does, can live for more than ten years and produce more than a dozen offspring in their lifetime. Coupled with a recent run of mild winters, which makes survival rates higher, this capacity for rapid expansion means that muntjac numbers will continue to grow.

Easy to miss

Muntjac can survive and even thrive in heavily urbanised areas without people realising they are there. Often the only trace of the deer is its small, black droppings, which are about 10mm (½in) long and 5–10mm (¼–½in) in diameter.

The muntjac is able to live in tiny patches of scrub in town parks and big gardens and has been present in some major cities for more than 20 years. Muntjac are to be found in the London suburbs and, since 1996, in every public park in Birmingham.

SPREADING OUT

The muntjac, an Asiatic deer species, originally from China, was established in Britain by the Duke of Bedford in 1894. He introduced several individuals into his park at Woburn, Bedfordshire, and began releasing them in 1901, but they probably didn't become established in the wild until the 1920s. In the 1940s and 1950s further releases took place in the Midlands, Kent and East Anglia, and more muntjac managed to escape from various zoos around the country.

Numbers increased and the deer spread out until the separate groups linked up to form a continuous distribution from Devon to Kent, north to Norfolk and west into Wales. Further releases led to muntjac turning up on islands and coasts and in parts of Scotland. By the early 1990s, muntjac had been seen in all but five counties in England and were present in many parts of Wales.

MUNTJAC FACT FILE

The introduced muntjac barely reaches the knees of a man of average height. Its antlers are inconspicuous – and grown only by the males (bucks) – but the dark face markings and rounded back are distinctive.

NAMES
Common name: Reeves's (or Chinese) muntjac, barking deer
Scientific name: *Muntiacus reevesi*

HABITAT
Dense woodland (deciduous and mixed); farmland; increasingly suburban parks and gardens; anywhere with a dense shrub layer

DISTRIBUTION
Widespread in central, southern and eastern England; spreading in Wales; scattered localities in northern England; yet to become widespread in Scotland

STATUS
More than 40,000 individuals; increasing rapidly

SIZE
Height 48–52cm (19–21in) at shoulder, does slightly smaller; length 90–100cm (36–40in); weight, bucks about 15kg (33lb), does about 12kg (26lb)

KEY FEATURES
Small stature; back humped; coat glossy chestnut colour in summer, buff below, duller in winter; 'V' shaped ridge on forehead, marked by dark stripes; antlers short, spiked, grow from 'stalks' of bone covered in skin and hair, called pedicles; tusks in upper jaw

HABITS
Skulking and elusive, especially during daylight

VOICE
Loud dog-like bark, often repeated many times

FOOD
Mostly leaves, buds and shoots of shrubs, especially bramble; nuts and fruits in autumn; grass in winter, spring and early summer; herbaceous plants chiefly in spring and early summer

BREEDING
Throughout the year; gestation averages 210 days; single fawn, twins very rare

YOUNG
Large, creamy white spots on brown coat disappear within two to three months

SIGNS
Loose groups of 20 or more small, black, oval droppings, usually around 10mm (½in) long and 5–10mm (¼–½in) in diameter

The pale-spotted coat of a muntjac fawn makes it almost invisible in dense undergrowth, where it will lie up quietly for most of the first few weeks. The buff spots fade after 8–12 weeks, by which time the fawn will be ready to venture into the open with its mother.

The rounded back and hindquarters are higher than the shoulders.
Cast in May or June, the short antlers grow again during the summer.
Pedicles (furry stalks) are present all year round.
Large scent glands below the eyes are rubbed against trees to mark out territory.
Dainty feet support short, sturdy legs.

Distribution map key

Present

Not present

The droppings, deposited in scattered groups of 20 or more, are easily overlooked and soon lost among the vegetation or fallen leaves.

However, muntjac may draw attention to themselves by making loud barking noises. The sharp call travels a long way, especially on still nights, but because it sounds like a dog barking, most people take no notice. Muntjac are often killed by traffic, but again escape notice since they look scarcely bigger than a dog or cat lying by the road.

Muntjac are often nocturnal and do not form large groups like some other deer. A single deer might be seen in the headlights of a car, or glimpsed fleetingly as it rushes across a parkland track. The cloven footprints of muntjac, which can be numerous in damp places, are only 15–25mm (⅝–1in) long and easily missed. At 12–15kg (26–33lb), muntjac are light animals and their weight does not result in deep footprints unless the ground is very soft. One good clue to their presence is that the tiny, pointed footprints are just

▲ The muntjac's tongue is extremely mobile and so long that it can stretch up and lick the corner of its eye. Females lack the prong-like horns seen in males and their faces are marked by a broad dark blaze right down the middle to the black nose.

◀ Male muntjac shred branches and saplings by thrashing them with their antlers. Afterwards they may also strip the bark with their incisors, leaving a characteristic twist of bark at the top.

Mutual grooming

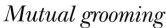

Although muntjac are solitary animals by nature, a fawn will often remain with its mother until she produces her next baby. Grooming behaviour occurs between mothers and fawns and is also seen between bucks and does.

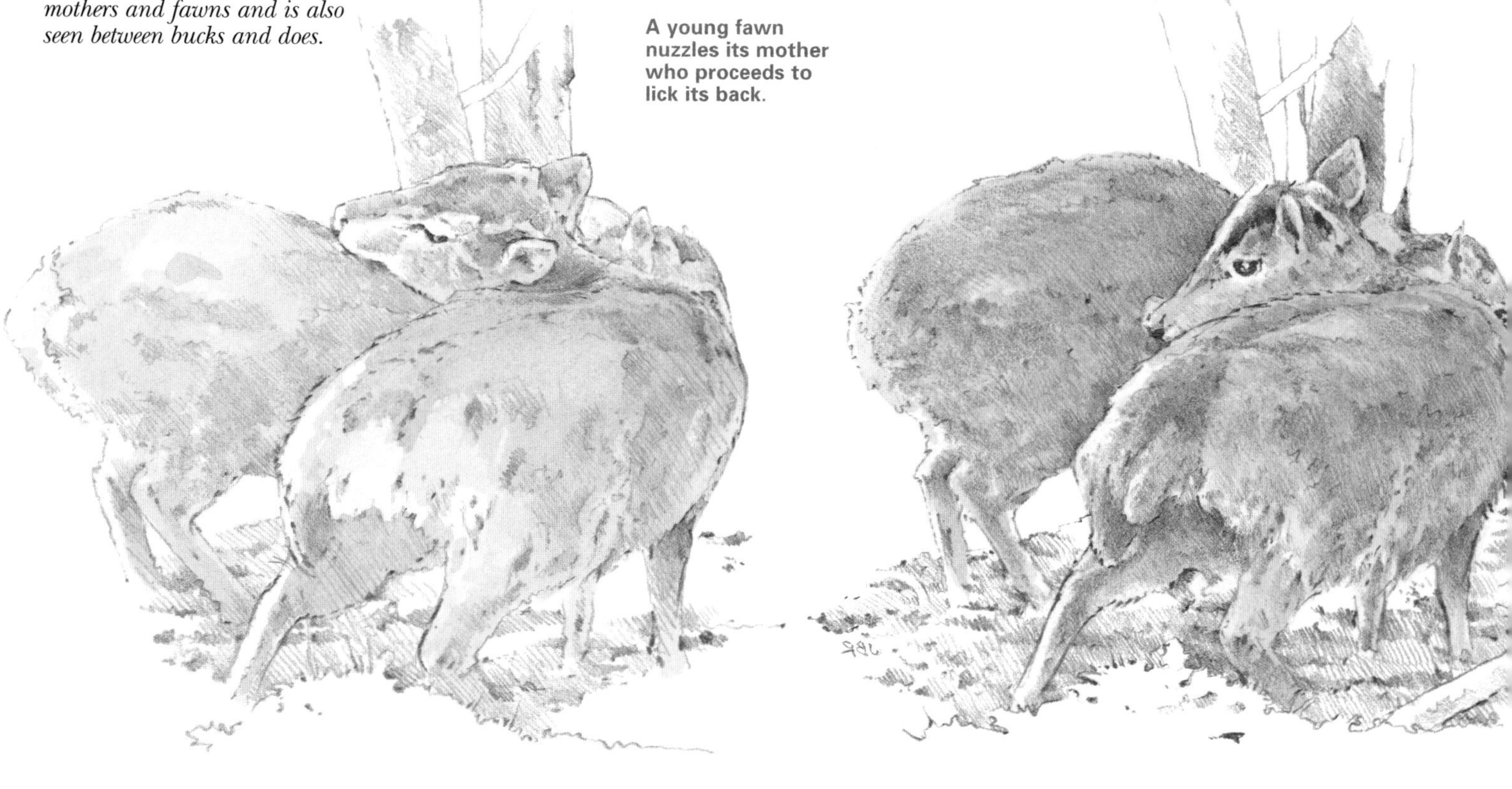

A young fawn nuzzles its mother who proceeds to lick its back.

Grooming not only helps maintain fur, but reinforces the bond between individuals.

FIGHTING TUSKS

Muntjac bucks have prominent tusks, a feature that is unusual in deer. These are enlarged canine teeth that project downwards from the upper jaw, well below the lower lip, and are easily visible even when the mouth is closed. The tips of the tusks are very sharp indeed and the rear edge is curved and also extremely sharp.

These tusks can inflict severe wounds, especially when the bucks fight, which they will do to establish ownership of territories and females. They do not confine their contests to a rutting season, as happens with other deer species in Britain. Fights between bucks involve vicious slicing at each other's throat with their tusks. For defence, they have thick skin around the neck to protect against the slashing action of a rival's tusks. One or both tusks may be broken in the course of battle and to reduce the risk of this happening, each tusk is embedded in a deep socket that has a rubbery attachment to the tooth. This allows the tusk a certain amount of movement, a few millimetres each way, without which it would easily snap off.

Nevertheless, most older males have broken tusks. This may also result from using these teeth to strip bark from trees, an activity indulged in by bucks to mark their territory as well as to feed. Females also have a canine tooth in their upper jaw but it is smaller and does not project beyond the lip.

This male's tusks are 2cm (¾in) long, but some individuals may have tusks up to 4.5cm (1¾in) long. Cornered muntjacs have been known to injure humans.

30cm (12in) apart, while sheep and other deer – which also have cloven hooves – take larger strides and their footprints are usually more than 50cm (20in) apart.

With a clear sighting, the muntjac is easy to recognise. The deer appears short and rounded, often with an arched back and prominent hindquarters. The animal stands about 50cm (20in) high at the shoulder, which is often held lower than the hips. Apart from a pale buff underside, the coat is a bright foxy red in summer and darker brown in winter. Muntjac moult around Easter time, when the coat can look ragged. They moult again in the autumn, but this time the change is less noticeable.

When the muntjac runs, it does so with a bounding gait. Normally the tail is tucked away between the legs, out of sight, but when alarmed it may lift its tail, which then appears to be surprisingly long and is pure white underneath.

Unlike most other male deer, which have large and spreading antlers, the muntjac's antlers are no more than short spikes with no side branches. They usually measure 6–8cm (2½–3in) long. In addition, unlike other deer, the antlers do not grow from a broad base – the coronet – pressed flat on the animal's head. Instead they emerge at the tips of long furry stalks called pedicles. These are longer than the antlers and very prominent – even at times of the year when the antlers are not present – and give the muntjac a distinctive profile.

As in all other deer, except reindeer, only males grow antlers and these are cast off and regrown each summer. To begin with, the antlers have a covering of soft, velvety skin, which rubs off by about

After attending to her offspring, the doe lowers her head to receive reciprocal licking behind the ears from her fawn.

Young females often stay near their mother's range, although young bucks tend to wander to new areas. They may travel more than 10km (6 miles) from where they were born to set up a new territory.

SCENT AND TERRITORY

Making a mark

To mark out their territories muntjac rub scent directly on to trees and the ground. Valuable information can be gathered about which deer have passed that way from scent left on tree bark and prominent twigs.

▶ **Muntjac have very large scent glands just below the eyes. These are as big as the eyes themselves and may be opened deliberately, when they look like a large wound on each side of the face.**

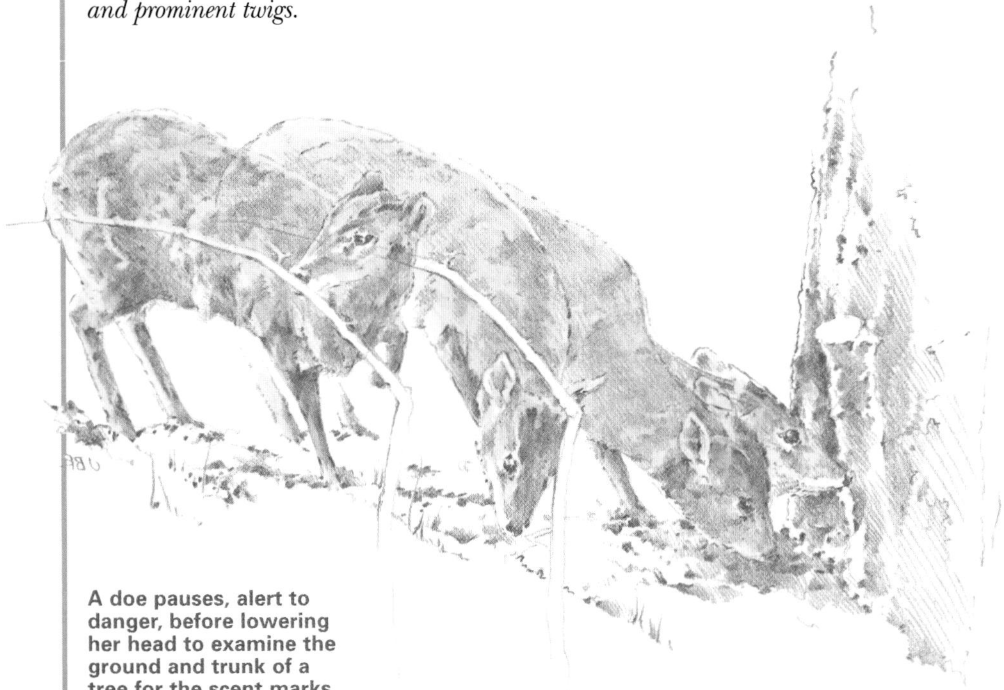

A doe pauses, alert to danger, before lowering her head to examine the ground and trunk of a tree for the scent marks of other muntjac.

As with other species that live in dense cover, muntjac rely heavily on scent to communicate with each other. They have huge scent glands on their faces and foreheads, which they rub against bushes and tree bark to leave markers. They also have glands between their toes that leave scent on the trails they use. Scent is important in establishing territorial boundaries.

Muntjac usually live alone, not even in family groups – apart from mothers and young – and never in social herds. The bucks range over 20 hectares (50 acres) or more, with the biggest having the largest territories, enabling them to meet and mate with more females. Does use smaller home ranges that often overlap.

September to expose the hard, whitish spikes. Unlike other deer, muntjac bucks are able to breed even while their antlers are regrowing.

Solitary habits

Muntjac do not pair up, and after mating the bucks go in search of new partners. Both sexes may use the same home range for several years, but after about four or five years the bucks are less able to defend their patch against fitter younger animals – often because their tusks are broken and they cannot defend themselves in a fight. Displaced bucks may have to move to a less favourable area.

Under the protective safety of night, muntjac overcome their natural timidity and may move up to 25m (80ft) out from cover. They do not like the cold or the rain, and in bad weather are likely to remain under cover all the time. Muntjac are herbivores but do not spend much time nibbling grass unless it is the only food available. However, in spring and early summer they may spend a week or

Unlike other deer, muntjac breed throughout the year. Females mate again soon after giving birth, normally producing a new baby every seven months. This means that many does are continuously pregnant for the whole of their life after reaching maturity at about six months old.

◀ Deep snow can be a problem for muntjac because it prevents them from getting at food. They can survive on their fat reserves for a while but persistent snow can result in many of them starving to death.

▶ A single fawn – twins are extremely rare – is born after a seven-month pregnancy. It may find itself in lush summer vegetation or bare woodland, yet more than half survive the first few weeks of life.

two grazing. They are mainly browsers, with teeth that are modified to shred large quantities of leaves. These are swallowed and digested with periods of 'chewing the cud', just like cows and sheep.

Muntjac like variety, often sampling several dozen plant species in the space of a few months. They are particularly fond of bramble but will also eat the leaves of climbing plants such as honeysuckle, ivy and old man's beard. They can consume plants that are unpalatable to other animals, such as cow parsley and ferns. They like flowers, including rosebay willowherb and primroses, and in gardens take pansies, lupins and roses – a particular favourite. Fortunately, they do not normally cause much trouble among farm crops, but they can wreak havoc on vegetable plots by eating cabbages and parsley. They love bluebells, too, and are in danger of completely eradicating them in some places.

In the autumn, muntjac seek out acorns, beech mast and conkers, and they also eat various kinds of fungi. This continues until there is nothing much left to eat except dead leaves and dry bark.

Tree damage

If muntjac are allowed to browse young trees and shrubs, they may create a serious problem for the future, because if all the young tree saplings are nibbled down, the woodland will be unable to rejuvenate. In time this leads to an open environment, with no replacement for older trees as they die off, which is damaging not only for the trees but for the wildlife that depends upon them, including the muntjac itself. Where hazel is coppiced, for example, the muntjac nibble off the new shoots, preventing proper regrowth. After a year or two the rootstock will die, which means that there is one less hazel shrub to produce nuts for birds and small mammals. Hazels are also important habitats for insects, which make up the diet of many species of birds.

WILDLIFE WATCH

Where can I see muntjac?

- Muntjac are particularly numerous in the Thetford area of Norfolk, and in wooded parts of Cambridgeshire, Hertfordshire and Warwickshire.
- Free-ranging muntjac are easily observed in many country parks, including Woburn Park in Bedfordshire and the South Lakes Wild Animal Park in Cumbria.
- In order to see wild muntjac, visit an area where they are known to live early in the morning. Listen for their loud, dog-like barks and the rustling of the foliage as they forge a path through the undergrowth.

A muntjac deer may sometimes be seen at dusk, feeding on grass, brambles, ivy and yew.

The pied wagtail

This unmistakable bird can be regularly seen in city parks and town centres, running along the ground on its slender legs, then darting after insect prey with sudden dashes and graceful swoops.

A long, constantly twitching tail, eye-catching black and white plumage and a distinctive '*tchizzick*' flight call ensure the pied wagtail is unmistakable.

Wagtails, together with pipits, belong to a family of birds called Motacillidae. The pied wagtail, *Motacilla alba yarrellii*, is found throughout the British Isles and is most common in the north and west, especially in areas of mixed farmland. Livestock attracts the flies and insects on which wagtails mainly feed and where arable farmland predominates – as in the eastern half of England and much of the south-east – the pied wagtail has become scarcer. The loss of farm ponds and old farm buildings and walls, which provide nesting sites, also causes the birds to look for new territories, which they often establish in parks and open spaces in towns and cities. The birds are regularly seen in man-made environments where adjoining areas provide both insect food and suitable nesting recesses.

Pied wagtails like to be near water, be it a fast-flowing river, canal, pond or puddle. This is reflected in one of the bird's many nicknames, water wagtail. It is also known as washtail, nanny washtail and washerwoman. These names may have come from the similarity between the constant up-and-down movement of the bird's tail and the vertical movement of the wooden paddle once used by washerwomen to beat the dirt out of clothes. Other common nicknames are dishwasher and willy wagtail.

Small, dark and handsome

The male pied wagtail in breeding plumage is a striking sight. His crown, upperparts, throat and upper breast are completely black, contrasting with a white mask and belly. His wings are also black, except for double white wingbars. When the tail is twitched up and down, or 'wagged' – hence the name – the clean white edges to the black tail feathers are especially noticeable.

DID YOU KNOW?

Throughout the month of June, roads winding through deciduous woodlands are often visited by large numbers of pied wagtails. The birds are attracted by the feast of plump caterpillars that litter the ground. The caterpillars fall from the overhanging boughs to lie helpless in the road, providing a free-for-all for wagtails with young to feed. This may seem to be a somewhat dangerous way to find a meal, but these nimble birds are usually able to skip out of the way of oncoming traffic very easily.

The short grass of a lawn provides a rich supply of insects for pied wagtails that choose to nest in an urban setting. Birds with beakfuls of grubs are a familiar sight in most town parks and on playing fields.

PIED WAGTAIL FACT FILE

True to its name, the pied wagtail has striking black-and-white plumage and a habit of twitching its long tail. It also moves its head backwards and forwards as it walks. These characteristic movements make this bird easy to recognise, even from a distance.

● NAMES
Common name: pied wagtail, water wagtail, willy wagtail, washerwoman, dishwasher
Scientific name: *Motacilla alba yarrellii*

● HABITAT
Wide range of open areas, from farmland to city parks; often near water

● DISTRIBUTION
Resident throughout Britain, most abundant in north and west; northern breeders move south and west for winter

● STATUS
Estimated 300,000 occupied territories in Britain; 130,000 in Ireland

● SIZE
Length 18cm (7in); weight: 19–27g (¾–1oz)

● KEY FEATURES
Male has black crown and upperparts, white mask and belly; throat and breast black in summer, reduced to narrow bib in winter; wings black with double white wingbar; tail black with white outer feathers; female greyer with reduced black markings; juvenile brownish grey with buff tinge to white parts

● HABITS
Chases insects mainly on ground with sudden dashes and swoops; often seen on tarmac and near water

● VOICE
Distinctive *'tchizzick'* flight call; song an unobtrusive, warbling twitter

● FOOD
Mainly small insects, especially flies and midges; insect larvae and caterpillars; occasionally crustaceans, snails, spiders, seeds

● BREEDING
Eggs laid mid-April to late July; usually 2 broods per year, occasionally 3

● NEST
Bulky cup of moss, grass, twigs and rootlets lined with wool, hair and feathers; built by female; sited in a recess, crevice or among ivy on a wall, bridge, bank or rock face; will also occupy open-fronted nestboxes as well as garden sheds and other outbuildings

● EGGS
5–6 off-white eggs with dark greyish brown speckling; incubated by female for 13–14 days

● YOUNG
Fed by male; fledge in 14–16 days

Pied wagtail nestlings stay in the nest until they are quite well grown and often return there to roost at night after they have fledged. Even at this stage, they clearly resemble their parents in terms of plumage pattern and profile.

The dark and slender bill is adapted to catching flying insects.

The males have a black back with white fringes and tips to the wings.

In summer the black bib merges with the black cap.

The long black tail with white outer tail feathers is constantly wagging up and down.

The belly is white all year round.

The legs are relatively long and dark.

Distribution map key

Present all year round

Present during summer months

Not present

PIED WAGTAIL CALENDAR

JANUARY • FEBRUARY

Small flocks of wagtails forage for food, but the mating urge soon takes over, especially in mild winters. Males start to seek out and defend territories.

MARCH • APRIL

Pairs are formed and the first nests built by the females. Eggs are laid in mid-April and incubated by females until the chicks hatch two weeks later.

MAY • JUNE

This is a hectic time for the adults as the chicks grow fast and fledge at two weeks old. Parents start a second brood straight away if the conditions are right.

JULY • AUGUST

By mid-August, most second broods have fledged and young birds (like this one) are out and about. Most adults start to moult in mid-August.

SEPTEMBER • OCTOBER

Families break up and wagtails begin to feed and roost communally. They often feed in fields and areas of open ground where they find abundant prey.

NOVEMBER • DECEMBER

Southern breeders are sedentary, but many others will move south for winter. Look for roosts on buildings or in trees and listen for the *'tchizzick'* call.

Water wagtail

A fast-flowing river with pebble-lined beaches and prominent rocky outcrops on which it can perch is ideal for the pied wagtail. If the weather conditions are not suitable for flying insects, the wagtail may wade through the shallows looking for food.

Stalking slowly through the water, the current swirling gently around its feet, this pied wagtail is hunting for aquatic insects and tiny snails.

The bird pauses, tilting its head on one side as if to listen for prey beneath the burbling water.

In flight, the long black tail and white outer tail feathers of the pied wagtail are among the bird's most striking features. At rest the tail feathers are folded in so that just a thin white edge is visible.

NESTING SITES

Pied wagtails like deep recesses in which to nest, preferably with a small opening, and they will tuck themselves into old stone walls, wood piles or anything that creates a safe nook – a stack of pallets, wooden boxes or even a pile of scaffolding poles will do.

They take fairly readily to open-fronted nestboxes of the kind that robins often occupy. Also like robins, wagtails may nest in obscure corners in outhouses such as garden sheds, greenhouses or workshops.

Pied wagtails have been known to build their nests in the most unlikely and inconvenient places. A car left unattended for any length of time, especially with the bonnet up, is an attractive nest site for a pied wagtail. Birds nesting under the bonnet have even been known to stay put when the vehicle is started up and moves.

◄ Many farmers check the engine bays of tractors and other mechanical equipment that has not been in use for a while, just in case a wagtail nest is hidden inside.

▼ A neglected window ledge in an old shed provides a perfect level nesting site for a pied wagtail. This bird has successfully raised a large brood of noisy youngsters.

As with so many other songbirds, the female is rather plain by comparison. Her duller plumage is an effective and necessary camouflage when she is at her most vulnerable on the nest. Overall, the female has much less black in her plumage, especially on the crown and breast, and her back is much greyer. Outside the breeding season, the male also becomes more drab, his black breast reduced to a horseshoe-shaped bib.

Breeding activity

By late March, the males are on their territories, establishing ownership and advertising for a mate with their unobtrusive, twittering song. A male pied wagtail may hold the same territory for several years and even re-use the same nest site each year. However, the pair bond lasts for the duration of the breeding season only and his mate will change from year to year.

In courtship, one or two males will chase a desired female in undulating flight. Once a pair have bonded, the

In fact, the wagtail has spotted something edible and is taking a closer look. With a sudden dart forward it plunges its head under the water.

Any exposed rocks that are covered with a furry coating of damp moss may harbour invertebrate prey.

The wagtail scrutinises the rock and pokes its narrow, pointed bill into likely crevices.

WHITE, YELLOW AND GREY WAGTAILS

The pied wagtail is a subspecies of *Motacilla alba.* Another subspecies is the white wagtail, *M. alba alba.* Common in continental Europe, the white wagtail is a regular spring and autumn passage migrant in Britain and Ireland. It looks somewhat like a female pied wagtail, but has a paler grey back and rump. In autumn, it may be confused with the young pied wagtail, which also has a pale grey back. The white wagtail breeds in the Channel Islands and occasionally in Scotland.

The white wagtail can be difficult to distinguish from the native pied wagtail. It is most easily identified by the lack of a join between the black cap and bib and the pale grey back.

The yellow wagtail is a summer visitor to Britain, where it breeds, and a regular passage migrant in Ireland, where it does not. In breeding plumage, the male is spectacular, with bright yellow underparts and olive upperparts. Females, young and non-breeding males are duller. Yellow wagtails draw attention to their presence with a prolonged, musical *'tswee-eep'* flight call. Their movements on the ground are characteristic of the family – a brisk walk or run, often with short flutters to catch flying insects.

Yellow wagtails breed in lowland pasture, marshes and on cultivated fields, often in the vicinity of water. The female lays four to six speckled eggs in a simple nest made of grass and rootlets lined with fine stems, hair and wool. The nest is sited in a hollow in the ground, usually well hidden against a tussock. The eggs are incubated by the female for 11–13 days and the young fledge at around 16 days old. In the south it is quite common for yellow wagtails to have a second brood.

◀ Yellow wagtails arrive in Britain from early April onwards. They are most often seen on coastal marshes and wet meadows, where there is likely to be an abundant supply of insects.

Outside the breeding season, yellow wagtails are gregarious and can often be heard calling as they fly overhead or feed on insects disturbed by the feet of grazing cattle. They eventually gather in large roosts in reedbeds on the south coast, where they feed on aphids to prepare for their return migration. By late September, most of them will have left for Europe.

The grey wagtail is the least abundant wagtail in Britain and Ireland. In common with the yellow wagtail, it has yellow underparts, but it also has a much longer tail and attractive blue-grey upperparts. In the breeding season, the male has a white stripe above and below the eye and a black throat. The grey wagtail moves very elegantly, whether in flight or on the ground, the very long tail giving it a particularly slender, elongated profile. Once the breeding plumage is lost both sexes are much duller. The juvenile grey may look very like a young pied wagtail, but the very long tail and the primrose suffusion on the undertail coverts are constant features that can help identification of the species. The grey wagtail's usual call is a *'tzitzi'*, reminiscent of the pied wagtail's *'tchizzick'* call but more penetrating and explosive. Outside the breeding season, the grey wagtail moves to lowland habitats near water, including coastal marshes, farmyard ponds and canals. Unlike the other two species, it is usually solitary.

▼ Seldom seen far from water, the grey wagtail breeds in upland areas, preferring to be near fast-moving, rocky or gravelly streams. It builds its rather untidy nest on ledges or in cavities in walls and banks.

female builds her ample and somewhat untidy nest. As she collects twigs, plant stems, roots, dead leaves and moss, the male follows her around, calling out encouragement. She lines the nest with hair, wool and feathers and lays a clutch of five or six pale bluish or greyish white eggs, which are evenly freckled with greyish brown markings.

The female completes most of the incubation over the following two weeks, but once the chicks have hatched the

During the breeding season male pied wagtails are extremely territorial. They will even become agitated at the sight of their own reflection in a mirror and spend time displaying to the mystery 'rival'.

▶ Occasionally pied wagtails become the hapless parents of a cuckoo baby. However, their choice of sites near human settlement usually means that this happens less often than it does to more rural species.

▼ While sitting on the nest, the female is tended by her mate. The male brings her beakfuls of insects, mainly adult flies and any larvae he can find.

male provides food for the hungry brood. No sooner has the first brood of youngsters fledged than a second clutch is laid. In very good years there may even be a third brood.

Roving flocks

By late summer the breeding season is over and, after the moult, the birds start to prepare for winter. Pied wagtails that live in relatively mild parts of the country, such as the south and west, tend not to move far. Indeed, many males will maintain their territories throughout the winter. Elsewhere, pied wagtails congregate in loose flocks, often numbering several hundred birds, and go in search of food and safe roosting sites. These transient roosts, usually near water, may number three or four thousand birds. The settling beds of sewage farms are a favourite location. The birds circle round and round above the roost site, calling to each other. They gradually circle lower until they are reassured that all is well, before dropping in squadrons to the roost site.

Pied wagtails are not exclusively rural birds in the winter, however, and it is not unusual to hear a babble of their chattering calls in town centres. Huge assemblies of wagtails may seek a safe roost for the night under the glass roof of a shopping arcade, for instance.

Wagtail survival

Studies show that in most nests three or four wagtail chicks from each brood will survive to fledging. Since wagtails produce two and sometimes three broods each year, this may seem like a lot of youngsters, but it is important to take into account both the number of failed nests and the mortality of birds during their first winter. Complete brood failure is usually the result of a raid by a terrestrial mammal predator, such as a stoat or weasel. Avian predators are less of a factor in the loss of nestlings, simply because wagtail nests are usually sited deep enough in a hole or crevice to thwart the efforts of a crow or magpie.

As for winter mortality, it is not surprising that a ground-feeding bird with a fondness for human habitation is an easy target for cats. Large numbers of roosting birds also attract birds of prey, such as hobbies and sparrowhawks. The pied wagtails' alarm calls warn of the presence of any such avian predator but inevitably some birds are taken.

The other principal cause of pied wagtail mortality is lack of food during bad spells of weather. This means that of sometimes ten or 12 young produced by one pair of pied wagtails in one summer, it is unlikely that more than one or two will survive until the following year.

WILDLIFE WATCH

Where can I see wagtails?

- Pied wagtails are extremely widespread, occurring in both rural and urban habitats. In the breeding season, they often choose to nest in buildings, including sheds, outhouses, walls and suchlike. Being primarily ground feeders, they are often seen on open grassy areas, including playing fields, lawns, pastures and grassy roadside verges, and after rain, anywhere with puddles.

- Outside the breeding season, transient roosts are often formed on rooftops in towns, in trees near water and in reed-beds. Sewage farm settling beds are a particular favourite. Listen out for the *'tchizzick'* call and follow the birds to their roost site.

- In the summer yellow wagtails can be found in any suitable farmland habitat in Britain. They are easiest to see along arable field margins, in water meadows or on mixed farming pasture, dodging the feet of cattle.

- From July to September, yellow wagtails often gather near reedbeds in coastal areas. Here they fatten up before setting off on their migration south. Listen out for their distinctive *'tswee-eep'* call.

- Grey wagtails are restricted to upland rivers and streams in the breeding season. They favour clear, clean mountain streams. Search boulders or rocks on or near the water's edge, and look out for a flash of primrose yellow and a very long tail twitching up and down. In the winter, an occasional bird may be found on a coastal marsh, sewage farm or even by a city park lake.

The swift

Perfectly adapted to flying long distances, the swift spends most of its life in the air. These birds arrive in May for a short summer stay to breed before returning to their southern winter quarters.

On warm evenings in July, the peace of urban parks may be suddenly broken as the air becomes filled with the shrill screams of swifts that seem to have appeared from nowhere, swooping and wheeling through the sky. Then, just as suddenly as they arrived, the swifts are gone. A close observer may have watched them circling higher and higher in the sky, until they disappear into the darkening hues of night.

During summer swifts are a common sight in towns and villages. They appear after the swallows and martins, sometime between late April and early May, and are a sign that spring has well and truly arrived. Swifts build their nests near human habitation, in the eaves of houses, churches and other buildings that offer dark, sheltered crevices. After breeding, they depart before the swallows and martins in the autumn. The young leave as soon as they have fledged and the adults follow shortly afterwards. Most birds will have gone by early September.

Swifts are capable of climbing to 3000m (10,000ft) in pursuit of insect prey. At these great heights, they soar and spiral on steady wings, and are even able to sleep while remaining in flight.

Swifts are superbly adapted for life in the air, with extraordinarily long, sickle-shaped wings that they use in a series of extremely fast, shallow wingbeats interspersed with short glides. Their bodies are torpedo-shaped for rapid flight and their mouths gape widely to catch prey as they twist and turn in the air. Their eyes are set deep in feathers, with a set of bristles providing additional protection against airborne debris that could blind them if it got in their eyes. It is an incredible fact that once a young swift leaves its nest it may not land again for up to four years. Swifts sleep, eat, drink and even mate without landing. They only leave the air to nest.

Despite appearances, swifts are not related to swallows and martins. Indeed, they are probably most closely related to hummingbirds. Unlike the perching birds, swifts have small, weak legs, hence the family name Apodidae, meaning 'no legs'.

TOWER SWIFTS

Most of what is known about breeding swifts derives from an ongoing study at a nesting colony situated in the ventilators of the tower at Oxford University's Museum of Science. The study began in the late 1940s, when the ventilators were replaced with glass-backed nesting boxes. This enables scientists to observe the birds at close quarters throughout the breeding cycle.

SWIFT FACT FILE

Superficially similar to those other aerial feeders, swallows and house martins, the swift is distinguishable by its colour, its voice and the way its long, curved wings beat rapidly in flight. During the summer, dense, swirling flocks of swifts are often seen over towns and countryside.

● NAMES
Common name: swift
Scientific name: *Apus apus*

● HABITAT
Spends most of its life in the sky; found over all types of land but especially villages, towns and cities where churches, houses and other buildings provide plenty of nest sites; often hunts flying insects over water

● DISTRIBUTION
Throughout Britain and Ireland; most abundant in eastern and southern England, scarcer in western and northern parts

● STATUS
Population estimated at 100,000 breeding pairs in Britain and Ireland

● SIZE
Length 17cm (6½in); wingspan 40–45cm (16–18in); weight 35–50g (1¼–1¾oz), arriving birds and non-breeders are heavier, parents feeding young are lighter

● KEY FEATURES
Slim, round-headed bird; plumage dark brown, appears black, with pale chin and throat patch; wings long, narrow, sickle-shaped; tail shallowly forked

● HABITS
Spends almost entire life on wing; never alights on ground voluntarily; soars in screaming groups

● VOICE
Shrill '*sree*' in communal display flight, also used at the nest; the call is a complex series of trills and whistles that differ between the sexes

● FOOD
Flying insects, especially flies, aphids and small airborne spiders

● BREEDING
Birds arrive from March to early May; egg-laying starts late May, most young fledged by late July, early August in poor weather; depart mid-August, depending on weather conditions

● NEST
Shallow cup of grass, straw and feathers cemented with saliva; nests added to in successive years; favours holes and crevices under eaves of houses and old buildings, occasionally on cliffs, holes in tall trees or in nestboxes

● EGGS
1–4 elongated, dull white eggs, laid at 2 day intervals; adults share incubation for 18–23 days; one brood per year

● YOUNG
Both parents feed young in nest for 37–56 days depending on the weather; young are independent on fledging

Distribution map key

Present during summer months

Not present

Wings are very long, narrow and scythe-shaped, with a proportionately very long outer wing, or 'hand'.
A fringe of bristles protects the eye from airborne debris.
A small, whitish patch shows the position of an expandable throat pouch.
Dark underparts distinguish swifts from swallows and martins.
Tiny feet are hardly ever used.
The tail is short and shallowly forked.

Behind the minute bill lies an enormous gape – the mouth opens almost from ear to ear and is an effective trap for flying insects.

Mating on the wing

Every aspect of the swift's biology is dedicated to flight. These birds are such skilled aviators that they are capable of doing almost everything on the wing – even mating.

They look helpless but swift nestlings are remarkably resilient. When poor weather causes fluctuations in their food supply, these frail creatures are able to enter a state of torpor until food is plentiful again.

The male begins by flying in front of his mate with his wings held in a deep V.

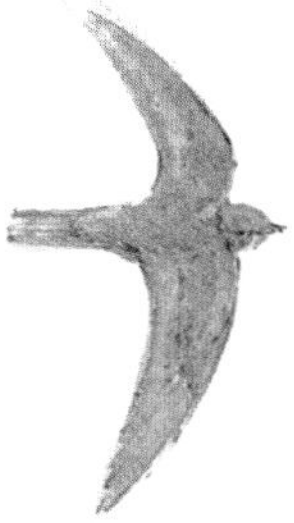

If the female is receptive, she will fly in a slow, shallow glide, her wings held downwards in a sharper V.

The male manoeuvres to place himself above his mate.

Mating takes place in this shallow dive. The male may use his feet to steady himself against his mate's back.

SWIFT CALENDAR

MARCH • APRIL

A few swifts reach Britain in March and early April but most birds start to arrive from late April onwards. Small numbers are regularly recorded at coastal bird observatories.

MAY • JUNE

Numbers peak in mid-May, by which time many birds will have returned to their colonies. Nesting gets under way immediately, with the first eggs laid during late May. They hatch in June.

JULY • AUGUST

In an average season, the young remain in the nest for six weeks. A protein-rich diet ensures they grow strong enough to migrate south as soon as they fledge in early August.

SEPTEMBER • FEBRUARY

Most swifts will have left Britain by September and many will have already reached their winter quarters in Africa. They will begin their return journey to Britain in the following February.

▼ The swift's tiny feet have needle-sharp, forward-pointing claws that provide a strong grip on minute holds, enabling the bird to hang from vertical surfaces. In this position, the very long curved wings cross over at the tip.

The primary feathers provide the forward power required for flight and their extra length makes the swift one of the fastest birds in the sky. They can reach speeds of more than 96km/h (60mph) and possibly twice this in a dive or when fleeing from a bird of prey.

After mating, the male brings his wings forward to slow his speed and lifts clear of his mate.

Conserving body heat is particularly important for a bird that flies at high altitudes for long periods of time, and the swift's tiny legs and feet minimise the heat lost through its skin. In any case, the swift needs its feet only to scramble in and out of its nest site. The feet have three needle-sharp front toes and a hind toe that swings forward and enables the birds to cling to the walls or cliff faces where they build their nests.

Identifying swifts

It is easy to recognise swifts in flight by their dark-coloured underparts. Swallows have a pale underbelly and dark throat patch, while house martins are pure white beneath with dark wings. In sand martins the white underside is dissected by a brown throat band.

Swifts can also be distinguished by their behaviour. They never perch on roofs and wires in the manner of swallows and martins. You might spot martins collecting mud from puddles, but a swift will never voluntarily land on the ground. Its legs are so short and its wings so long that it finds it difficult to take off again. Swallows and martins rarely fly as high as swifts, which circle up into the sky until they are almost out of sight. Their calls are also different. The screaming call of the swift is unmistakable.

Homing instinct

As summer warms up, the returning adults prospect for nest sites. Swifts tend to re-use nests and many of the mature birds return to the same site year after year. Swifts can live for more than 20 years, whereas most birds of their size are lucky to live for seven or eight. Swifts have been seen literally banging their heads against the wall of a renovated building,

Hatching is staggered, so the oldest nestling is always bigger on emergence than the youngest. When times are hard, the oldest and strongest offspring will have a great advantage over its smaller, weaker siblings.

vainly trying to reclaim their usual nest site by entering a cavity that is now blocked because the builders did not leave them a suitable gap. In an effort to avoid this problem, a campaign was started in 1996, supported by the RSPB and the British Trust for Ornithology, to provide information to property owners, builders and architects about how to make allowances for swifts when carrying out restorations.

Where nest sites have been lost, people sometimes put up nestboxes for swifts. The traditional design, which fits under the eaves, is the shape and size of a large shoebox with a hole underneath since swifts much prefer to fly into their nest from below. In Holland, specially adapted roof tiles that incorporate a nest cavity have been tested with great success. The latest nestboxes fit snugly on the wall of a building and even incorporate a space at the back for roosting bats. Elevation and orientation can be critical in siting the nestboxes and swifts may not take up residence for the first two or three seasons.

Once they have chosen a nest site the birds spend a little time settling in before egg-laying begins. Frequent scuffles and fights occur as other swifts attempt to intrude. Given that swifts do not start breeding until they are three or four years old, there are always plenty of non-breeding birds in a colony. This makes it difficult to estimate the

Swifts are meticulous parents, carefully turning their clutch. The eggs are unusually resistant to chilling, so cold weather merely delays the incubation process rather than spelling death for the developing chicks.

ALPINE SWIFT

In the swift family 92 species are divided into 19 genera. The common swift belongs to the genus *Apus* and occurs throughout Europe. Three other *Apus* species breed in continental Europe and two are occasionally seen in the British Isles – the alpine swift, *Apus melba*, and the pallid swift, *Apus pallidus*.

The alpine swift is easy to distinguish from the common swift. It is noticeably the largest European representative of the family and is paler and longer-winged. It also has a more shallowly forked tail and a conspicuous white belly and throat. As its name suggests, it is a mountain species, preferring hilly areas that provide updraughts on which it can soar. However, it can also be seen in cities in southern Europe where there are suitable nest sites – Zurich cathedral has a breeding colony that is reputed to be as old as the building itself.

The presence of the alpine swift is often first announced by its distinctive voice. Like common swifts, the birds dash about in screaming parties, but the word screaming does not do them justice. Their calls, which are somewhat reminiscent of a falcon's cries, consist of a bubbling trill that rises and falls in pitch.

Visiting individuals are recorded in Britain about half a dozen times in most years. They are most likely to be seen at coastal sites and their appearance is often associated with inclement weather further south. This suggests that they have been swept round the edge of a weather system. Since they seem to be expanding their breeding range, especially into France and Germany, the number of alpine swifts recorded in Britain may increase in the future.

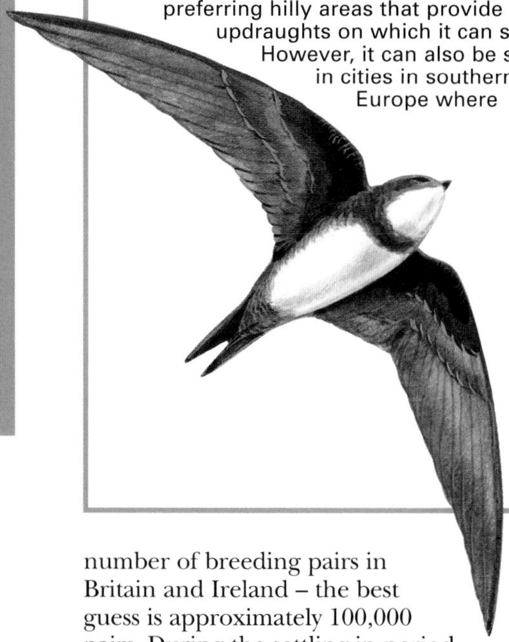

◄ The alpine swift is distinguished by its large size and its white underparts and brown breast-band. At first glance, distant birds can look like small falcons.

► In spring, weather systems may force alpine swifts as far north as southern England. The birds may pause to rest on sea cliffs or rock faces.

number of breeding pairs in Britain and Ireland – the best guess is approximately 100,000 pairs. During the settling-in period, pair bonds are reinforced by a behaviour known as allopreening, in which each bird preens the other.

In many cases, if the birds succeed in returning to the same site, nest building simply means repairing the old structure. The nest is an untidy construction of feathers, grass and straw, collected by both male and female in flight as the lightweight material floats up into the air. The structure is glued together with saliva, for which the swift is equipped with an enlarged salivary gland.

Survival strategy

Usually two or three eggs – rarely, one or four – are laid at two-day intervals, longer if the weather is bad, so that there is always an age difference between the chicks. This staggered hatching means that if food becomes scarce, the older and stronger chicks are guaranteed the lion's share because they are able to out-compete their weaker siblings. This allows at least one or two healthy chicks to fledge rather than the whole brood starving, which may happen if insufficient food is distributed equally. If food is plentiful, however, all the chicks will live. Both parents share the tasks of incubation, feeding and brooding.

Swift chicks are unusually resistant to chilling. If a period of bad weather affects the availability of insects on the wing, the young in the nest will go hungry for a time but rather than this meaning disaster for the brood, the chicks enter a state of torpor. In this condition, they can resist starvation for several days, living on their fat reserves and retarding their rate of development. They can lose as much as 50 per cent of their body weight and still recover. Their body temperature can drop from its normal 41°C (106°F) down to as low as 25°C (77°F) during the night, and then pick up again the next day. Such a temperature drop would be fatal for most other birds.

Swift nestlings are blind and naked, with gangly limbs and an oddly proportioned body. They emerge from the eggs after two-and-a-half to three weeks and then spend around six to eight weeks in the nest. Young swallows fledge in half the time or less, but swifts have to

Adult swifts gather insects to feed to their young, storing them in an expandable throat pouch. This parent bird's pale-coloured throat bulges conspicuously as it returns to the nest.

◀ The chicks cluster around an adult begging to be fed. The young must use their own saliva as a solvent to break down the insect ball, as it may have hardened in the adult's throat as it returned from its feeding flight.

be fully independent once they fledge. The extra time spent in the nest allows the youngsters to develop the long, strong feathers needed for migration. Swallows continue to feed their young even after they have departed the nest, but young swifts are on their own from the moment they take their first flight. They set off on their migratory journey south almost immediately.

To turn a naked, helpless hatchling into an efficient flying machine requires lots of protein-rich food, and this is the burdensome task of both parents during the fledging period. All prey are taken in flight. The tiny prey are transferred to the bird's throat pouch, where they form a pellet called a bolus. There can be anything between 250 and 1000 individual insects in each ball. Studies undertaken by ornithologist David Lack and his team at the Museum of Science tower in Oxford showed that, in fine weather, a brood of two chicks will be fed about 15 times in a 10-hour period. So, in a fine summer, a single brood of chicks may consume 300,000 insects or more in just 40 days.

Swifts, especially young in the nest, are hosts to a large and formidable-looking parasite called the louse-fly. It takes a blood meal from its host every five days. An individual is likely to have anything from six to 35 of these parasites. Surprisingly, the swift does not appear to be unduly harmed, although nestlings will suffer if they are heavily infested, especially during a period of poor feeding.

▼ On summer evenings in July or early August swifts can be seen over cities, towns and villages. Scan the skies and listen for their screaming calls as clouds of birds whirl round buildings where colonies are located.

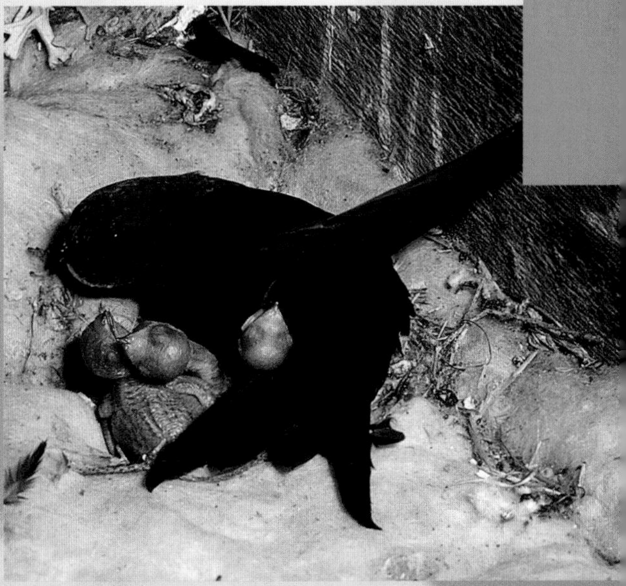

▶ Despite their grace in the air, swifts are remarkably ungainly when forced to land. Brooding the chicks in the nest can be an uncomfortable business, as the swift's long wings and short legs make moving about difficult.

WILDLIFE WATCH

Where can I see swifts?

- Small flocks of swifts may be seen from coastal bird observatories from late April onwards as they arrive for the summer, but remember that swifts often fly so high they are out of sight. In late summer and early autumn, parties of swifts gather at coastal sites for the return flight, and are often to be seen feeding on insects over suitable stretches of water.

- When the weather is cool, wet or windy, swifts can be seen hawking for insects in much lower level flight. Not only does poor weather make soaring flight very difficult, it also drives flying insect prey nearer to the ground.

- The concentration of insect prey is likely to be greater near water than anywhere else. For example, at least 80,000 swifts were seen together in June 1980 over Hanningfield Reservoir in Essex. The swift's dull, sooty-brown colour is also easier to see against the water.

- Look out for swifts near housing estates. In Crewe, Cheshire, parties of more than 1000 swifts have been seen over one housing development. Older houses may have convenient gaps between walls and eaves, allowing birds access to the horizontal timbers where most of their nests are to be found.

Recognising damselflies

They may not be as flamboyant as dragonflies, but damselflies have their own understated appeal. Summer is the season to see these attractive insects on the wing.

A visit to a local pond or lake in summer would not be complete without the sight of several graceful little damselflies flitting over the surface of the water in search of the small flying insects that consitute the main part of their diet. They also frequent canals and rivers, and may even visit gardens with no ponds during late spring and summer.

The damselfly's large compound eyes provide it with excellent vision, enabling it to locate its prey by sight. It often catches prey insects in flight, using the basket-like arrangement of its legs.

Males and females of the same species may have different coloration or markings from one another. Furthermore, several different colour forms of the same species may also occur. Newly emerged damselflies, particularly males, may not acquire the colours typically seen in maturity for several days.

Courtship displays

The courtship behaviour of most damselfly species is enchanting to watch. Groups of males flutter above the water, on the lookout for passing females. Once a male has found a willing female, he woos her with vibrating wings before grasping her thorax with the claspers at the tip of his abdomen. He will then transfer sperm to a storage apparatus and the female collects this by arching her abdomen in a graceful curve.

Females lay their eggs in or near water. Some simply drop their eggs on to the surface, while others insert them into plant stems, sometimes submerging themselves in order to do so. The larvae, called nymphs, usually hatch in late summer or autumn and can be found in ponds, lakes and canals until the following spring, when they will leave the water and metamorphose into adults.

Underwater nymphs

Most damselfly nymphs lurk among aquatic vegetation where they stalk small invetebrate prey. Some species remain among the debris or gravel on the bottom, especially in flowing water. They are all sensitive to pollution and prefer to live in clean water.

Damselfly nymphs are superficially similar to the nymphs of mayflies. The immature stages of both insect groups have three projections at the tail end, which function as gills for breathing and also help the larvae to swim. In mayflies these projections are like fine threads while in damselflies they are flat and paddle-like.

WILDLIFE WATCH

Where can I see damselflies?

- Although the greatest number of damselfly species is found in the southern half of Britain, they occur almost anywhere in lowland areas where there are suitable aquatic habitats for their larval stages. Adults are quite often seen in gardens and parks in summer.

- Most damselfly species are associated with standing water or water where there is a slow flow. Lakes and ponds are ideal, as are flooded gravel pits. A good range of damselflies can be found on heathlands, where their larval stages inhabit boggy pools.

- Most adult damselflies are on the wing between May and August.

- Some species of damselfly are distinctive enough to be recognised on the wing but most need to be studied when at rest for confident identification.

  Visit suitable damselfly habitats on cool, overcast days when the insects are unlikely to be flying. Search among the marginal vegetation for resting individuals, and take a good look at them first through close-focusing binoculars.

Damselflies are light enough to land on the surface of ponds. This is a blue-tailed damselfly – both males and females have the sky-blue patch on the tail.

EASY GUIDE TO SPOTTING DAMSELFLIES

WHAT ARE DAMSELFLIES?

- Damselflies are classified in an order of insects called the Odonata, the group to which dragonflies also belong. Damselflies are placed in the suborder Zygoptera.

- A total of 21 species has been recorded in the British Isles, but several are scarce while two are now extinct.

The damselfly's widely spaced eyes emerge on both sides of the head, giving it a distinct hammer-head appearance.

- Adult damselflies have delicate, slender bodies with clearly segmented abdomens. As with dragonflies, damselflies are brightly coloured; males are brighter than females.

- The life cycle of damselflies involves incomplete metamorphosis – there is no pupal stage. Eggs are laid in or close to water and from these larvae (nymphs) emerge.

- Two beautiful species in the genus *Calopteryx* are known as demoiselles.

HOW CAN I IDENTIFY DAMSELFLIES?

- Damselfly identification relies partly on a study of the arrangement of veins in the wings. For this, dead specimens are usually needed. Fortunately, however, most British damselfly species have distinct markings on the abdominal segments, which are often brightly coloured. These features are usually enough to allow accurate identification in the field. It helps to learn the key segments to look for and to use binoculars that focus in close-up.

- The shape of the coloured wing marking is important in male demoiselles and the colour of the wings is crucial in females. For blue damselflies, note the colour of the eyes and legs, and the colours and markings on the abdominal segments, particularly the last three. The time of year, location and habitat are also important clues.

- Adult damselflies have two pairs of wings that are about the same size and shape. In most species, the wings are transparent, with clear dark veins. Male demoiselles' wings are all or partly dark with iridescent veins. At rest, damselflies hold their wings closed above the body or only partly open. Their flight is relatively weak and fluttering, especially compared with that of dragonflies.

- The nymphs are aquatic and can be distinguished from those of dragonflies by the three flattened gills that project at the tail end. They are predators and, like the much larger, broader dragonfly nymphs, catch their prey with jaws located on an extendible 'mask' under the head.

- When damselflies mate, the male and female become joined at the tips of their abdomens to form a 'wheel' or 'heart' shape. They often fly united in this way.

Distribution map key

Present — Not present

BANDED DEMOISELLE *Calopteryx splendens*

In both sexes the thorax and abdomen are greenish blue with a metallic sheen. The male's wings are clear with a thumbprint mark the colour of which ranges with age from brown to blue. The female's wings have a metallic, very pale greenish sheen and a small pale marking near the tip of each wing, largest on the forewings.

The banded demoiselle is fond of resting on waterside vegetation. This enables it to save energy as it watches for potential mates.

- SIZE
Up to 45mm (1¾in) long

- HABITAT
Slow-flowing rivers or canals with muddy bottoms and plenty of waterside vegetation

- DISTRIBUTION
Throughout lowland Britain and Ireland; most common in southern England

- FLIGHT SEASON
Mid-May–September

BEAUTIFUL DEMOISELLE *Calopteryx virgo*

A green thorax and abdomen with a metallic sheen are common to both sexes. The male's wings are brownish blue to violet depending on age. The female's wings are uniformly very pale reddish brown or purplish brown, without an obvious sheen; each has a small pale marking at the tip.

Male beautiful demoiselles often settle on ferns close to water. In heathland areas, gorse bushes are favoured.

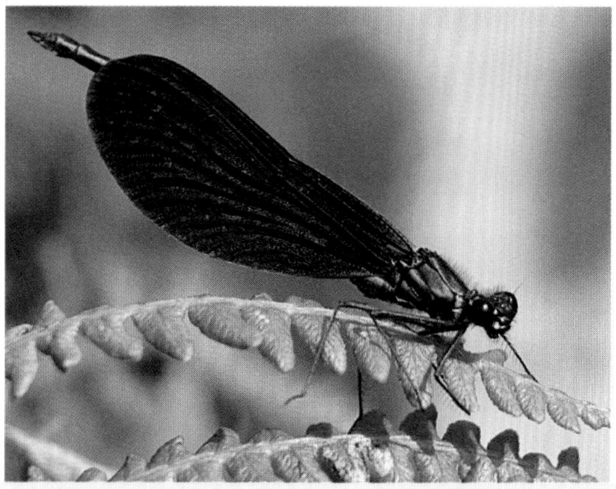

- SIZE
Up to 45mm (1¾in) long

- HABITAT
Clear, fast-flowing streams with gravelly beds and bordered by vegetation

- DISTRIBUTION
Mainly southern and western counties of England and Wales; scattered up to the Lake District

- FLIGHT SEASON
Late May–late August

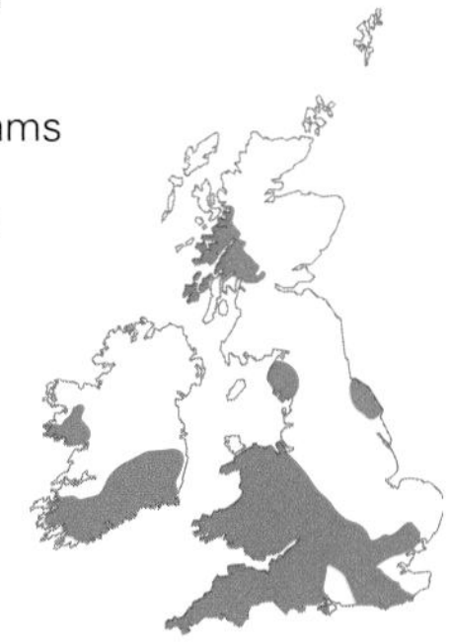

RED-EYED DAMSELFLY *Erythromma najas*

As its name indicates, the red-eyed damselfly has striking red eyes. Its head, thorax and abdomen are mainly dark, although the tip of the abdomen is sky-blue in the male. This feature is absent in the female. A robust insect, this damselfly is relatively fast and powerful in flight.

An emergent waterside plant provides a resting site for a red-eyed damselfly. Males fly regular circuits in search of females and food.

- **SIZE**
  Up to 35mm (1⅜in) long
- **HABITAT**
  Ponds and lakes, especially with waterlilies
- **DISTRIBUTION**
  Southern half of England; most common in the Midlands, Norfolk Broads, Surrey and Sussex
- **FLIGHT SEASON**
  Mid-May–mid-August

LARGE RED DAMSELFLY *Pyrrhosoma nymphula*

The abdomen and eyes of this relatively large damselfly are mostly deep red. There are variable amounts of black at the joints between the abdominal segments and the thorax is mainly black, bordered with red lines on the upper surface. Mainly black females with yellow lines on the thorax also occur.

Often the first of its kind to be encountered each spring, the large red damselfly is tolerant of a close approach by observers.

- **SIZE**
  Up to 36mm (1½in) long
- **HABITAT**
  Freshwater, including garden ponds, lakes, canals and ditches; tolerant of mildly brackish conditions
- **DISTRIBUTION**
  Throughout British Isles, including most Scottish islands
- **FLIGHT SEASON**
  Late April–late September

EMERALD DAMSELFLY *Lestes sponsa*

This is smaller than the superficially similar *Calopteryx* species, and the wings are clear in both sexes. Males have a metallic green sheen to head, eyes, thorax and abdomen. Females are a uniform duller green. Newly emerged individuals are paler. The abdomen acquires a bluish 'bloom' with age and maturity.

With a weak, fluttering flight, the emerald damselfly spends much of its time perching.

- **SIZE**
  Up to 38mm (1½in) long
- **HABITAT**
  Ponds and shallow margins of overgrown lakes and ditches
- **DISTRIBUTION**
  Most common in lowland Britain, especially south-east England; vulnerable to waterplant clearance
- **FLIGHT SEASON**
  Late June–late September

WHITE-LEGGED DAMSELFLY *Platycnemis pennipes*

A delicate little insect, the white-legged damselfly's most distinctive features are its pale legs. The hindlegs, especially in males, have swollen feather-like, white sections. Both sexes are creamy when newly emerged. The female becomes pale green with age, the male a pale blue, in both cases with darker markings.

The white-legged damselfly often rests on marshland plants at some distance from open water.

- **SIZE**
  Up to 36mm (1½in) long
- **HABITAT**
  Slow-flowing muddy streams, rivers and canals with plenty of waterside vegetation; intolerant of pollution
- **DISTRIBUTION**
  Southern and central England and Welsh border counties only
- **FLIGHT SEASON**
  Late May–mid-August

COMMON BLUE DAMSELFLY *Enallagma cyathigerum*

The mature male common blue damselfly has a striking blue body with dark patches at the joints between the abdominal segments. A club-shaped mark occurs on the upper surface of the second abdominal segment. The female has a greenish black body and a short spine projecting from the underside of the abdominal tip.

Brightly coloured as an adult, when immature the common blue can be mistaken for the white-legged damselfly.

● SIZE
Up to 32mm (1¼in) long

● HABITAT
Slow-flowing streams, garden ponds and canals with emergent and marginal plants

● DISTRIBUTION
Throughout British Isles

● FLIGHT SEASON
Mid-May–mid-September

AZURE DAMSELFLY *Coenagrion puella*

Males and females vary in appearance. The mature male is sky-blue with dark bands between the abdominal segments, and has a dark 'U'-shaped mark on the upper surface of his second abdominal segment. The female is dark with narrow, greenish lines on the thorax and at abdominal segment joints.

The azure damselfly, once called the common coenagrion, prefers sheltered ponds, such as those found in many gardens.

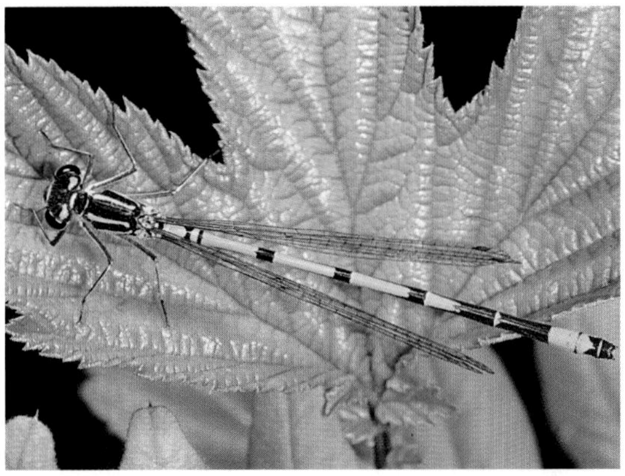

● SIZE
Up to 33mm (1⅜in) long

● HABITAT
Overgrown ditches, garden ponds and streams

● DISTRIBUTION
Throughout much of British Isles, but especially in southern counties

● FLIGHT SEASON
Mid-May–late August

VARIABLE DAMSELFLY *Coenagrion pulchellum*

Another species that is variable in appearance, the mature male has a blue and black abdomen, with a black mark, roughly shaped like a cross-section through a wine glass, on its second segment. Mature females have more black than blue on the abdomen, with segments eight and nine mostly black.

Although the variable damselfly sometimes consumes small prey on the wing, it often returns to a perch, such as a flowerhead, to eat.

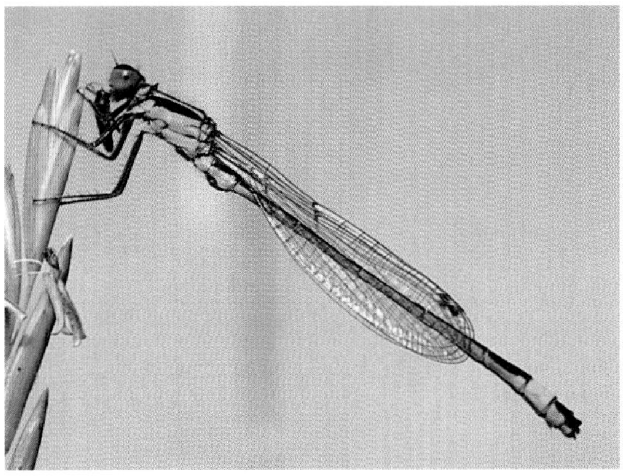

● SIZE
Up to 33mm (1⅜in) long

● HABITAT
Overgrown ponds and ditches with plenty of waterside vegetation

● DISTRIBUTION
Increasingly scarce; scattered throughout Ireland, southern and eastern England and a few places in Wales and Scotland

● FLIGHT SEASON
Late May–early August

BLUE-TAILED DAMSELFLY *Ischnura elegans*

Sometimes also known as the common ischnura, this is one of Britain's most abundant damselflies. The abdomen of both sexes is dark, except for the eighth segment, which is light blue. The thorax is marked with sky-blue lines in most individuals, but in some females the dividing lines can be green, orange, pink or violet.

Seen from the side, the tip of the abdomen of this species stands out like a little blue beacon.

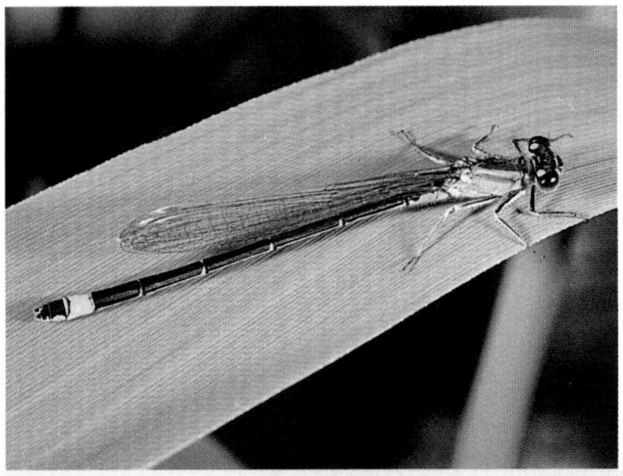

● SIZE
Up to 31mm (1¼in) long

● HABITAT
Freshwater including slow-flowing streams, canals, lakes, garden ponds, ditches, flooded gravel pits

● DISTRIBUTION
Throughout British Isles

● FLIGHT SEASON
Early May–early September

The ladybird

Sometimes called the gardener's friends because of their appetite for aphids, ladybirds eat immense numbers of these insects during their short lives and are a familiar sight on flowerbeds and vegetable plots.

Ladybirds are a promiscuous family of beetles. Research on the common two-spot ladybird has shown that on every sunny day up to half the population is likely to be mating. Each female may mate an average of 20 times during a May to July breeding season. Such intense activity is the reason why ladybirds are among the few groups of insects to suffer from a sexually transmitted disease in the form of a blood-sucking mite. This lives under the ladybirds' wing cases and moves from insect to insect as they mate.

A female ladybird may lay between 200 and 1000 eggs over the three-month mating period. Adults and larvae have the same diet, most species eating aphids or other sap-sucking plant pests, which they consume at an impressive rate. For example, a seven-spot larva will eat about 500 aphids in the few weeks it takes to develop, while the adult ladybird will consume over 5000 in its brief lifetime of around a year at most.

Ladybird mating sessions are lengthy, with the male and female locked together for nine hours or more.

From larva to adult

Ladybird larvae pupate after three to four weeks of voracious feeding. The metamorphosis within the pupa takes around ten days, after which the adult ladybird emerges. The new adult is usually yellow and unspotted, gaining its final adult colours over the next day or two.

Some ladybirds produce only females because they are infected with a bacterium that kills male embryos before they hatch from the egg. Those not infected produce young of both sexes but the female offspring of infected females produce only females in their turn, since the bacteria are transferred to the next generation in the eggs.

Unlikely though it may seem, this unattractive-looking larva will develop into a colourful, winged ladybird. Both adults and larvae are natural predators of aphids.

Range of colours

Ladybird colours vary greatly. The most common combination – the one most associated with the name – is red with black spots, a pattern found in several species. Others are black with red spots, yellow and black, or maroon or orange with white spots. The striped ladybird is a rich chestnut brown colour with creamy yellow spots and stripes, while the larch ladybird is brown, and usually completely unspotted.

Not only do species differ from one another, but individuals within the same species may show great variation in colour and the number of spots. For example, the Adonis ladybird can have anything from three to 15 spots, while the 24-spot ladybird may have from zero

EGGS

Ladybirds are not fussy about where they lay their eggs. All that is required is that they are near an abundance of aphids for the grubs to feed on when they hatch out. One exception to the rule, however, is the 24-spotted *Subcoccinella*, which is vegetarian and feeds directly on legumes so must lay its eggs on an appropriate plant.

Eggs are usually laid on the underside of leaves close to aphid colonies.

The 22-spot ladybird is unusual because, unlike most of its relatives, it does not feed on live prey. Instead, it feeds on mildew and its mouthparts are adapted for this purpose.

to 26 spots, and rarely has exactly 24. Most of the two-spot ladybirds are red with two black spots. However, in many parts of Britain, some two-spots are black with four or six red spots, and other patterns occur more rarely. The 10-spot ladybird displays even greater diversity, with individuals sporting assorted patterns as well as an array of background colours.

Ladybird habitats

Some ladybirds thrive in a variety of habitats while others are more choosy. The two-spot, seven-spot and 14-spot ladybirds are common in gardens, where they will live on a wide variety of plants if insecticides are not used to excess.

Several species, including the eyed, striped, cream-streaked, pine and 18-spot ladybirds, favour needled conifers, particularly Scots pine. The mildew-feeding orange and 22-spot ladybirds prefer sycamore and hogweed respectively, and the water ladybird lives in wetlands, especially reedbeds.

Two rarer species have unusual choices of habitat. The scarce seven-spot lives close to wood ants' nests, while the five-spot occurs in significant numbers only on unstable river shingles in west Wales and the Spey Valley in Scotland.

Cannibalism and biting

One of the ladybird's less attractive habits is cannibalism. Larvae eat eggs, other larvae or pupae, and adults will eat any other stage of ladybird they come across, particularly when their normal food is scarce. This cannibalism extends to their siblings – in each batch, the first larvae to hatch will consume any unhatched eggs as soon as their mouthparts have hardened.

Ladybirds can also bite humans, although they do so rarely. During the last great ladybird explosion, which occurred in 1976, there were numerous reports of holiday-makers being bitten by ladybirds. In fact, the beetles were starving to death, having consumed all the aphids available. Dispersing to seek more, they eventually reached the coast, where, in desperation, they tried anything that might be edible – including people. When a ladybird starts feeding it injects digestive enzymes into its prey to soften it up. Every time a ladybird bit a person it left behind a trace of enzyme, which produced a stinging reaction and a tiny bump. Ladybird population explosions on the scale of 1976 are a rarity – the one before that was in 1959.

Warning signals

The bright colours of most ladybirds are defensive, acting as a memorable warning to vertebrate predators, particularly birds, that ladybirds are highly distasteful. The yellow fluid that ladybirds produce from pores in their legs when disturbed, in a process known as 'reflex bleeding', also deters predators, both smelling and tasting pungently acrid. The defence is generally successful, and few birds prey on ladybirds.

Less common species, such as this orange ladybird, may visit the garden from time to time, especially if sycamore trees grow nearby. The orange ladybird is widespread in the southern half of England and Wales.

However, ladybirds have many other enemies, including predatory beetles, spiders and ants. More insidious are parasitoids – insects that lay their eggs inside another species of insect where they hatch and develop. In Britain, parasitoids of ladybirds include a number of flies and a small wasp, *Perilitus coccinellae*. The female wasp reproduces asexually, laying a single egg inside an adult ladybird. The egg hatches into a larva that hijacks the nutrients of the ladybird but does not kill it. Once fully fed, it paralyses the ladybird and burrows its way out, making a cocoon underneath its host. Here it is protected by the ladybird's warning coloration and reflex bleeding.

Other enemies of ladybirds include nematode worms, pathogenic fungi and, of course, man. Untold numbers of ladybirds are killed by the indiscriminate use of pesticide sprays.

Britain's largest species of ladybird, the eyed ladybird, is found in a variety of settings. Its favourite habitat, though, is open conifer woodland and it can often be found on plants at ground level.

WILDLIFE WATCH

How can I encourage ladybirds in my garden?

- Both adult and larval ladybirds are beneficial in the garden because of the large numbers of aphids and other damaging insects that they consume. Encourage them by avoiding the use of chemical pesticides.
- Most British ladybirds hibernate over the winter as adults, so make sure the garden has plenty of winter refuges. Leaving a wild patch of garden is a good way of doing this.
- Most ladybirds emerge from hibernation in April or early May. After mating and egg-laying, the adults gradually dwindle in number. Within a couple of weeks, however, the larvae will be on the rampage and adults will appear again in force by July.

Recognising snails

A summer shower brings out snails in abundance, revealing their different shell shapes and colours. Slowly and smoothly, they slide along the ground, leaving silvery trails in their wake.

Snails are fascinating creatures. The main part of the snail's body, containing most of the delicate internal organs, remains permanently inside the spiral shell. The only part of the body on view is the muscular foot, with the head at the front end.

Most British snails have two pairs of retractable tentacles, with eyes at the tips of the longer ones. However, a few species, such as the round-mouthed snail, have a single pair, with an eye at the tip of each. Snails' eyes are simple, merely enabling them to discern light and dark, but they are able to recognise the shadow of an approaching bird, which prompts them to retract their soft bodies into their shells. This strategy gives them a degree of protection, although some birds, such as song thrushes, have learned to break open snail shells by banging them on stones.

Courtship dance

Snails are hermaphrodites – each individual bears both male and female sexual organs. When two snails meet they carry out a short preparatory routine, circling one another until ready to mate. The mating process is unusual. Each snail possesses a muscular sac containing a pointed dart made of chalk. As they mate they shoot these darts deep into each other's foot, enabling them to exchange sperm. The snails separate and each one lays around 40 fertilised eggs in shallow depressions in the soil. After about a month the young snails hatch, miniature versions of their parents.

Most small snails mature in a year and die soon after breeding, although some may live for a second season. The large species take several years to mature and fewer than half of adults die each year. Some may even live for more than ten years.

These Roman snails are performing a courtship ritual. They usually mate on warm, damp nights in summer.

WILDLIFE WATCH

Where can I find snails?

- Most snails enjoy a moist, although not necessarily wet, habitat and do not like direct sunlight. They are most likely to be active at night and after summer showers, when they may come out in the daytime to feed and mate.
- Most British snails are herbivorous and are found wherever there is a suitable source of plant food – in parks, fields and gardens, woods and hedgerows, on sand dunes and along river banks. In Scotland many are found mainly near the coast.
- The Roman snail and the round-mouthed snail are found only in habitats where the soil is rich in calcium, so their ranges are restricted to the chalk and limestone regions of southern England.

EASY GUIDE TO SPOTTING SNAILS

WHAT ARE SNAILS?

● Snails are molluscs, a group of animals that also contains slugs, mussels and octopuses. They belong to the class Gastropoda, which includes many marine species, such as whelks and winkles. Britain has around 80 species of land snail.

● At the base of the shell is an opening through which the snail extends its foot in order to move. Most snails protect themselves from drying out by secreting a film of mucus that hardens to form a tough covering, the epiphragm, over the opening.

● Snails move around on their muscular foot, which secretes a sheet of mucus or slime. At the head end of the foot, on the underside, is the snail's mouth. The snail uses a ribbon-shaped tongue (radula) armed with rows of tiny teeth to rasp at food before swallowing it.

HOW CAN I IDENTIFY SNAILS?

● The key characteristic of snails is the coiled shell, which displays a variety of shapes and textures, the main examples of which are shown here.

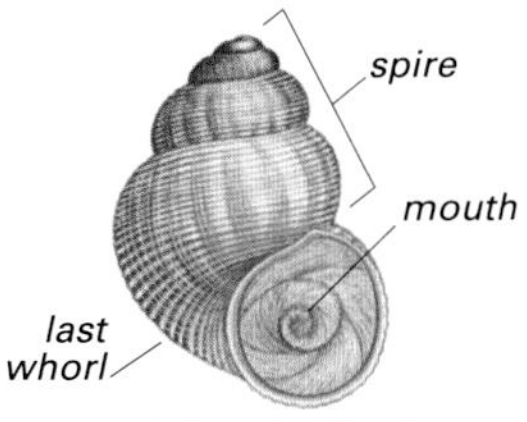

Coiled and ridged as in the round-mouthed snail

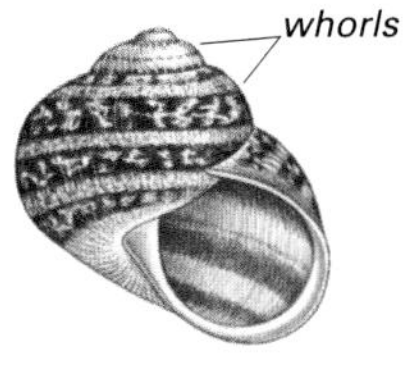

Coiled and smooth as in the garden or common snail

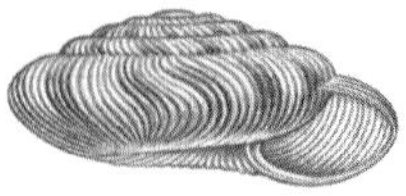

Flattened and ridged as in the rounded snail

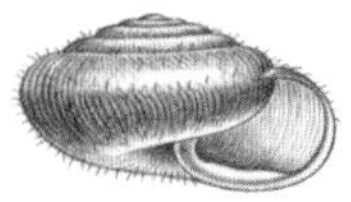

Flattened and hairy as in the hairy snail

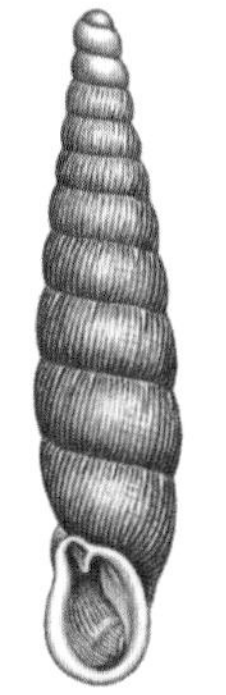

Very elongated as in the two-toothed door snail

ROUND-MOUTHED SNAIL *Pomatias elegans*

This is the only British land snail that has a round, calcareous plate, known as an operculum, attached to the foot. When the snail withdraws into its shell, which has 4½–5 whorls, this plate fits neatly into the shell's mouth, protecting the delicate body from drying out.

Active mostly at night, this snail, also called the land winkle, is quick to withdraw into its shell if disturbed.

● SIZE
Up to 16mm (¾in) across by 12mm (½in) high

● COLOUR
Violet-grey to yellowish with broken dark bands

● HABITAT
Woods, hedges and hillside screes

● DISTRIBUTION
Chalk and limestone

AMBER SNAIL *Succinea putris*

The thin, translucent shell has 3 whorls, the last one making up most of the shell. The foot is usually a pale yellowish brown but can be dark grey. Found in the same habitats is Pfeiffer's amber snail, *Oxyloma pfeifferi*, which usually has a darker, less translucent shell and a darker body, although the two can easily be confused.

With tentacles extended, two amber snails make their way across a leaf by the waterside.

● SIZE
Up to 17mm (¾in) high

● COLOUR
Greenish yellow to amber

● HABITAT
Always by water; often on waterside plants

● DISTRIBUTION
Common but rare in mountains

ROUNDED SNAIL *Discus rotundatus*

Many fine ribs occur on the upper surface of this species' shell, which has 5½–6 whorls and virtually no spire. Very similar and as common is the dwarf snail, *Punctum pygmaeum*, but its shell has just 3½ whorls and is tiny, about a quarter of the size of the rounded snail.

These snails have round shells when viewed from above. Seen from the side, the shell is flattened, allowing the animal to retreat into tight crevices.

● SIZE
Up to 7mm (⅜in) across

● COLOUR
Yellow-brown with reddish stripes

● HABITAT
Almost anywhere damp and sheltered

● DISTRIBUTION
Common but mainly coastal in northern Scotland

GLOSSY GLASS SNAIL *Oxychilus helveticus*

The glass snail – also known as the Swiss snail – has a thin, semi-transparent, glossy shell, with a low spire and 5 whorls. The foot is greyish, often with deep blue markings. Similar, but smaller, with a pale yellowish brown or greenish shell, is the garlic glass snail, *Oxychilus alliarius*, found throughout the British Isles.

The attractive blue colouring shows up clearly when the foot is fully extended.

SIZE
Up to 10mm (½in) across

COLOUR
Translucent orange-brown

HABITAT
Damp, shady places along hedges, in woodland and among rocks; often in parks

DISTRIBUTION
England and Wales

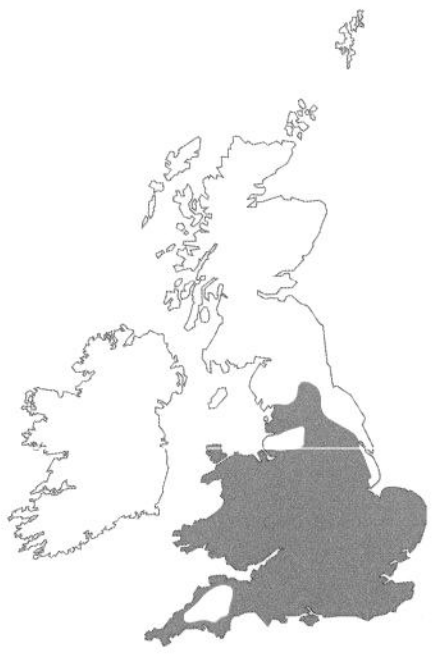

TWO-TOOTHED DOOR SNAIL *Clausilia bidentata*

This is the only commonly encountered land snail in which the shell is much longer than it is broad. Finely ribbed, the shell has 12–13 whorls and may be blackish rather than reddish brown. It bleaches with age so often appears much paler. The two teeth in the shell's mouth are visible with a hand lens.

Small groups may be found beneath stones or on bark. The young are pyramid-shaped and elongate as they grow.

SIZE
Up to 3mm (⅛in) across by 12mm (½in) high

COLOUR
Dark reddish brown with white specks

HABITAT
Moist places in woods, hedges, among rocks and on old walls

DISTRIBUTION
Abundant, but scarce in Scotland

POINTED SNAIL *Cochlicella acuta*

Easily recognised by its ice-cream-cone shaped shell, the pointed snail has 8–10 whorls, which increase regularly in size from the point downwards. In dry weather the snails become inactive and large groups may be found together, hanging from grass stems and other herbage.

When hanging from a plant stem, the snail's mouth is closed to help prevent its body from drying out.

SIZE
Up to 7mm (¼in) across by 20mm (¾in) high; occasionally larger

COLOUR
Chalky white with irregular dark lines

HABITAT
Sand dunes and coastal grassland

DISTRIBUTION
South and west coasts; inland in southern Ireland

SILKY SNAIL *Monacha (or Ashfordia) granulata*

The broadly cone-shaped shell is thin, slightly glossy, with 5–6 whorls and is covered in oblique rows of persistent straight hairs with a bulb-shaped base. This snail is often found feeding on decaying, rather than fresh, plant material.

A mainly pale, pinkish grey body helps distinguish the silky snail from the hairy snail, which often occurs in the same locations.

SIZE
Up to 9mm (⅜in) across by 7mm (¼in) high

COLOUR
Off-white to pale brown

HABITAT
Woods, hedges and marshy areas

DISTRIBUTION
Common; scarce in Scotland and Ireland

HAIRY SNAIL *Trichia (or Hygromia) hispida*

The top of the adult hairy snail's shell is much more flattened than that of the silky snail, and the curved hairs are much less persistent, being easily rubbed off with age. Snails from cooler, damper situations tend to be the hairiest. The hairy snail's shell has 6–7 whorls.

Brown is the most common colour for the hairy snail. This fully grown snail has retained most of the hairs on its shell.

SIZE
Up to 12mm (½in) across by 6mm (¼in) high

COLOUR
Dark brown to cream; often patchily hairy

HABITAT
Under logs, stones and moss

DISTRIBUTION
Abundant; absent from high mountains and very dry sites

STRAWBERRY OR RUDDY SNAIL *Trichia (or Hygromia) striolata*

Although young strawberry snails are slightly hairy, by the time they reach adulthood the hairs have all worn off. The flattened shell has 6 whorls and a blunt spire and is somewhat translucent, coarsely and irregularly ridged.

A strawberry snail, with tentacles extended, moves across the dead leaves on the floor of a beech wood, displaying the characteristic ribbing on its shell.

SIZE
Up to 14mm (⅝in) across by 9mm (⅜in) high

COLOUR
Creamy yellow to dark reddish brown

HABITAT
Damp and shady places, often in parks and gardens

DISTRIBUTION
Abundant in most regions

COPSE SNAIL *Arianta arbustorum*

The glossy, thick-walled shell of this medium-sized snail has a regular, cone-shaped spire and a narrow dark band running around the 5–6 whorls. Larger snails tend to have a more flattened spire than smaller individuals. Active on dewy, summer mornings, the copse snail leaves a conspicuous slime trail.

The body of the copse snail is always very dark in colour, which helps identification.

SIZE
Up to 28mm (1⅛in) across by 22mm (⅞in) high

COLOUR
Dark brown to yellow-buff, randomly flecked

HABITAT
Damp places in meadows, scrub and hedges

DISTRIBUTION
Patchily abundant; scarce in Ireland

SANDHILL SNAIL *Theba pisana*

In dry, summer weather this introduced Mediterranean snail congregates in large numbers on sand-dune vegetation so that the whole area can appear to be covered in hoar frost. The thick-walled shell has 5½–6 whorls and the spire is slightly raised with a blunt top. It has darker spiral bands that vary in intensity.

The variety of shell colour and pattern is noticeable when these snails cluster together.

SIZE
Up to 25mm (1in) across by 20mm (¾in) high

COLOUR
Off-white, yellowish, reddish yellow or orange-brown

HABITAT
Sand dunes and dry, exposed coastal sites

DISTRIBUTION
Scarce

BROWN-LIPPED OR GROVE SNAIL *Cepaea nemoralis*

Brown-lipped and white-lipped snails can be difficult to tell apart, especially as they share the same habitat. The lip around the brown-lipped snail's shell mouth is dark brown, and the shell colour, usually yellow, may be variable. The 5½ whorls sometimes have narrow dark bands running around them.

A brown-lipped snail cuts a hole into a leaf as it feeds. The brown lip encircling the mouth-opening can be clearly seen.

- **SIZE** Up to 25mm (1in) across by 22mm (⅞in) high
- **COLOUR** Usually yellow but can be white, pink or brown
- **HABITAT** Hedges, woods, scrub, grassland and sand dunes
- **DISTRIBUTION** Abundant, but scarce in much of Scotland

WHITE-LIPPED HEDGE SNAIL *Cepaea hortensis*

With a thinner, slightly more flattened shell than the brown-lipped snail, this species has the same colour variations, banding and number of whorls. The distinguishing feature is that the mouth has a thickened white lip – although, confusingly, this can be brown.

Both these white-lipped snails have the pale-coloured lip that gives the species its name.

- **SIZE** Up to 17mm (⅔in) high by 20mm (¾in) across
- **COLOUR** Usually yellow but can be white, pink or brown
- **HABITAT** Hedges, woods, scrub, grassland and sand dunes
- **DISTRIBUTION** Common, but scarce in much of Scotland

GARDEN OR COMMON SNAIL *Helix aspersa*

The garden snail's shell is roughly globular with a very large mouth. It has 4½–5 whorls and up to five spiral bands, which can be quite broad, often dotted with white flecks. These snails have an apparent homing instinct and may often be found together in large groups beneath stones.

Size and shell pattern easily distinguish this adult and juvenile common snail from any other species.

- **SIZE** Up to 40mm (1½in) across by 35mm (1⅜in) high, or more
- **COLOUR** Brown, occasionally yellow, with dark, spiral bands
- **HABITAT** Parks and gardens; hedges, woods, sand dunes and rocks
- **DISTRIBUTION** Scarce in or absent from mountains

ROMAN OR EDIBLE SNAIL *Helix pomatia*

The largest British species, the Roman snail has a roughly globular shell with 5–6 whorls, up to five rather indistinct bands and a large mouth. It was reputedly eaten by the Romans in Britain, hence its name.

Pictured in a beech wood, this mature Roman snail has lost some of the glossy coating from its shell.

- **SIZE** Up to 50mm (2in) across by 50mm (2in) high
- **COLOUR** Creamy white to yellowish brown
- **HABITAT** Woods, hedges, tall grass and scrub
- **DISTRIBUTION** Chalk and limestone areas only

Black garden ants

A close look at these common insects of parks and gardens reveals a system of complex communities that have an important ecological role to play.

Black garden ants are social insects that live in underground nests made up of many chambers and tunnels. Most parks contain at least one black garden ant nest, typically under a paving stone or in a rockery. The colony is highly organised and contains many thousands of individuals, most of which are workers. Ant society is made up of three castes – the queen, winged males and workers. The wingless worker ants are sterile females and they perform most of the duties within the colony. They look after the queen, tend the nursery, collect food and enlarge or repair the nest as necessary. They also defend the community against predators.

◀ Black garden ants, *Lasius niger*, are attracted by sugar-rich fluids and workers swarm over the flowers of plants such as sycamore, collecting sweet nectar and pollen. They also gather fat-rich seeds.

The search for food

Worker black ants travel up to 5m (16ft) from the nest to collect food for the rest of the community. As part of their foraging activity they may enter houses, where they invade kitchens in search of sugary foods. Although these raids are a nuisance, black garden ants are harmless to humans. In fact, they offer a service because they kill and eat all kinds of small insects, many of which are regarded as pests in parks and gardens and other cultivated plots. These include wireworms, flies, moths and sawfly larvae.

Ants have poorly developed eyes because they spend much of their life underground. They live in a world of taste, touch and smell, which they sense using their antennae. Ants leave scent trails by depositing drops of liquid on the ground from their abdomens. The scent trails act as invisible highways along which the worker ants travel to and fro. When two ants meet, they gently tap each other's antennae, using scent to determine each other's identity. Each colony has its own distinctive smell, so ants from rival nests are easily detected.

In summer, the larvae destined to become queens are given a special food produced by a few worker ants. This is rich in chemicals that encourage them to develop into fully reproductive adults. As they mature, the new queens outgrow their tiny guardians.

Apart from a brief mating flight, the queen spends her life deep within the nest. She is the only ant in the colony capable of laying eggs, which she does at a steady rate throughout her life. The worker ants clean and tend the eggs, then feed the larvae as they hatch.

For most of the year, the queen lays fertilised eggs, which develop into workers. For a short time, however, she lays unfertilised eggs, which develop into

Worker ants keep busy within the nest continually turning eggs and moving them from one chamber to another so that they remain at the right temperature. They feed the grubs on sugars and liquefied insects.

winged males. These remain in the nest and are cared for by the workers until they are needed. In summer, some of the 'worker' larvae are fed a special liquid that enables them to become queens. The role of the winged males is to mate with these new queens to form new colonies.

Mating flights

In late summer the ants swarm. Males and virgin queens from neighbouring nests launch into a special mating flight while hundreds of worker ants mill around on the ground. Mating takes place on the wing and only the strongest males stand a chance in the strenuous chase. The queens receive enough sperm to last a lifetime, which may be several years. After mating the males die and the queens bite off their own wings since they no longer need them.

Each queen may now start a new colony. Sometimes she will enter an existing nest of the same species – several queens often cooperate in the same nest – but more often she hides under a stone and emerges in spring to dig a new small chamber and lay the first of her eggs. The queen feeds the developing larvae with saliva. This first batch of worker ants will care for the next generation of eggs, expand the nest and search for food. Unlike the colonies of some social insects, such as common wasps, the ant colony survives the winter.

Hunters and farmers

Worker ants forage for a wide variety of food, which they carry back to the nest in their jaws. Ants are strong for their size and can carry objects several times larger than themselves, such as a dead wasp.

They are particularly attracted by sweet food, such as nectar from flowers and tree sap. As well as foraging, black ants also herd and 'milk' aphids, collecting the sweet-tasting honeydew. Ants sometimes keep aphids in special chambers in the nest, where they feed on plant roots and provide a handy supply of honeydew. The workers may even collect aphid eggs in the autumn and keep them in the nest during winter. In spring, the ants take the eggs out and place them on suitable plants close to the nest. They will eat the aphids if the population builds up beyond a certain level.

A worker ant may stroke an aphid's abdomen with an antenna to stimulate the aphid to excrete more honeydew. The precious liquid is taken back to the nest and fed to the queen and her larvae.

WILDLIFE WATCH

Where can I see black garden ants?

- Most gardens in the British Isles harbour black ant colonies, often under paving slabs or in rockeries. They also occur widely in grassland, heaths, open woodland and parks.
- On warm days, lines of black ants can be watched going about their daily business. The trail will lead to and from a source of food.
- On hot, sultry days in summer, black ants swarm, often just before or after a violent thunderstorm.

▲ Worker ants labour cooperatively to herd batches of aphids together and collect their sweet honeydew. They may even protect the aphids from their many predators, such as ladybirds and lacewing larvae.

► On a humid summer day, the winged queens leave the nest and are pursued by the winged males. Many of the ants will be eaten by birds that take advantage of this brief but bountiful supply of food.

Large umbellifers

The flat flowerheads of large umbellifers are associated with waysides and the wilder parts of parks and gardens. The tiny individual flowers attract numerous insects, their shallow shape allowing easy access to the nectar.

The familiar cow parsley and hogweed of hedgerow and wayside belong to the family *Umbelliferae* (now changed to *Apiaceae*), along with parsley, carrots and parsnips. The name umbellifer refers to the plants' flat-topped flowerheads ('umbels'), where many small flowers cluster together on stalks of equal length. There are 60 species of umbellifers in the British Isles, most of which have white flowers, although some are yellow or pink. One species, the sea holly, has blue flowers.

The large umbellifers are for the most part perennial, with substantial fleshy rootstocks producing several leafy shoots. Stems are erect and often hollow. The leaves, which sheath the stem at the base, are divided one or more times into smaller leaflets or narrow segments.

The individual flower parts comprise a tiny outer whorl (calyx) of five sepals (below the petals), five petals, five male filaments (stamens), and a two-part ovary. The ovary is topped by a nectar-secreting disc and two pollen-catching stigmas. The stamens mature early, promoting cross-pollination by visiting flies and beetles. When the ripe fruit dries out, it splits into two fruitlets (mericarps).

The stems, leaves and seeds of umbellifers are often aromatic or resinous when bruised and contain chemicals that deter grazing animals.

Poisonous plants

The umbellifers include several highly poisonous species. For instance, hemlock contains the deadly alkaloid coniine. Hemlock water-dropwort, which contains a complex alcohol, is also poisonous and has caused several fatalities in Britain. These two plants are similar in appearance to the relatively innocuous cow parsley, so care should be taken with identification.

Giant hogweed is notorious for causing painful skin burns. Chemicals in its sap sensitise skin to sunlight, creating large blisters that are slow to heal.

Conversely, some of these aromatic chemicals have given other umbellifer species an attractive flavour. Carrots are grown for their swollen roots, while many other edible species were once popular. Sweet cicely is still sometimes used to flavour gooseberry and other dishes, while fennel, with its sweet aniseed taste, is used to make tea as well as in cookery.

▲ The outer petals on the outermost flowers of an umbel are often enlarged to increase the visibility of the flowerhead to pollinating insects.

◀ In spring and summer cow parsley thrives on roadsides, in hedgerows and woodland margins. Its delicate flowers, a froth of white blooms, gave rise to its common name of Queen Anne's lace.

UMBELLIFER FACT FILE

● **Wild angelica**
Angelica sylvestris
Habitat and distribution
Naturalised on watersides, in marshes, damp woodlands and shady hedgerows
Size 50–250cm (1ft 8in–8ft) tall
Key features
Robust, often purplish, perennial with stout, hollow stems; leaves glossy, with large basal sheaths, divided into oval, toothed leaflets; flowers white or tinged pink, umbels domed, 3–15cm (1¼–6in) across, 20–30 stalks; fruits oval, flattened, 4-winged
Flowering time
June–September

● **Cow parsley**
Anthriscus sylvestris
Habitat and distribution
Woodland margins, hedgerows, roadsides and other shady places
Size 50–150cm (1ft 8in–5ft) tall
Key features
Hairy perennial with hollow green or purplish stems; leaves pale green or flushed purplish, feathery, emerging in late autumn, divided into toothed segments; flowers white, umbels 2–6cm (¾–2½in) across, 8–12 stalks; fruits smooth, 6–9mm (¼–⅜in) long
Flowering time
April–June

● **Sweet cicely**
Myrrhis odorata
Habitat and distribution
Native of the mountains of southern Europe, established on roadsides, woodland margins and grassy places, mostly from Staffordshire northwards
Size 40–120cm (1ft 4in–4ft) tall
Key features
Similar to cow parsley but leaves are white-flecked, smell of aniseed when bruised; fruits narrow, sharply ridged, rough, about 2cm (¾in) long
Flowering time
April–June

● **Wild carrot**
Daucus carota
Habitat and distribution
Dry grassland and on roadside verges, especially on limestone cliffs and banks or on the coast. Scarcer in the north and west
Size 30–150cm (1–5ft) tall
Key features
Rough-hairy perennial with tough, slender stems and a thin whitish taproot; leaves divided into small, narrow leaflets; flowers white, umbels domed, 3–7cm (1¼–2¾in) across, with a ruff of slender bracts, 20–40 stalks; fruits prickly, held in concave heads
Flowering time
June–September

Wild angelica
Angelica sylvestris

Sweet cicely
Myrrhis odorata

Wild carrot
Daucus carota

Cow parsley
Anthriscus sylvestris

The flower umbels of wild carrot are often pale pink before they bloom in well-rounded, white domes. The leaves and roots smell of carrots, but wild carrot roots are nothing like the thick, orange taproots of the cultivated variety.

UMBELLIFER FACT FILE

● **Hogweed or cow parsnip**
Heracleum sphondylium
Habitat and distribution
Common in hedgerows, roadside verges, grassland, waste and cultivated land
Size 50–300cm (1ft 8in–10ft) tall
Key features
Tall, robust, hairy biennial with stout, hollow, grooved stems; leaves large, divided into deeply lobed, coarsely toothed leaflets; flowers white or pinkish, umbels 5–20cm (2–8in) across, 15–30 stalks; fruits oval, flattened, winged with dark streaks
Flowering time
May–November

● **Giant hogweed**
Heracleum mantegazzianum
Habitat and distribution
A native of the Caucasus now naturalised alongside streams, roadsides and on wasteground
Size 2–5m (6½–16ft) tall
Key features
Similar to hogweed but stems up to 10cm (4in) thick; leaves up to 1m (3ft) long on stalks of same length, smell resinous when bruised; umbels domed, 20–100cm (8in–3ft) across, 50 or more stalks
Flowering time
June–August

● **Hemlock**
Conium maculatum
Habitat and distribution
Abundant in south and east in patches on roadsides, waste ground, stream banks and around farm buildings
Size 80–250cm (2ft 8in–8ft) tall
Key features
Hairless biennial with hollow, purplish spotted stems; leaves feathery, divided into finely toothed segments, unpleasant smell when bruised; flowers white, umbels 2–6cm (¾–2½in) across, 10–20 stalks; spherical, wavy-ridged fruits, 3mm (⅛in) long
Flowering time
June–August

● **Hemlock water-dropwort**
Oenanthe crocata
Habitat and distribution
Widespread but patchy on watersides and in wet ditches
Size 50–150cm (1ft 8in–5ft) tall
Key features
Robust, branched, hairless perennial with hollow stems; glossy large leaves divided into broad-lobed leaflets; flowers white or greenish, umbels 5–10cm (2–4in) across, 15–25 stalks; fruits cylindrical, ribbed
Flowering time
June–August

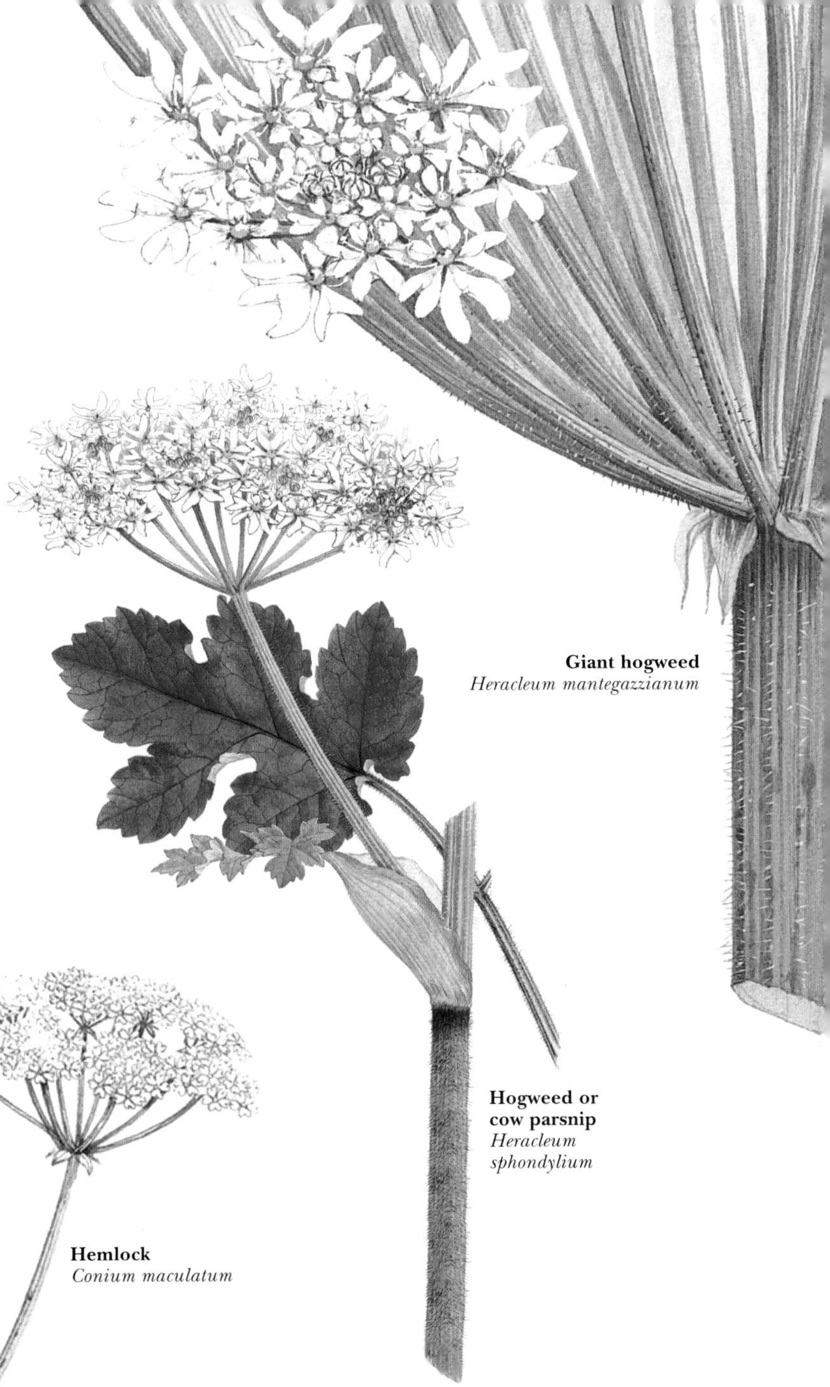

Giant hogweed
Heracleum mantegazzianum

Hogweed or cow parsnip
Heracleum sphondylium

Hemlock water-dropwort
Oenanthe crocata

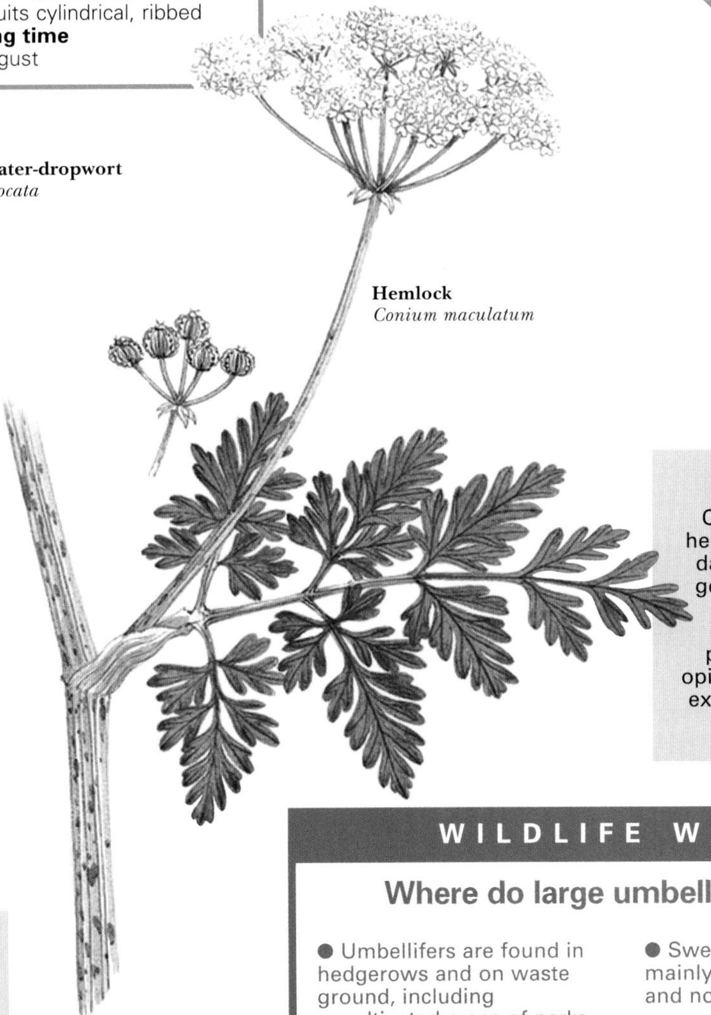

Hemlock
Conium maculatum

DID YOU KNOW?

One old herbal called hemlock a 'naughtie and dangerous herbe'. The government of ancient Athens famously employed hemlock, probably mixed with opium to remove pain, to execute the philosopher Socrates in 399BC.

DANGER!

Always cover your skin when handling or walking through giant hogweed and other large umbellifers on a sunny day – even a light brush against a leaf may cause some burning.

WILDLIFE WATCH

Where do large umbellifers grow?

● Umbellifers are found in hedgerows and on waste ground, including uncultivated areas of parks and gardens. They also grow in marshy ground, on watersides and near the sea.

● Sweet cicely occurs mainly in northern Britain and northern Ireland.

● Hemlock and giant hogweed grow on waste ground, often by roads and by streams and rivers.

Index

Page numbers in *italic* refer to illustrations

Acknowledgments

Photographs: Front cover NHPA/Ernie Janes, inset BC/A Purcell; Back cover OSF/M Birkhead; 1 WW/R Revels; 2-3 Woodfall Wild Images; 4 (t) NP/O Newman, (b) FLPA/F Merlet; 5 FLPA/M Withers; 6-9 NP; 10-11 Woodfall Wild Images/Jan Godwin; 12(t) FLPA/Hans Schouten/Foto Natura, (b) NP/Paul Sterry; 13(tr) Laurie Campbell, (clu) PW, (cl,br) NV/Heather Angel; 14(tr) PW, (c) unknown, (b) NV/Heather Angel; 15(tr) NP/NA Callow, (br) NP/Paul Sterry, (clu) NV/Heather Angel, (cl) PW; 16(tl) BC/Dr E Pott, (br) NV/Heather Angel; 17(tl) OSF/F Skibbe, (tr) Andrew Gagg, (cl) BC/H Lange, (br) FLPA/E&D Hosking; 18(tl) Andrew Gagg, (tr) OSF/T Nyssen, (cr) OSF/RL Manuel, (bl) Dave Aplin, (br) Ardea/David Dixon; 19(tc) BC/Dr E Pott, (cr) Andrew Gagg; 20(t) NV, (blu,br) NP/Paul Sterry, (bl) NP/O Newman; 21(tl,c) NP/Paul Sterry, (tr) NP/Geoff du Feu, (b) NP/NA Callow; 22(sp) FLPA/M Withers, (bl) FLPA/Martin Smith; 23(tr) FLPA/SC Brown, (cru) FLPA/Chris Newton, (cr) NHPA/AP Barnes, (br) NV/Heather Angel; 24(tl) FLPA/R Tidman, (tr) FLPA/H Clark, (cl) FLPA/R Wilmhurst, (cr) unknown; 25(tl) FLPA/Tony Wharton, (cr) FLPA/W Wisnieski, (c) FLPA/R Wilmhurst; 26(tr) FLPA/G Laci, (sp) NP; 27(tr) FLPA/MB Withers, (br) unknown; 28(tl) FLPA/D Middleton, (c) FLPA/P Perry, (cr) FLPA/R Tidman, (br) FLPA/W Meinderts; 29(tl) FLPA/R Wilmhurst, (cl) FLPA/RP Lawrence, (cr) FLPA/GE Hyde, (bl) FLPA/I Rose; 30(tr) Garden Matters, (bl) NV/Heather Angel; 31(tl) NV/Heather Angel, (tr,br) Midsummer Books/AJ Beer, (bl) NV/D Cattani; 32(t) NV/Heather Angel, (cl) FLPA/D Hosking, (b) NV/Heather Angel; 33(tl) WW/M Hamblin, (tc,tr) WW/B Glover, (b) NV/Heather Angel; 34(bl) Windrush/D Tipling, (sp) FLPA/J Watkins; 35(tl) FLPA/R Tidman, (tr) Windrush/R Brookes, (cr) BC/G McCarthy, (br) FLPA/J Hawkins; 36(tl) BC/G McCarthy, (tr) WW/T Rasanen, (bl) FLPA/Danny Ellinger/Foto Natura, (br) NHPA/Manfred Danneger; 37(b) Collections/Colin Underhill; 38-39 NHPA/Hellio & Van Ingen; 40(t) Ardea/L&T Bomford, (b) FLPA/G Laci; 41(tr) OSF/R Jackman, (b) Ardea/D Avon; 42(tl) OSF/R Jackman, (tr) BC/Jane Burton, 43(tl) OSF/R Jackman, (tc) Ardea/L&T Bomford, (cr) OSF/R Jackman; 44(tl) FLPA/G Laci, (tr,bl) NHPA/S Dalton, (br) OSF/R Redfern; 45(tr) BC/Kim Taylor, (cr) OSF/R Jackman, (b) Ardea/Ian Beames; 46(tl) OSF/M Hamblin, (b) NP/O Newman; 47(tl) OSF/M Hamblin, (tru) Midsummer Books, (br) Andy Rouse; 48(r) BC/Kim Taylor; 49(tr) WW/J Robinson, (b) BC/Jane Burton; 50(c) OSF/A Shay, (b) NHPA/S Dalton; 51(tr) OSF/T Bomford, 52(tl) OSF/D Boag, (tr) Aquila/W Walter, (bl) BC/Kim Taylor, (br) WW/R Revels; 53(bl) OSF/M Reid, (br) NHPA/S Dalton; 54(t) RSPB/R Wilmhurst; 55(tr) FLPA, (b) Ardea; 56(tl) FLPA/R Wilmhurst, (tc) Aquila/A Cardwell, (tr) OSF/M Hamblin, (cl) Mike Read, (c) NP/P Newman, (cr) Aquila/MC Wilkes; 57(tl) Aquila/C Smith, (tr) FLPA/R Wilmhurst, (br) Dave Bevan; 58(tr) BC/Kim Taylor, (cl) OSF/J Sierra, (cr) FLPA/R Wilmhurst, (bl) Aquila/RT Mills; 59(tl) Dave Bevan, (tr) Ardea/John Daniels, (b) Mike Read; 60(tl) Aquila/M Lane; 61(tr) Aquila, (b) NP/Paul Sterry; 62(tl) BC/R Glover, (tr) David Chapman; 63(tr) NP/F Blackburn, (c) FLPA/MB Withers, (br) Aquila/AT Moffett; 64(tr) Aquila/RT Mills, (cl) OSF/D Tipling, (c) BC/G McCarthy, (bl) BC/F Furlong, (bc) Aquila/A Moffet; 65(tr) FLPA/J Watkins, (cr) David Chapman, (b) OSF/M Tibbles; 66(tr) David Chapman, (c) OSF/D Boag; 67(tr) OSF/M Hamblin, (b) NP/Paul Sterry; 68(cl) David Chapman, (cr) Aquila; 69(tr,c) NP/H Clark, (cl,cr,bc) FLPA/E&D Hosking, (bl) BC/C Varndell, (br) OSF/M Birkhead; 70(tr) FLPA/E&D Hosking, (cl,cr) Aquila/MC Wilkes, (bl) NP/EA Janes; 71(tl) NP/R Tidman, (tr) Aquila/MC Wilkes, (bl) Aquila/R Glover; 72(t) BC/Kim Taylor, (b) OSF/D Thompson; 73(tl) OSF/D Thompson, (tr) OSF/J Cook, (c) NP/Paul Sterry, (b) BC/J Cook; 74-78 PW; 79 NP/Geoff du Feu; 80(tl,cr) NP/Geoff du Feu, (tr) BC/Kim Taylor, (b) NP/NA Callow; 81(tl) OSF/S Littlewood, (tr) BC/Kim Taylor, (b) NP/NA Callow; 82(tl,tc,tr) NV/Heather Angel, (bl,br) NP/SC Bisserot; 83(tr) FLPA/R Wilmhurst, (c) FLPA/MJ Thomas, (bl) BC/J Grayson; 84(tl) NP/A Cleave, (cr) NP/Geoff du Feu, (cl) NP/WS Paton, (br) Midsummer; 85 NHPA/Stephen Dalton; 86 NPL/George McCarthy; 87 BC, 88(tr) Windrush; 89(tl,c) Windrush, (tr) NP; 90(tl) NP; 91(tr) BC; 92(cr) Andy Rouse; 93(tr) FLPA/M Clark, (b) BC/G Langsbury; 94(tl) FLPA/J Tinning, (tr) FLPA/M Clark; 95(tr) BC/R Maier, (br) OSF/M Birkhead; 96(tr) OSF/S Osolinski, (b) NHPA/J Blossom; 97(tl) FLPA/M Clark, (tr) OSF/S Osolinski, (b) Windrush/D Mason; 98(b) BC/C Varndell; 99(tr) Aquila/B Speake, (c) Aquila/R Wilmhurst; 100(tl) Aquila/D Owen, (tc) FLPA/M Jones, (tr) Aquila/B Speake, (cl) Windrush/D Tipling, (c) BC/G Langsbury, (cr) FLPA/E Hosking; 101(tl) NP/H Clark, (tc) Alistair Baxter, (cr) Aquila/MC Wilkes; 102(tc) FLPA/R Brookes, (cl) FLPA/R Wilmhurst, (cr) BC/D Green, (bl) Windrush/BR Hughes; 103(tl) Windrush/D Green, (tr) FLPA/BS Turner; 104(t) FLPA/F Merlet; 105(c) FLPA/E&D Hosking, (bl) Ardea/S Roberts; 106(tr) OSF/D Bromhall, (cl) Aquila/RA Hume, (c) Windrush/J Hollis, (bl) FLPA/R Wilmhurst, (bc) Aquila/JM Simon, (br) NP/WS Paton; 107(tl) NHPA/S Dalton, (tr) WW/J Robinson, (bl) Aquila/MC Wilkes; 108(tl) Midsummer, (tr) Aquila/P Castell, (b) OSF/D Bromhall; 109(tl) OSF/D Bromhall, (cr) Aquila/MC Wilkes, (c) BC/Kim Taylor; 110(b) BC/A Purcell; 111(t) BC/F Labhart, (c) OSF/T Leach, (b) David Chapman; 112(t,b) PW, (cu) BC/A Purcell, (c) NP/TD Bonsall; 113(t) BC/G Dore, (cu) NP/NA Callow, (c) NP/Paul Sterry, (b) NP/TD Bonsall; 114(t) FLPA/B Borrel, (bl) OSF, (br) FLPA/L West; 115(tl) NP/Geoff du Feu, (tr,b) BC/Andy Purcell; 116(b) PW; 117(cu,b) Ardea/JL Mason, (c) PW; 118-120 PW; 121(t) OSF/G Kramer, (b) NV/Heather Angel; 122(tr,cr) NP/NA Callow, (bl) NP/EA Janes, (br) NPL/PW; 123(bl) BC/J Grayson, (br) OSF/J Wilson; 124(br) FLPA/L Batten.

Illustrations: 37(t), 47(tr,cr), 117, 124-126 Midsummer Books; 50-42-3, 51, 56-57, 62-64, 68-69, 88-91, 94-96, 100-101, 106-107 John Ridyard; 84(br), 117(t), 124-125 Ian Garrard; 108(tl) Tim Hayward.

Key to Photo Library Abbreviations: BC = Bruce Coleman Ltd, FLPA = Frank Lane Photo Agency, NHPA = Natural History Photo Agency, NI= Natural Image, NP = Nature Photographers, NPL = Nature Picture Library, NSc = Natural Science Photos, NV = Heather Angel/Natural Visions, OSF = Oxford Scientific Films, PW = Premaphotos Wildlife, WW = WW Wild.

Key to position abbreviations: b = bottom, bl = bottom left, blu = bottom left upper, br = bottom right, bru = bottom right upper, c = centre, cl = centre left, clu = centre left upper, cr = centre right, cru = centre right upper, cu = centre upper, l = left, r = right, sp = spread, t = top, tl = top left, tlu = top left upper, tr = top right, tru = top right upper.

Wildlife Watch

Gardens & Parks in Summer

Published by the Reader's Digest Association Limited, 2005

The Reader's Digest Association Limited
11 Westferry Circus, Canary Wharf
London E14 4HE

We are committed to both the quality of our products and the service we provide to our customers, so please feel free to contact us on 08705 113366, or via our website at: www.readersdigest.co.uk

If you have any comments about the content of our books you can contact us at: gbeditorial@readersdigest.co.uk

Reader's Digest General Books:
Editorial Director Cortina Butler
Art Director Nick Clark
Series Editor Christine Noble
Prepress Accounts Manager Penelope Grose

This book was designed, edited and produced by Eaglemoss Publications Ltd, based on material first published as the partwork *Wildlife of Britain*

For Eaglemoss:
Editors Marion Paull, Celia Coyne, Ben Hoare, John Woodward
Art Editor Phil Gibbs
Consultant Jonathan Elphick
Publishing Manager Nina Hathway

Printed and bound in Europe by Arvato Iberia

CONCEPT CODE: UK 0133/G/S
BOOK CODE: 630-005-1
ISBN: 0 276 44053 6
ORACLE CODE: 356200006H.00.24